Inclusive Leadership

by Shirley Davis, PhD

Inclusive Leadership For Dummies®

Published by: **John Wiley & Sons, Inc.,** 111 River Street, Hoboken, NJ 07030-5774, www.wiley.com

Copyright © 2024 by John Wiley & Sons, Inc., Hoboken, New Jersey

Published simultaneously in Canada

For general information on our other products and services, please contact our Customer Care Department within the U.S. at 877-762-2974, outside the U.S. at 317-572-3993, or fax 317-572-4002. For technical support, please visit https://hub.wiley.com/community/support/dummies.

Wiley publishes in a variety of print and electronic formats and by print-on-demand. Some material included with standard print versions of this book may not be included in e-books or in print-on-demand. If this book refers to media such as a CD or DVD that is not included in the version you purchased, you may download this material at http://booksupport.wiley.com. For more information about Wiley products, visit www.wiley.com.

Library of Congress Control Number: 2024935004

ISBN 978-1-394-19723-1 (pbk); ISBN 978-1-394-19724-8 (ebk); ISBN 978-1-394-19725-5 (ebk)

SKY10071033_032724

Table of Contents

Introduction

"**I**f you are a leader and no one is following you, you're just taking a walk."

This is one of my favorite quotes to live by and one that I coach leaders all over the world. The reality is, at the core of effective leadership is the expectation that you meet the needs of a new generation of talent that brings different ways of working, thinking, believing, and behaving; that you demonstrate the kind of skills and competencies that engender followers; that you grow others into effective leaders; and cultivate the kind of work environment that brings out the best in others and drives high performance. Today, effective leadership begins and ends with inclusive leadership. And successful organizations recognize that in order to attract and retain top talent, enhance the employee experience, drive innovation and creativity, and meet the changing needs of their customers, they must have inclusive leaders who are knowledgeable and skilled at working across differences.

I have been preparing to write this book all of my personal and professional life because of the experiences I've had, the challenges I've overcome, and the expertise and knowledge that I have acquired. Writing this book is a labor of love because it is my life's work of more than three decades as a corporate executive, certified HR and leadership consultant, a global workforce expert, a Toastmasters International Golden Gavel recipient, and an inductee into the Inclusion Hall of Fame. And on a personal note, I am a woman of color, a single mom, a person of faith (licensed and ordained minister), a big sister to three brothers, a daddy's girl, a movie buff, a dog mom, an HGTV junkie, and a world traveler. This intersectionality of my life has produced a myriad of life lessons that have shaped and formed me into the person I am today and how I see and experience the world. Although it wasn't an easy road, it led me to my destiny of writing this book. I share my experiences throughout this book because, as I discover with live audiences around the world, it is still the experience of many others who may be members of the same communities that I am part of and who may share some of my same diverse characteristics and attributes. This is important because storytelling has become an important bedrock of inclusive leadership as a way to demonstrate greater trust, increase psychological safety, and build deeper and more meaningful relationships — all of which are lacking today.

About This Book

Inclusive Leadership For Dummies helps leaders successfully navigate the nuances and complexities of a changing, global, and more diverse workforce and create a culture where all talent can thrive. It provides you with the knowledge, tools, and strategies to ensure that all employees are treated fairly, and feel included, valued, safe, and can do their best work. It contains answers to the many questions that leaders ask and the plethora of concerns and misnomers that exist, and it demystifies inclusion to make it practical, understandable, and implementable. There is something here for all levels of leader. It speaks directly to people leaders, senior and executive leaders, and middle managers. It also speaks to emerging and aspiring leaders and to seasoned long-term leaders.

However, this book is not designed to be a blanket prescription for implementing strategies and tips. Every organization is at (and in) a different place, working at a different pace, and has varying degrees of resources, complexities, and levels of commitment. Therefore, this isn't a one-size-fits-all reference guide. Use it to find information, ideas, and guidance for where you are and to help you get to where you want to go on your inclusion journey. Use it to evolve your own thinking and behaviors, and get comfortable with disruption, difference, and change, so toss out the one-size-fits-all leadership approaches, because the workforce is not a monolith — it's a rich and beautiful tapestry made up of people from all backgrounds, cultures, skills, and experiences.

I cover topics relevant for CEOs, executives, board members, and general staff, such as the business case for inclusive leadership, assembling and leading diverse and hybrid teams, demonstrating empathy, authenticity, and transparency, dealing with conflict, communicating inclusively, and much more. To help you navigate the content, I've divided this book into five parts:

>> **Part 1: Getting Started with Inclusive Leadership.** In this part I lay the groundwork with the basics of what effective and inclusive leadership looks like and why it is a relevant business need.

>> **Part 2: Developing the Skills to Lead Yourself.** This part focuses on you, the leader within. It's a jumping off place for how to be effective in leading others by first knowing how to lead yourself.

>> **Part 3: Leading Others.** After doing the internal work in Part 2, this part helps you to hone the skills necessary to lead others effectively.

>> **Part 4: Cultivating a Culture of Inclusion and High Performance.** This part brings in the accountability factor. It details ways to measure your progress

and success in the area of inclusion and equity, and how to continue to influence positive change.

>> **Part 5: The Part of Tens.** This part highlights additional lessons, strategies, and food for thought in your role as an inclusive leader.

Foolish Assumptions

You know what they say about making assumptions, but while it might be a common idiom, in this case allow me to make a few in an effort to best serve your needs. While writing this book I assumed the following:

>> You chose this book because you recognize that today's talent and the future generation expects to work for an inclusive leader.

>> You may not have been through any significant training on this topic and are curious about what it means and how to be more inclusive.

>> You are an emerging or aspiring leader, or have recently taken on a new role as a leader, or are a seasoned leader, and understand the importance of upskilling and reskilling so that you remain relevant, competitive, and effective.

>> You have some reservations and maybe even a little resistance as to why this topic is so important, and you want clarity and some practical insights.

Icons Used in This Book

Throughout this book, icons in the margins highlight certain types of valuable information that call for your attention. Here are the icons you'll encounter and a brief description of each:

TIP

This icon alerts you to helpful hints that may save you time, effort, stress, embarrassment, and money while implementing inclusion initiatives and developing into an inclusive leader.

REMEMBER

This icon marks information that's especially important to know. To siphon off the most important information from each chapter if you're in a hurry, just read through these icons and skim the rest of the text for useful tidbits.

TECHNICAL STUFF

This icon marks information of a more technical or data-driven nature that is essential crunchy reading for those who like to dig a little deeper and discover the details behind the headlines. Other readers may simply prefer the headlines!

WARNING

Watch out! This icon marks important information that may save you headaches, time, and money, and helps you hurdle those obstacles that appear where you least expect to find them.

Beyond the Book

In this book I provide a plethora of ideas on inclusion and leadership that gives you a solid foundation from which to lead. But there's more. You can access additional resources and tools online at Dummies.com. Check out this book's online Cheat Sheet. Just go to www.dummies.com and search for "Inclusive Leadership For Dummies Cheat Sheet."

If you, your team, or other leaders in your organization need additional resources, education, training, or any consulting services on the topics discussed in this book, be sure to reach out to me at www.drshirleydavis.com. I also encourage you to get a copy of my book *Diversity, Equity, & Inclusion For Dummies* (John Wiley & Sons, Inc., 2022) so that you have a companion book with even more tips, tools, and strategies. Additionally, I've developed a LinkedIn learning course to complement this book: *Inclusive Leadership.* There you will see and hear me share more of my strategies and tips for being a more inclusive leader.

Where to Go from Here

If you are new to the topic of inclusion, I recommend that you start at Chapter 1 to understand the basic terms leaders need to know and Chapter 3 to help you understand the business case behind inclusive leadership. This book is not linear, so feel free to access it like a workbook or reference guide, perusing the Table of Contents for a list of all the great topics covered and selecting the ones that best meet your needs now.

The world continues to change and situations arise that require leaders to have the knowledge and insight to act appropriately and immediately — and this book provides both. You may need to know how to use inclusive language to avoid making others feel minimized, insulted, or disregarded. If so, jump to Chapter 13. If you a working on establishing a more psychologically safe work environment, go to Chapter 11. If you want to assess your own level of effectiveness as an inclusive leader, Chapter 4 will help you. And if you have some consternation about coaching and giving feedback to someone who is different from you, Chapter 12 gives great tips for how to do so. These are just a few examples, but my point is that this book encompasses all you need to know about leading more inclusively.

It is not my expectation that after reading this book you will be an expert on inclusive leadership — that takes years of practice, learning, and achieving success. However, I do hope that I answer many of your questions and clear up confusion about inclusion and leadership. It is my desire that you are better positioned to treat all talent as unique and valued members of your team and to show a measurable impact of how being a more inclusive leader has made the lives of those you work with and lead more welcoming, trusting, and enriching. In fact, I hope that you can earn the title that too few leaders have, and that is "Best boss ever." It is one that I hold with the highest regard and work hard every day with my team to maintain. I hope you will too.

1

Getting Started with Inclusive Leadership

Discover the basics of what effective and inclusive leadership looks like, how it is changing, and why it is a relevant business need.

Uncover the changing needs, expectations, and ways of working, thinking, and communicating with the new generation of talent today and in the future. Identify the skills and competencies that they look for in a leader.

Explore the many benefits that inclusive leadership offers and discover ways that you can drive greater worker performance, engagement, creativity, and retention.

Assess your strengths and areas for improvement in demonstrating inclusiveness as a leader. Identify ways that you can further develop into the kind of leader we all want to work for.

Chapter **1**

Establishing the Basics of Leadership and Inclusion

'm so glad that you're holding a copy of this book! It means that you are serious and curious about learning the nuts and bolts of leading more inclusively. It means you realize that as the workforce becomes more global, diverse, hyper-connected, and work gets done in different ways and from different locations, the need for more inclusive leadership is imperative.

You may have heard that we have a leadership gap, an accountability gap, and an inclusion gap. Most organizations are still reporting that they are making slow progress in their culture transformation efforts; a few report that they are making steady progress; and far fewer are making substantial progress. The main reasons are because transformation is hard, especially if your organization is rigid, hier-archical, risk-averse, and predominantly homogeneous. The other reasons are because of a lack of training and education, and the pace of change. Leaders say that they can't keep up and have not invested in their skill building at the same pace that change is happening. It can feel like a vicious cycle or like Groundhog Day but it cannot continue if organizations want to remain competitive, want to become great places to work, and want to achieve sustainable success.

REMEMBER

Now more than ever, inclusive leadership must become the new normal. It must become a leadership responsibility and a performance expectation that is as common as managing projects and serving customers. From the boardroom to the C-Suite (the group of high-level executives within a company, typically having titles that begin with "Chief"), to the front lines, leaders must shift their mindsets, and adopt new skillsets in order to meet the demands of the global changing marketplace, workplace, and the communities in which they do business.

This chapter introduces you to the fundamentals of leadership and inclusion, and acts as a stepping off point for what you'll discover in other chapters. It explains why these are critical in driving high performance for the changing workforce, and it acts as the basis from which to develop and demonstrate the skills and competencies that top talent are demanding.

Knowing Why Inclusive Leadership is Important

I work with organizational leaders all around the world and, over the past few years, my firm has conducted hundreds of organizational audits, staff focus groups, listening sessions, and training programs to assess the employee experience and the state of the workplace culture. What we have found to be the most common denominator among those thousands of workers is a lack of inclusive leadership. Organizations today are dealing with some significant workplace issues — everything from the inability to attract top diverse talent, to working amid a hybrid work environment, to low employee engagement, to decreased trust, to high turnover.

REMEMBER

From Price Waterhouse's 2023 *Global CEO Survey* that is published each year (https://www.pwc.com/us/en/library/ceo-survey.html), to Bain & Company's recent report on *The Fabric of Belonging: How to Weave an Inclusive Culture* (https://www.bain.com/insights/the-fabric-of-belonging-how-to-weave-an-inclusive-culture/), to numerous research studies from the Society for Human Resource Management (www.shrm.org), there are common workplace and people issues that all organizations are dealing with and the top two solutions to most of them are the need for more inclusive leaders and the need to transform workplace culture to be more welcoming, respectful, and equitable. Other common inclusion issues, thankfully covered in this book, include:

>> Attracting and increasing the pipeline of diverse talent (see Chapter 12).

>> Assessing the employee experience (see Chapter 15).

- >> Dealing with flexible work and connecting with a remote and hybrid workforce (see Chapter 10).

- >> Tracking the rise of artificial intelligence (AI) and automation's impact on future skill gaps (see Chapters 2 and 20).

- >> Responding to social, economic, geopolitical and social justice issues at work (see Chapter 20).

- >> Embracing mental health, and ensuring emotional well-being (see Chapter 20).

- >> Acting as an ally, advocate, and sponsor (see Chapter 17).

- >> Fostering a psychologically safe workplace (see Chapter 11).

- >> Upskilling and reskilling for the future of work (see Chapters 2 and 20).

- >> Having tough and uncomfortable conversations (see Chapters 13 and 14).

TIP

These are not in any particular order but I encourage you to consider which of them are you dealing with as a leader, and which of them is your organization facing. Keep these at the top of mind and jot down tips and strategies as I address them.

Also recognize that if these issues are not dealt with, they will compromise your chances of attracting top talent and keeping what you currently have. Today's top talent has options about where and how they work and the type of leader that they want to work for. And they are revealing their expectations and experiences in talent management research studies published by global consulting firms, in the hundreds of staff surveys and focus groups my firm has conducted as well as on worker platforms such as Glassdoor.com and Google reviews, and in online chat rooms on social media.

TECHNICAL
STUFF

Unfortunately, feedback reveals that inclusive leaders seem to be elusive beasts in the workplace safari. According to research by Korn Ferry, only 5 percent of leaders worldwide demonstrate inclusive characteristics. According to Bain & Company's research, fewer than 30 percent of employees feel fully included — a finding that holds across industries, geographies, and demographic groups, including members of racial, gender, or sexual orientation majorities. In that same study it found that inclusive organizations have an easier time attracting talent across demographics: Approximately 65 percent of people across identity groups view an inclusive environment as "very important" when considering new roles.

Moreover, respondents in more inclusive organizations are much more likely to feel free to innovate and to feel comfortable challenging the status quo —and the gains in creative thinking are much higher as inclusion increases in an organization, compared with the gains from increasing diversity alone. This is a compelling business case for why we all need to focus on this topic right now, and you'll find out more in Chapter 3. I mentioned at the start of this chapter that we have a leadership and inclusion gap — these studies affirm that notion.

I get it. Becoming an inclusive leader isn't as easy as it sounds. Inclusive leadership is much more than having a title, giving a hug, and being nice. It requires a paradigm shift, an openness to different ways of doing things, leaning into some discomfort, and demonstrating courage to embrace the unfamiliar. Many leaders have neither the basic foundational knowledge about inclusive leadership, nor an idea of what workers expect in their leaders today.

Becoming an inclusive leader means leaning into some discomfort and demonstrating courage to embrace the unknown and the unfamiliar. It requires intentionality. It demands an openness to different ways of thinking and doing things. It also means adopting new skillsets and broadening your knowledge base. So while we all have a lot to learn, with commitment and dedication and using this book as your resource, you can get there.

LEADING LIKE AN EAGLE

I believe that we can learn a lot about inclusive leadership from eagles. I believe that there are important parallels between the features, attributes, and characteristics of eagles and the qualities of effective and inclusive leaders. Consider the following parallels:

- **Having great vision.** One of the most striking features of eagles is that they have exceptional vision. An eagle's eyesight is four to eight times stronger than that of an average human. They can focus on things more than three miles away and are rarely distracted, which is a demonstration of their visionary capabilities. Similarly, inclusive leaders are visionary leaders who communicate a compelling picture of the future that inspires their team and promotes commitment to their goals. Inclusive leaders will see the vision through to completion and will not lose focus even in times of change. I talk a lot more about this in Chapter 5.

- **Navigating stormy turbulence.** Eagles fly higher than all other birds due to their superior strength, and they love to fly during storms. They are known for their remarkable ability to not only endure but thrive in stormy weather. The inclination of eagles to soar through storms can be attributed to several factors. First, they use the winds gathered by a storm to fly even higher while most other birds are taking shelter and waiting for fairer skies. Second, their mastery of flying in storms is attributed to their strong wings and agile maneuvering capabilities. And third, the choice of eagles to fly in storms may also be linked to their predatory instincts. Storms can disorient prey and make hunting more accessible for eagles. Relative to inclusive leaders, they are not afraid of turbulence, uncertainty, or the storms of life because instead of battling them, they take them in stride and move forward. In the realm of inclusive leadership, storms or challenging situations represent diversity, adversity, and varying perspectives within a team or organization. Inclusive leaders harness the strength derived from diverse viewpoints, enabling their teams to rise above challenges with collective resilience. They are also able to navigate their team through these disruptive times and to seize opportunities that others might overlook. For more on these traits, check out Part 2.

- **Exhibiting fearlessness.** The eagle is renowned for its unconquerable spirit, demonstrating a steadfast determination to persevere, irrespective of the strength or size of its prey. Eagles are tremendously territorial. If another bird gets too close, the eagle fights ferociously. Even when faced with the most daunting challenges, they relentlessly protect their territory. Similarly, inclusive leaders must choose their battles, but when the fight matters, they can model themselves on an eagle's tenacity. For me, this is always important when it comes to values. My beliefs in inclusion and the inherent dignity of every human being on my team and among the clients I serve are unshakeable. See Chapter 14 on dealing with conflict and Chapter 5 for getting clear on your purpose, vision, and values.

- **Being attentive and nurturing.** Eagles have well-deserved reputations for ferocity but are in fact very attentive parents to their eaglets — in fact, they are among the gentlest birds in the animal kingdom when related to their young. When teaching an eaglet to fly, an eagle will first model the way, only encouraging their young to glide on the wind when they're ready. When ready for flight, the parent eagle hovers just below, ready to catch them if necessary. Inclusive leaders who face all their challenges with strength and audacity can learn a lot from eagles in this regard. They should pay attention to their staff, encourage them to grow, let them fly on their own, but never force them to do something that would compromise their health or safety. I cover more on this topic in Chapters 7 and 12.

There are several more attributes that I could include but I think you get the point and can understand why eagles have long been admired for their ability to develop and train, their exceptional vision, and their mastery of flight, and their caring nature. These abilities make them extraordinary leaders in the avian world and if we can learn and develop some of these same skills, we too can be extraordinary leaders in our organizations.

Summarizing Key Workforce Shifts

Workforce predictions for 2030 and beyond are quite informative. Major global consulting firms have conducted extensive research on the future of work and how it will impact workers and leaders. The research findings provide insight into how dramatically different things will be and what new skills, habits, and behaviors people need to adopt in order to remain relevant, competitive, and sustainable.

The workforce is becoming increasingly more diverse with an aging population, multiple generations in the workforce at the same time with the younger generation making up over half of the working population, and more women attending and graduating college yet nowhere near parity in pay or representation in senior leadership roles or heads of corporations. Racial diversity is growing in many nations. According to a recent survey conducted by Pew Research Center (https://www.pewresearch.org/global/2019/04/22/how-people-around-the-world-view-diversity-in-their-countries), approximately 69 percent of people surveyed across 27 nations said their respective nations have grown more diverse over the last 20 years. Close to half of survey respondents say that they favor a more racially diverse nation.

The workforce is also becoming increasingly more digital. Automation and artificial intelligence (AI) are replacing human tasks. This move changes the skills people need to succeed in the workplace. Price Waterhouse's *Workforce of the Future* report (https://www.pwc.com/gx/en/services/workforce/publications/workforce-of-the-future.html) indicates the following:

>> Thirty Seven percent of workers are concerned that automation puts their jobs at risk.

>> Seventy Four percent of workers are ready to learn new skills or retrain.

>> Sixty percent of workers think long-term employment won't be an option for the future.

>> Seventy Three percent of workers think technology can't replace the human brain.

A few more notable predictions about the future workforce of 2030 and beyond include:

>> Our world is rapidly growing older. According to the United Nations Department of Economic and Social Affairs, people aged 65 or older is projected to reach 1.5 billion by 2050.

>> Artificial intelligence may replace jobs humans once held and create jobs that didn't exist before.

>> Employers may recruit global, contract-based workers instead of employing full-time workers. Traditional offices and corporate headquarters may go by the wayside.

>> Traditional retirement will peter out as workers continue working as long they can.

>> Workers will demand more comprehensive benefits and "best place to work" environments, which may lead to job hopping.

Understanding Inclusive Terminology

Even as I write this book, things are changing so rapidly that it's time to update a few things that I wrote my previous first book, *Diversity, Equity, & Inclusion for Dummies* (John Wiley & Sons, Inc., 2022). I continue to be amazed at how much I still need to learn even after over 30 years, as new terminology, strategies, and resources are introduced.

REMEMBER

The important thing to remember is that it is a marathon and not a sprint. Everyone is on their journey; they just happen to be at different mile markers along the way. An important place to start on this journey is understanding the common terminology associated with inclusion so that you have a working knowledge and can at least hold a conversation about it. I only focus on key definitions as there are many and I could write another book on terminology alone!

Belonging

Belonging is a fundamental human need — the desire to feel a sense of security, safety, and acceptance as a member of certain groups. Belonging is what allows employees to feel like they can be their authentic selves without fear of punishment or without having to cover up and be someone they're not. Workers report that when they feel belonging, they can be more productive.

If this definition sounds a lot like the ones I introduce for diversity and inclusion, keep in mind one of the mantras that Diversity, Equity, and Inclusion (DEI) professionals use to distinguish the three:

Diversity is having a seat at the table; inclusion is having a voice; and belonging is having that voice be heard.

BIPOC

The term *BIPOC* gained a lot of traction and visibility over social media following national protests for social justice and equity. The term describes any group of people native to a specific region — people who lived in a given region before colonists or settlers arrived. It's used to acknowledge that not all people of color face equal levels of injustice. BIPOC stands for Black and Indigenous People of Color and is pronounced "by-poc." Here's a breakdown:

>> *Black* can refer to dark-skinned peoples of Africa, Oceania, and Australia or their descendants — without regard for the lightness or darkness of skin tone — who were enslaved by white people.

>> *Indigenous* refers to ethnic groups native to the Americas who were killed en masse by white people.

>> *People of color* is a term primarily used in the United States and Canada to describe any person who is not white.

Diversity

Simply put, *diversity* is the collection of unique attributes, traits, and characteristics that make up individuals. They include values, beliefs, experiences, backgrounds, preferences, religion, behaviors, race, gender, abilities, socioeconomic status, physical appearance, age, and so on. Some of these traits are visible, and many others are invisible.

TIP

For decades, I've been defining diversity as being comparable to an iceberg (see Figure 1-1). Scientists say that 90 percent of what makes up an iceberg is invisible or below the waterline, and only 10 percent is above it. Think about diversity. People can only see about 10 percent of visible traits that make you diverse. The rest is invisible (beneath the surface). Sometimes you can see the diversity, and sometimes you can't.

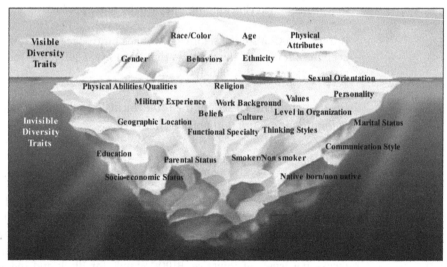

FIGURE 1-1:
The diversity iceberg.

Courtesy of Dr. Shirley Davis.

REMEMBER

You can have diversity and not have inclusion. Diversity just is. Diversity is the human aspect, and everyone is diverse. But inclusion is the environment and the atmosphere people experience and work in. And that's where the work continues. Recruiting and hiring top diverse talent isn't enough; you must create an inclusive work environment where those people feel valued, respected, and treated fairly and have equal opportunity to succeed. To discover more about what diverse talent needs, check out Chapter 2.

Think about DEI as a continuum with inclusion as the final phase toward sustainability and business outcomes. In the workplace, diversity without inclusion fails to attract and retain diverse talent and doesn't encourage diverse employees to bring their full selves to work, thereby failing to motivate their participation and do their best work.

In short, diversity is easier to measure because humans in all varieties merely exist; however, inclusion is a practice. Diversity can and has been legislated in various policies throughout various locations and organizations. Inclusion often results from a commitment to practicing this type of behavior.

Diversity also has different meanings within various cultural contexts. For example, the U.S. perspective of diversity suggests all the various ways you can see or describe people. But in some European countries, diversity leans more toward gender differences. In Middle Eastern countries, diversity often speaks to religious beliefs.

Equity and Equality

Although the terms *equity* and *equality* may sound similar, implementing one versus the other can lead to dramatically different outcomes for marginalized or underrepresented people. Here's how I define them. *Equality* is defined as each person or group of people being given the same resources or opportunities. On the other hand, *equity* recognizes that each person has different circumstances and allocates each the exact resources and opportunities they need to reach an equal outcome. You can find out more on how to apply an equity lens in Chapter 18.

Equity is the process, and equality is the outcome. In other words, equity is essential to achieving true equality. And a diverse organization isn't automatically an inclusive one, and an inclusive organization isn't automatically an equitable one.

Recognizing DEI as separate and complex, though related, concepts is an important step for leaders to achieve a diverse, equitable, and inclusive workplace culture. Leaders need to understand that diversifying a workforce doesn't automatically result in new hires feeling welcome, which suggests that inclusion should be a goal that organizations assign resources to. And their focus on equity needs to be based on the knowledge that not all employees or potential employees have access to the same resources and that they should structure strategies and resources accordingly.

Implicit bias

Bias is a tendency or inclination that results in judgment without question. Often, biases are unreasoned and based on inaccurate and incomplete information. Everyone has bias. It's part of the human makeup; you need bias to protect you from danger. Biologically, people are hard-wired to prefer people who look like them, sound like them, and share their interests. But when left unchecked, biases can have a negative impact in every interaction.

Implicit bias (also referred to as *unconscious bias*) is an unconscious opinion, positive or negative, that you have about a group or person. Implicit biases are the attitudes or stereotypes that are taught and developed early in life, and they strengthen over time, affecting your understanding, actions, and decisions without your knowing it.

With the vast amount of diversity that makes up the global workforce — including more women, people of color, LGBTQ people, veterans, introverts and extroverts, immigrants, people with different abilities/thinking styles/personalities, and people from five generations to name a few — the level of complexity and potential conflicts that can arise from unconscious bias is sure to increase. Leaders make decisions in the workplace every day, from sourcing to promotions to creating business strategy and beyond. Whether they recognize it or not, implicit bias enters into every one of these decisions. To find out more about implicit bias, as well as other types of biases and how you can deal with them, head to Chapter 6.

Inclusion

I describe *inclusion* as the degree to which an employee perceives that they're a valued member of the work group and encouraged to fully participate in the organization. At the base level, diversity efforts are concerned with representation of various groups; however, don't confuse that with creating an inclusive environment. To find out how inclusive you are, take the assessment provided in Chapter 4.

Intersectionality

Intersectionality refers to complex ways in which people hold many marginal group affiliations at the same time. These identities can combine, overlap, or intersect in a person or group, resulting in multiple, interdependent systems of discrimination or oppression (for example, descriptors of my identity include a woman of color, a mom, a movie buff, a corporate executive, a world traveler, a speaker, and a Human Resources professional). Thus, the intersectional experience of one person or group is greater than the sum of the individual forms of discrimination or disadvantage.

Microaggressions

The term *microaggression* describes when someone says something, does something, or makes a decision that makes you feel minimized, trivialized, invisible, or overlooked. We are all guilty of microaggressions and I provided advice in Chapter 6.

Ever heard these statements: "Wow, you speak English really well," or "You are very articulate," or "You must be really good at math or science" (said to someone of Asian descent)? While these statements are often intended as compliments, they are actually microaggressions that stem from our biases. Discover more about microaggressions in Chapter 6.

Neurodiversity

The concept of neurodiversity is newer in the inclusion space but not the medical and social science fields. *Neurodiversity* is a term that was introduced in 1998 by an autistic sociologist named Judy Singer. It comes from a number of brain studies that reveal that people who think, learn, and process information differently than others have brains that are wired that way. Advocates seek to set the record straight that people who are neurodiverse are not suffering from a disease or dysfunction. Rather, the idea is that people should expand their understanding of what's "normal" in terms of brain function — that many things that have been considered problems are actually just differences.

Phobias and -isms

WARNING

In the simplest terms, *-isms* are forms of oppression and discrimination.

Following are some of the most common -isms:

>> **Ableism:** Discrimination or prejudice against people with disabilities.

>> **Ageism:** Prejudice or discrimination on the grounds of a person's age.

>> **Antisemitism:** A certain perception of Jews, which may be expressed as hatred, hostility, or prejudice.

>> **Classism:** Prejudice against or in favor of people belonging to a particular social class.

>> **Heterosexism:** Discrimination or prejudice against non-heterosexual people based on the belief that heterosexuality is the only normal and natural expression of sexuality.

>> **Racism:** Prejudice, discrimination, or antagonism directed against a person or people on the basis of their membership in a particular racial or ethnic group, typically one that's underrepresented or marginalized.

>> **Sexism:** Prejudice, stereotyping, or discrimination — typically against women — on the basis of sex.

A *phobia* is an unreasonable or excessive fear or hatred of something or someone. While there are many phobias, several are specific to DEI. Examples include:

>> **Homophobia:** Dislike, fear, or hatred of or discomfort with people who are attracted to members of the same sex.

>> **Islamophobia:** Dislike or hatred against anyone practicing or perceived to be a practitioner of Islam because of their religious affiliation.

>> **Transphobia:** Dislike or discrimination against trans people or gender nonconforming people because of their gender identity.

>> **Xenophobia:** Dislike of people from other countries or anyone deemed "foreign" because of their immigrant or visitor status.

REMEMBER

Belief in these many -isms and phobias influence our biases in our everyday life, including the workplace. Recognizing and understanding these beliefs is an important step in our inclusion journey so that we become aware of what not to do and what to do more effectively.

Looking at Leadership Models and Frameworks

Leadership was once defined by traditional hierarchies and a command-and-control approach but has been undergoing a profound transformation in response to the dynamic and rapidly evolving nature of today's globalized and diverse landscape.

REMEMBER

Effective leadership today cannot be one size fits all. It must be flexible and situational. Getting the best performance out of others requires using different approaches and behaviors to meet the needs of the individual. In other words, it means using a variety of leadership styles — at the right time and in the right way — to inspire and empower others to achieve more.

Some of the best-known and most utilized models and frameworks on leadership are included in this section, plus a few others that have gained more traction in recent years. Chapter 4 goes into more detail about them but it's important to be aware of the many frameworks and models that leaders use — those that have been vetted, tried, and proven to produce better outcomes. That way you have a path to becoming a more inclusive leader by learning and benchmarking what has worked well for others.

TECHNICAL STUFF

Ken Blanchard, one of the most well-known authorities, speakers, and authors on leadership (having written more than 60 books on the topic), developed the *situational leadership* model. It is one of the oldest frameworks for leadership styles (he first described it in 1969) but is still relevant today. Some of the most common leadership styles laid out in his model include:

>> **Directing.** Directing is the basic level of leadership style used nearly for all new employees who need guidance and direction. With this style you tell people what they have to do, how to do it, why it needs to be done, and when it needs to be done.

>> **Coaching.** Coaching is used for those who demonstrate some competence but still need some guidance, consistent check-ins and feedback for improvement. This is the basis of creating strong commitment in the future.

>> **Supporting.** Supporting is used when followers are competent in the job but somewhat inconsistent in their performance and not as committed to the end goal. This style will guide them towards achieving sustained performance.

>> **Delegating.** Delegating is used for the follower who feels fully empowered and demonstrates strong skills and strong commitment. They are able to work and progress on their own. The job of the leader here is to monitor progress and still be part of some decision.

TECHNICAL STUFF

Kurt Lewin, a German–American psychologist made significant contributions to the understanding of group dynamics and leadership. His leadership model (1939) is known for its emphasis on democratic and participative leadership styles. Another model called *transformational leadership* was popularized by leadership expert James MacGregor Burns (1978). It focuses on setting an uplifting tone at the top and helping team members find meaning in their work. This can be an effective strategy for business leaders seeking to motivate their teams towards reaching a common vision. Leaders who take this approach must keep their ego under control while encouraging followers to become more self-reliant. Also, they seek feedback from followers before making decisions based on what information is received. In 1947, German sociologist Max Weber established the idea of different leadership styles and described what would eventually become known as *transactional leadership theory*. Bernard Bass (1985) extended the work of Burns by further developing a *full range leadership model* which classified leadership styles into three types: transformational leadership; transactional leadership; and laissez-faire leadership. *Servant leadership* (or *selfless leadership*), popularized by Robert K. Greenleaf (1970), is an approach to management in which leaders prioritize the needs and relationships of their team members before themselves. This is done in an attempt to increase employee engagement and build trust, which in turn increases performance and productivity.

Another and newer model that I use for consulting and training global leaders was developed by Deloitte. It outlines six signature traits of an inclusive leader which I affectionately call the Six Cs:

>> Commitment

>> Courage

>> Cognizance of Bias

>> Curiosity

>> Cultural Intelligence

>> Collaborative

These six traits represent a new way of thinking, leading, and working inside of organizations, and across differences. It requires intention, education, and accountability. Find out more, and assess yourself, in Chapter 2.

A few newer leadership models are also gaining traction:

>> *Adaptive leadership* involves the ability to respond effectively to change and uncertainty. Leaders who practice adaptive leadership are flexible, open to new ideas, and adept at guiding their teams through evolving circumstances. The past decade has seen an acceleration of technological advancements, global crises, and societal shifts, making adaptive leadership increasingly vital as leaders navigate the unpredictable landscape. This involves embracing agility and resilience to steer their organizations through rapid transformations.

>> *Authentic leadership* is characterized by leaders being true to themselves, transparent, and genuine in their interactions. Authentic leaders build trust through honesty and consistency, creating an environment where team members feel comfortable expressing their opinions. More information can be found in Chapter 7.

>> *Inspirational leadership* involves motivating and influencing others through a compelling vision or purpose. Inspirational leaders inspire their teams to

achieve beyond expectations, fostering a shared sense of purpose and commitment.

>> *Digital leadership* involves the effective use of technology to drive innovation, collaboration, and organizational success. Digital leaders are proficient in leveraging digital tools and data to make informed decisions and adapt to the fast-paced, technology-driven business landscape. Learn more about leading in a digital age in Chapters 2 and 20.

REMEMBER

Leadership is an ever-evolving skill, so in order to succeed you must be adaptable and open to learning new styles and approaches for bringing out the best performance in others.

TIP

MAKING SURE YOU A.C.T.

As you read this book, I encourage you to Assess, Commit, and Take Ownership and Action, or A.C.T. Try this after completing each chapter:

- Assess your effectiveness on the skills that workers say they want, on your readiness to respond to the demographic shifts, on your ability to work effectively across differences and to foster a workplace culture of inclusion, belonging and high performance. Consider where you have the biggest knowledge gaps, blind spots (biases), and areas that are your strengths.

- Commit to a continuous learning process by taking on board the tips discussed in this book. Solicit input from your colleagues, direct reports, and trusted advisors on your growth and acquisition of new skills, competencies, attitudes, and behaviors related to inclusion. Be open to this feedback and commit to making the necessary adjustments.

- Take ownership and take action. Check regularly to see how you have progressed and get a partner to hold you accountable. Be intentional about asking questions to seek understanding. Be intentional about becoming the best inclusive leader that you can be.

Remember, becoming an inclusive leader takes time, practice, and focus but when you A.C.T., you are taking the necessary steps to increase your effectiveness in business and in your career; you are positioned to help your team members reach peak performance; and you are contributing to your organization's success.

IN THIS CHAPTER

» Digging into the demographics of the future workforce

» Knowing what the changing workforce expects

» Sharpening your competencies and traits as an inclusive leader

» Confronting leadership challenges in a diverse workforce

» Reaping the benefits of employing top future talent

Chapter **2**

Revealing What the New Generation of Talent Needs at Work

For business leaders worldwide, understanding the shifting dynamics of the workforce is more important than ever. As the new generation of talent brings a unique set of expectations, those who adapt and embrace these changes are poised for greater success. To navigate the new workplace, leaders must deeply understand these demographic changes, what top talent expects, and the challenges and benefits of leading diverse teams. Although leading a multi-cultural, multi-generational workforce can be challenging, it can also provide immense rewards. This type of workplace brings a wealth of perspectives, creativity, and innovation, fostering a dynamic environment that can drive long-term growth and a brighter future.

In this chapter I detail the most significant workforce demographics that will disrupt and redefine the role of leaders. I outline what the new generation of talent seeks in their employment decisions and I identify the issues as well as the opportunities that leaders should be prepared to respond to with the new workforce.

Understanding the Workforce Demographics of the Future

Demographic trends in the workforce are noticeably shifting, which is influencing how companies conduct their operations. These continuing shifts will also have a profound impact on how businesses recruit and operate in the years ahead.

TECHNICAL STUFF

With that said, it is important to understand what the future workforce looks like in order to attract top talent and to gain a competitive advantage. In my book *Diversity, Equity, & Inclusion For Dummies* (John Wiley & Sons, Inc., 2022), I provide a comprehensive outlook of the myriad demographic trends and predictions up to 2030 and beyond that will redefine the workplace. It is worth documenting some of that research in this chapter also. Numerous studies have been published by global consulting firms and media outlets conducting extensive research on the future of work and how it will impact workers and leaders. The research findings provide insight into how dramatically different things will be and what new skills, habits, and behaviors people need to adopt in order to remain relevant, competitive, and sustainable.

REMEMBER

A few notable predictions include the following:

>> **According to the United Nations** (https://www.un.org/en/global-issues/ageing), **the population in nearly every country is growing older.** They state that by 2050, one in six people in the world will be over age 65 (16 percent), up from one in 11 in 2019 (9 percent). As a result, future businesses and offices will consist of older employees who work further into retirement ages.

>> **According to research published by the *New York Times*, 57 percent of Americans in their early 60s were still working prior to the COVID-19 pandemic.** This is in comparison to 46 percent of that age group two decades earlier. This decision to work longer is due to a number of factors. For one, life expectancy and health care costs are increasing. Another big influence is economic uncertainty and personal financial situations, such as a lack of necessary savings and investments, that affect the ability to retire. Making up around 25 percent of the workforce, this older generation values workplace visibility over remote work, they are often self-sufficient, and bring a level of competitiveness. They are also motivated by teamwork and company loyalty.

» **Racial minorities are the primary demographic engine of future growth in the United States, countering an aging, and soon-to-be declining white population.** The 2020 U.S. census data projected that the nation will become "minority white" in 2045. During that year, whites will comprise 49.7 percent of the population in contrast to 24.6 percent for Hispanics, 13.1 percent for blacks, 7.9 percent for Asians, and 3.8 percent for multiracial populations. Among the minority populations, the greatest growth is projected for multiracial populations, Asian populations, and Hispanic populations with 2018–2060 growth rates of 176, 93, and 86 percent, respectively. The projected growth rate for blacks is 34 percent. The new U.S. census projections also indicate that for under 18s (the post-millennial population), minorities outnumber whites as of 2020 (https://www.brookings.edu/articles/the-us-will-become-minority-white-in-2045-census-projects).

» **Racial diversity is growing in many nations.** According to a recent survey conducted by Pew Research Center (https://www.pewresearch.org/global/2019/04/22/how-people-around-the-world-view-diversity-in-their-countries/), approximately 69 percent of people surveyed across 27 nations said their respective nations have grown more diverse over the last 20 years. Close to half of survey respondents say that they favor a more racially diverse nation. Even though racial diversity is still growing in some nations, other nations (such as Trinidad and Tobago) already have a very diverse population.

» **Gender balance and pay gaps will improve, but not close.** In the coming decades, more women will hold leadership positions and the pay gap between male and female employees will improve, but not close. According to the World Economic Forum's *Global Gender Gap Report* (https://www.weforum.org/publications/global-gender-gap-report-2023/), the gap is 68.6 percent closed in 2023. However, the report states it will take 131 years to reach full parity if the current rate of progress continues.

» **Racial and ethnic board diversity will keep accelerating.** As the most diverse generations make up the majority of the workforce, one result will be a more inclusive board, meaning more racial representation at executive and leadership levels. Although it is unacceptably low today, younger generations will accelerate the pace. Between the data showing more diverse boards correlate to business success, the personal values of these generations, and private and public sector policy, these inclusive businesses will reap the rewards in coming decades.

» **Hybrid, more flexible work arrangements will remain in demand.** Although the future of work-from-home and hybrid work is still being redefined, flexible arrangements will be an expected norm. Businesses that embrace and effectively manage it, while prioritizing the wellbeing of their employees, will attract and retain better talent. Leaders will continue to evolve their managerial skills and policies to maximize productivity, even with workers at home on certain days of the week.

>> **Artificial intelligence, virtual reality, and smart technology will change office spaces and work functions.** With technology moving so rapidly, future office spaces will inevitably look different than today. Virtual reality (VR), artificial intelligence (AI), virtual assistants, and other smart technologies will continue to change how workers operate. VR will transform the way meetings are held, teams will connect in virtual spaces, while training, managing remote workers, and other aspects of operations will become more efficient.

>> **As AI rapidly advances and disrupts routine tasks, leaders will have more time to concentrate on strategic initiatives and improving productivity.** This technology will become more of an assistant, as it helps automate and speed up tasks. It will be the driving force behind marketing, operations, sales, coding, legal, distribution, and administrative work.

>> **There is also a likelihood that unforeseen events, societal changes, and economic conditions will also influence the next few decades of work.** Regardless, leaders must remain adaptable and responsive to handle whatever challenges come their way.

TIP

As the preceding bullet list shows, the global economy is experiencing dramatic transformation, altering workplace environments and practices worldwide. These types of changes are expected to continue over the next few decades as well. The question is "To what extent are you ready (to a great extent, to some extent, not ready at all), and to what extent is your organization ready?" Take a few moments and jot down the answer to these two questions and identify why you rated yourself as you did. Also, consider what steps you and your organization need to take to be more prepared.

So what do these dramatic demographic shift mean for leaders and organizations? Here are a few examples. Reflect on which of these you listed in your answer:

>> **Leaders must adapt to new ways of thinking, behaving, recruiting, developing, coaching, and rewarding their diverse workers.** For example, as the populations of many countries age, leaders will need to adjust their recruitment strategies and management approaches to accommodate an older workforce. This older generation has different life experiences and values than the younger workers. Additionally, when new laws and rulings are enacted by a country's highest court, leaders will need to adjust their practices and behaviors to ensure compliance. A recent example occurred in the United States when in 2023 the Supreme Court ruled that universities could no longer use race as one of the factors for student admissions and the impact it might have on the entering workforce. As a result, universities need to be

more diligent with their recruiting efforts. The Supreme Court's ruling spilled into the corporate sector and the political arena where certain legislators used this ruling as a basis to require corporations to do the same.

>> **Leaders must be able to attract younger talent by understanding their values and needs.** As Gen Z continues entering the workforce, they will soon surpass millennials as the largest generation working. As such, this group carries a different perspective on work, has very different values from the older generation of workers, and is pickier when it comes to who they work for. They are focused on diversity and sustainability, corporate culture, the meaning of their work, and balancing their job with their personal life. Because of this, recruiting and retention strategies may need ongoing adjustments.

>> **Businesses need to cater to flexible work and hybrid working demands.** The seismic shifts that the global pandemic brought upon the workplace will be felt for decades to come. With the exponential growth of remote and hybrid workers, many businesses have had to completely reimagine their offices and policies. Flexible work demands will continue to be a key driver of worker retention and engagement. In fact, a growing number are only interested in positions and companies that offer remote or flexible work arrangements. As a result, leaders need to balance these expectations with managing remote teams to attract and retain talent.

Addressing the Needs of the Changing Workforce

In addition to the examples in the previous section, a myriad of other ramifications exists that shifting workforce demographics are bringing. It is reshaping the way businesses operate and leaders manage. Adapting to these changes is critical for organizations to remain competitive, innovative, and inclusive in the evolving world of work.

TIP

The following checklist contains common practices that help you prepare for and meet the needs of the changing workforce:

>> **Assess your current internal workforce**

- Review the age distribution, education levels, and diversity of your current employees. Chapter 15 provides more details.

- Identify potential skill gaps or areas where demographic shifts may impact your workforce.

>> Upgrade recruitment strategies

- Update your recruitment strategies to source and attract a diverse range of candidates.

- Consider partnering with educational institutions or offering training programs to bridge skill gaps.

- Expand your reach beyond the traditional recruiting methods by establishing strategic alliances with organizations and community groups that cater to minority/underrepresented professionals.

>> Evaluate flexible work arrangements and offer multiple options

- Assess the effectiveness and utilization of your flexible work arrangements, including remote-work options, return-to-office policies, and inclusion activities for remote workers.

- Accommodate employees with family and caregiving responsibilities with flexible schedules.

- Provide flexible hours and shorter workweeks. Top talent prefers the freedom to set their own schedules and work hours. Working fewer days each week, such as opting for four-day work weeks with longer hours on those working days, is often an incentive to attract these candidates.

- Create an unlimited paid time off (PTO) policy regardless of age, gender, race, culture, or education level. A recent survey of over 2,000 workers found that 65 percent of respondents would like unlimited paid time off. So, consider creating an unlimited PTO policy and other attractive policies to stand out.

- Maintain authentic communication. Effective and transparent communication is a trait often seen in successful companies. It also has a major impact on the recruitment process and retaining of employees. Communicating inclusively is detailed in Chapter 13.

- Offering flexible work options tends to be both controversial and challenging for many leaders. Too often they believe that visibility equals value. But I have found that belief to be a fallacy. Just because the leader sees the worker in the office doesn't mean that they are adding value. They can be in their seats but playing video games, streaming a movie on their smart device, or on social media most of the day. Conversely, someone who is not in the office where they can be seen, does not mean that they are not productive. Some may travel for their jobs, be at the client sites, or do their best work at their home office. So as leaders, it's important to focus on productivity, results, and solutions rather than managing by "butts in seats."

» Offer ongoing development and education

- Provide opportunities for ongoing education and upskilling to retain and attract top talent.

- Encourage employees to pursue higher-level certificates and degrees.

- Offer mentoring and sponsorship opportunities (can be formal or informal). Learn more in Chapter 17.

» Conduct succession planning

- Develop a robust succession plan for key roles, especially those that may have fewer potential replacements.

- Consider mentorship and leadership development programs to prepare future leaders.

- Be intentional about ensuring that underrepresented talent is considered and not overlooked.

» Stay informed about external factors

- Consider demographic predictions and trends that may impact your industry and region. Find out more in Chapter 1.

- Continuously monitor changes in workforce and marketplace composition and adjust your strategies when needed.

- Stay updated on social, economic, technological, legal, and geopolitical issues that will affect workplace strategies and policies.

» Promote Diversity, Equity, and Inclusion (DEI)

- Prioritize DEI initiatives to enhance your employer brand and the employee experience. Read Chapter 3 for more on this.

- Ensure that your workplace is welcoming and supportive of employees from all backgrounds.

- Require leaders to attend learning and education programs to enhance their knowledge and understanding of DEI. It can also minimize your legal exposure when you have leaders who know how to deal with DEI issues.

- Conduct audits and assessments to ensure that equity, belonging, and inclusion are achieved. Chapter 15 outlines how to assess the employee experience.

- Involve the entire staff in fostering this kind of culture.

» Seek expert guidance

- Consult with HR professionals or DEI experts to develop customized strategies.

- Collaborate with industry associations and organizations to stay informed about best practices.

>> Strive to be an accessible leader

- Encourage and be open to communicating in multiple ways with your team. It can be face-to-face group meetings, virtually, one-on-one, via email, text message, letter, or phone call.

- Maintain an open-door policy.

>> Focus on employee engagement

- Engage with your employees to understand their true motivation, values, and needs. This includes employee engagement and inclusion surveys, focus groups, listening sessions, town halls, suggestion boxes, and observations by people leaders. More on this in Chapter 15.

- Conduct *stay interviews* to uncover what the staff enjoys about working for you, for the company, with their peers, what makes them want to stay with the company, how they see their future at the company.

- Seek feedback on topics such as workplace flexibility, career development, leadership effectiveness, compensation, equity, and inclusivity initiatives (to name a few).

>> Monitor legal compliance

- Ensure that your HR policies and practices comply with changing labor laws and regulations.

- Consult with legal counsel if needed to navigate complex issues.

- Take employee complaints and feedback seriously and work to bring a win–win solution.

>> Measure progress

- Establish key performance indicators (KPIs) to track the effectiveness of your DEI initiatives.

- Create a feedback culture. Ensure that all departments and employees are receiving both positive and constructive feedback to improve morale and productivity. Chapter 12 covers coaching and giving feedback.

- Regularly review and adjust your approaches based on feedback and measured outcomes.

- Celebrate the successes of others, recognize stand-out performers, and hold everyone accountable when they miss the mark.

- Conduct annual employee engagement and inclusion surveys, focus groups, or listening sessions and regular all-staff meetings to allow for the staff to share their experiences, opinion, and suggestions.

Honing the Competencies and Key Traits of an Inclusive Leader

While many of the tips shared earlier in this chapter are broad in nature and mostly focused on organizational activities, I want to share some personal leadership competencies that should be developed and demonstrated by leaders at any level.

WARNING

In order to meet the needs of the changing global workforce, leaders must be able to embrace the differences that workers represent and demonstrate behaviors that are inclusive and that will foster an inclusive work environment. Unfortunately, I find that too many organizations suffer from underdeveloped and ineffective leaders who still don't understand diversity nor do they demonstrate the key traits of inclusive leadership.

TIP

One of the most practical and useful global models that I use was developed by Deloitte. It outlines six signature traits of inclusive leadership (https://www2.deloitte.com/us/en/insights/topics/talent/six-signature-traits-of-inclusive-leadership.html). I affectionately refer to them as the Six Cs. These six traits represent a powerful capability highly aligned with diversity. Embodiment of these key traits enables leaders to operate more effectively in leading teams, within diverse markets, and enables them to better connect with diverse customers, access a more diverse spectrum of ideas, and enable diverse individuals in the workforce to reach their full potential. You can read about them in the nearby sidebar.

One best practice for how some of my clients have used this framework to integrate it into their leadership development and responsibilities was to take one of these Six Cs each month and be intentional about demonstrating it. I provided a toolkit with resources and ideas and they took action. For example, they started with the first one — Commitment — and for the entire month they took action to show more commitment to DEI. They took some of our courses or attended DEI activities that were being hosted inside of their organizations or in their local communities. They included a DEI topic on their team meeting agenda to raise awareness and to invite team dialogue about it with some helpful guidelines that I provided. And they took various assessments to identify where their knowledge and skill gaps were and I provided insights and debriefs to explain what it meant in the workplace. At the end of the month or quarter, I would conduct one-hour check-ins and debrief sessions with the leadership team and discuss impact and next steps. This practice of being intentional about being more inclusive has proven to be a gamechanger in many of my clients' workplaces. More importantly, it had significant personal impact to the leaders in their everyday lives.

ASSESSING THE SIX CS

Reflect on your own level of effectiveness for each trait and give yourself a rating on a scale of 1 to 5 (5 being very effective, 1 being not effective at all).

The first trait is Commitment.

Highly inclusive leaders are committed to diversity and inclusion because these objectives align with their personal values. They know that by committing their time, energy, and support to investing in people, they engender inclusive workplaces. By demonstrating this level of commitment, they empower and inspire others to achieve their potential. Rating ____

The second trait is Courage.

Inclusive leaders challenge the status quo and aren't afraid to call out deeply held and ingrained beliefs, attitudes, and behaviors that foster homogeneity. They are willing to have the difficult conversations and lean into their discomfort. Rating ____

The third trait is Cognizance of Bias.

Inclusive leaders understand that personal and organizational biases narrow their field of vision and preclude them from making objective decisions. They exert considerable effort to identify their own biases and learn ways to prevent them from influencing talent decisions. They also seek to implement policies, processes, and structures to prevent organizational biases from stifling diversity and inclusion. Rating ____

The fourth trait is Curiosity.

Inclusive leaders have an open mindset and a hunger for other perspectives and new experiences to minimize their blind spots and improve their decision making. Additionally, their ability to engage in respectful questioning, actively listening to others, and synthesizing a range of ideas makes the people around them feel valued and respected, and a sense of belonging. Inclusive leaders also refrain from making quick judgments, knowing that snap decisions can stifle the flow of ideas on their teams and are frequently marked with bias. Rating ____

The fifth trait is Cultural Intelligence.

Inclusive leaders have an ability to function effectively in different cultural settings. They also recognize how their own culture impacts their personal worldview, as well as how cultural stereotypes can influence their expectations of others. They know when and how to adapt while maintaining their own cultural authenticity. Rating ___

The sixth trait is Collaborative.

Inclusive leaders understand that collaboration is the key to team performance and success. As a result, they create a safe space in which all individuals feel empowered to express their opinions freely with the group without judgment or retribution. They also realize that diversity of thought is critical to effective collaboration; thus, they pay close attention to team composition and team processes. Rating ___

Scoring

The highest score you can receive is 30 points, so if you fall between 25–30 points you are doing well in demonstrating inclusive leadership. If you fall between 20–24, you are above average; and if you rated below 20 points you have work to do in developing and demonstrating these skills. After rating yourself, consider what one or two traits you will focus on improving in the next 90–120 days.

Tackling the Challenges of Leading a More Diverse Workforce

Leading diverse talent and workplaces can be very rewarding. It is, however, both an opportunity and a challenge for leaders. While diversity brings a wealth of perspectives, it also presents unique issues that demand attention and planning.

Let's take a look at some of these challenges and hypothetical workplace scenarios that exemplify these challenges.

Unconscious bias

Unconscious bias refers to the subtle and unintentional attitudes, stereotypes, or prejudices that people hold toward others. These are usually based on characteristics such as race, gender, age, and ethnicity and can have an enormous impact on workplace behaviors and decisions.

Where do these biases come from? Its sources may include past experiences, stereotypes, and mental shortcuts. And unfortunately, these factors can negatively impact everything from hiring employees to designing DEI initiatives.

Workplace scenarios that illustrate unconscious bias include age bias (when managers assign higher-visibility projects to younger team members) and beauty bias (where leaders favor attractive candidates). Other examples of unconscious bias include anchor bias (depending too heavily on initial piece of information received), weight bias (having negative perceptions about people due to their weight), and distance or proximity bias (where the manager favors those who are in the office versus virtual or remote employees). The latter is especially critical in this hybrid work environment.

REMEMBER

Companies and leaders must address these biases head on. They can do so by investing in unconscious bias training, creating more welcoming workplaces, and encouraging their employees to seek out diverse sources of talent.

Communication barriers

These barriers spring up when team members do not receive important, accurate company news or updates in a timely fashion. This often leads to missed deadlines, time and resources wasted, mistrust, the rumor mill, and employee and customer churn.

REMEMBER

With today's technology, there are many channels for team communication in the workplace, such as Slack, Teams, and Google Chat. Each team member may prefer one over another and may not use certain channels regularly. This, plus a plethora of social media and other communication channels, could prevent them from receiving the right messages in a timely manner. Other barriers include language issues, such as miscommunication due to spelling, accents, cultural contexts, or confusing phrases.

Cultural differences impeding teamwork

WARNING

As when working across cultures, it's essential to be sensitive to differences between races, religions, and countries. What might seem appropriate or necessary in your culture (for instance a firm handshake or direct eye contact) could be perceived as offensive by another.

These types of cultural differences can have a negative effect on teamwork and collaboration. Being aware of these complexities is often a challenge for leaders, but you should address them accordingly and encourage open communication among team members about cultural differences.

REMEMBER

Studies show that diversity leads to greater creativity and innovation compared to less diverse groups. In short, those that can navigate these differences and use them to get the most out of one another will see greater success.

Retaining diverse talent

There is no denying that many businesses struggle to attract and retain diverse talent. For example, women and minorities remain underrepresented in leadership positions. As such, it is crucial for leaders to retain diverse talent and teams throughout all departments and the board. Discover more in Chapter 3.

TIP

To ensure that all team members feel welcome in your workplace culture, be sure that inclusion is at the core of everything your company stands for. Make it a core part of your values, communicate regularly about your goals, and be sure to execute your initiatives.

REMEMBER

As part of your commitment to developing employees, providing options for employees to do so is also key. This could involve offering lateral movement into other departments or individual education funds or mentoring and sponsorship programs as ways for your diverse talent to advance. Showing this support demonstrates to your diverse talent that they are valued when trying to advance themselves further in their careers.

Developing inclusive leaders from within

Developing leaders from within the organization is a strategic and organizational approach that focuses on cultivating and nurturing talent from existing staff. This method not only fosters a sense of loyalty and commitment but also ensures a seamless integration of leaders who are already familiar with the company's culture, values, and objectives. By identifying and investing in potential leaders among current employees, organizations can tailor leadership development programs to address specific needs and align with corporate goals. This approach promotes continuity, boosts morale, and enhances organizational stability, creating a dynamic environment where individuals are empowered to grow, lead, and contribute to the company's long-term success.

Empathetic leaders can create an atmosphere in their teams where members feel safe to openly express themselves, making the entire group feel valued, increasing collaboration, improving performance and increasing engagement levels. I cover this in Chapter 8.

REMEMBER

Inclusive leaders must recognize and seek to address their own biases, while helping team members do the same. Inclusive leaders are committed to building an inclusive workplace for long-term success; therefore don't shy away from changing or revising outdated rules or working toward more equitable processes.

Recognizing the Benefits that Top Talent of the Future Brings

Leading a diverse workforce, although challenging, can be very rewarding. In fact, research shows that companies get the most benefits when upper management and lower management are more diverse.

REMEMBER

Here are just a few of the benefits your business will see as diversity improves across leadership roles:

>> **Enhanced innovation and creativity.** Teams composed of diverse talent ensure your business reaps the benefits of unique perspectives and ideas that can boost creativity and innovation. Teams composed of diverse talent are more likely to provide solutions to business problems than groups with similar backgrounds or experience.

Encourage your team to look for candidates from underrepresented groups and connect them with institutions that offer assistance. Also include an equity statement in the job description to boost chances of attracting minority applicants.

Research suggests that inclusive companies are 1.7 times more likely to lead their respective markets, which makes sense given that business leaders with diverse workforces can better understand and react faster to customer needs and market changes.

>> **Improved decision making.** McKinsey & Co, a multinational strategy and management consulting firm, reported that more diverse teams make quicker, better decisions faster (https://www.mckinsey.com/featured-insights/diversity-and-inclusion/diversity-wins-how-inclusion-matters). This was evidenced by companies in the top quartile for gender and ethnic diversity being 21 percent more profitable than those in the bottom quartile.

Why is that? Diverse teams consider perspectives from many different angles and perspectives. When you have a homogenous team, on the other hand, innovative thinking is often a challenge. Diversity really encourages new ways of thinking, and in many cases that is beneficial to the bottom line.

>> **Helping attract top talent.** Inclusion initiatives can offer many advantages when it comes to recruiting top talent. By eliminating discrimination and bias within hiring teams and senior leadership, diversity ensures that promising candidates receive the attention and opportunities they deserve. Without it, their skills or experiences are often overlooked.

Reaching out to groups or associations specializing in recruiting women, LGBTQ people, people with disabilities, or those from socioeconomically disadvantaged backgrounds helps expand your candidate pool further. Be sure to write inclusive job descriptions that eliminate some of the bias inherent in how roles are typically described.

>> **Improved employee engagement and productivity.** Business leaders and executives committed to diversity and inclusion understand that a well-trained, talented workforce can be an asset in the marketplace. When employees feel part of a cohesive group, they are more likely to engage with their work and contribute toward company success.

In fact, diverse businesses often have greater financial performance and engagement. In turn, this engagement can increase employee retention and contribute to business success.

Studies have shown that employees who are satisfied with their organization's commitment to diversity and inclusion are twice as engaged and deliver 57 percent more effort than uncommitted ones.

The new generation of talent will continue playing a pivotal role in workforce dynamics. Their values, experiences, needs, and expectations will continue to have an impact on the way businesses and leaders manage, recruit, and develop.

By understanding how demographics are changing, what top talent expects, and the challenges and benefits of leading a diverse and inclusive group of individuals, you set yourself up for success. On the other hand, ignoring these shifts or sticking to the status quo can be perilous for many reasons.

TIP

Want to gauge your understanding of what top talent expects and assess if you are using best practices in attracting and retaining talent? Use the self-assessment test in Chapter 4 as a starting point to identify areas for improvement and take proactive steps to improve your leadership practices.

Chapter **3**

Making the Business Case for More Inclusive Leaders

Throughout many parts of the world, the practice of inclusive leadership has led to greater innovation and business success. From well-known *Fortune* 500 brands to mid- and small-sized businesses alike, the positive impacts this type of leadership provides is undeniable and measurable. As it continues to gain acceptance, inclusive leaders will continue to shape the workplace landscape for years to come.

REMEMBER

The business case for inclusive leadership is compelling for all industries and sectors. It is not a one-size-fits-all concept; it requires a nuanced and adaptive approach to address the unique challenges faced by diverse and minority team members. Those that prioritize diversity and inclusion in their leadership teams gain a competitive edge in innovation, decision making, talent attraction, customer understanding, and financial performance, to name just a few perks.

Embracing inclusive leadership is not just the right thing to do. It is also a strategic necessity for sustained success and growth.

This chapter examines the compelling business reasons for why developing more inclusive leaders is key to success.

Accessing a Larger Talent Pool

When businesses prioritize inclusivity, they send a clear message that individuals from all backgrounds are valued. This approach attracts a broader range of candidates — those from different ethnicities, genders, abilities, ages, beliefs, and experiences. In short, a broader and varied talent pool becomes available, and they bring a wealth of skills and talents that can contribute to innovation, adaptability, reaching a broader customer–client base, and overall success in a competitive market.

REMEMBER

To tap into this wealth of potential, leaders must take deliberate steps both within their organizations and throughout the recruitment process. Here are a few important steps that can be taken externally and internally:

>> **External steps**

- **Partner with diverse networks and organizations with a high concentration of underrepresented talent.** These can include industry associations, community organizations, colleges and universities, vocational schools, and local agencies/ministries. This allows leaders to tap into a broader pool of potential candidates and build relationships with them in ways that they would not have without this kind of outreach.

- **Create diverse recruitment panels.** Candidates from underrepresented groups seek employers that will welcome them and enable them to develop new skills and to succeed, and they want to see people that look like them. When sourcing and recruiting talent, ensure that the hiring process involves individuals from diverse backgrounds, as not only minimizes biases in decision making but also signals to candidates that the organization is committed to diversity at all levels.

- **Write inclusive job descriptions.** Craft job descriptions carefully, avoiding language that might be exclusive or unintentionally biased (see Chapter 13). Use inclusive language that focuses on skills and competencies rather than specific demographics and preferences. This will make the opportunity more appealing to a broader range of candidates.

- **Use targeted recruitment events.** Attend and host events specifically targeting diverse talent pools. This could include career fairs, networking events, workshops focused on topics of interest by underrepresented groups, sponsoring minority conferences, and offering internships. All of these can be done in-person and/or online. By actively participating in these events, leaders demonstrate a commitment to diversity and attract candidates who might not otherwise consider the organization.

- **Encourage diversity in employee referrals.** If your organization incentivizes employee referrals, be sure to remind employees about the organization's commitment to attracting talent from all backgrounds, experiences, cultures, ethnicities, ages, and so sorth, and encourage them to think broadly when referring friends and colleagues. Implementing incentive programs for successful referrals can motivate existing staff to actively contribute to building a more inclusive workforce.

If your organization is very homogeneous, and you don't have an existing employee referral program, it might be best to not implement one. Employee referral programs tend to bring you more of what you already have. Once your workforce mirrors your community and customer base in terms of diversity, that is a better time to incentivize employee referrals.

>> **Internal steps**

- **Promote an inclusive culture.** This involves establishing values, policies, and practices that foster belonging, access to opportunities, equity, and inclusion for all employees. Ongoing learning and education programs that are designed to facilitate open dialogue and skill building can also be implemented to raise awareness, set expectations about expected behaviors, and promote a more inclusive mindset among staff.

- **Consider leadership representation.** Having diverse leaders in key positions is essential. When employees see leaders who share their backgrounds, cultures, gender, age, and experiences, they are more likely to feel inspired, empowered, and represented. This representation not only strengthens the leadership team's ability to make well-informed decisions but also contributes to a positive workplace culture. Leaders should also actively mentor and sponsor individuals from underrepresented groups to ensure a more inclusive leadership pipeline.

- **Utilize Employee Resource Groups.** Establishing Employee Resource Groups (ERGs) within the organization provides a platform for employees to connect based on shared identities, or life experiences. These groups can offer support, networking opportunities, and a sense of community. In turn, ERGs can serve as valuable sources for attracting diverse talent. Common ERGs include women, people of color, LGBTQ, working parents, interfaith, veterans/military personnel, people with disabilities, mental health advocacy, young and emerging professionals, and community impact/volunteerism. Find out more about ERGs in Chapter 17.

- **Introduce flexible work policies.** Recognizing and accommodating diverse needs, such as flexible work schedules, remote work options, and inclusive parental leave policies, can attract a broader range of talent. This demonstrates a commitment to the fact that all workers have unique needs and work differently, and acknowledges the diverse responsibilities individuals may have outside of work.

- **Be transparent in communication.** Open, honest, and transparent communication about the organization's commitment to diversity and inclusion is crucial. This can be communicated through internal channels, social media, and during recruitment processes, creating a positive image that appeals to a wider audience.

TIP

Reflect on the steps that you are currently taking to access a larger talent pool, particularly those in underrepresented and minority populations. List one or two areas where you can improve your efforts and include these in your recruitment strategy (see Chapter 10 for more about sourcing diverse talent).

Enhancing Financial Performance and Company Reputation

Numerous studies have demonstrated a positive correlation between diversity in leadership and financial performance. As a *Harvard Business Review* article called "Getting Serious About Diversity: Enough Already with the Business Case" (2020) states, "The case for establishing a truly diverse workforce, at all organizational levels, grows more compelling each year . . . The financial impact — as proven by multiple studies — makes this a no-brainer."

TECHNICAL
STUFF

The *Women in the Workplace 2023* study by McKinsey & Company (https://www.mckinsey.com/featured-insights/diversity-and-inclusion/women-in-the-workplace) conducted comprehensive research over five years on Diversity, Equity, and Inclusion (DEI) spanning over 1,000 companies in 15 countries (Brazil, Mexico, the U.K., the U.S., Australia, France, Germany, India, Japan, Nigeria, Singapore, South Africa, Denmark, Norway, and Sweden). It analyzed five indicators of DEI practices (representation, leadership accountability, equity, openness, and belonging) and found that companies with gender diversity in executive leadership were 25 percent more likely to achieve above-average profits than companies who didn't have as much gender diversity in the *C-Suite* (high-level executives within a company).

In short, the greater the gender diversity representation within executive leadership, the greater potential to outperform financial goals. This financial advantage has been observed in companies such as TIAA, U.S. Bank, AbbVie, Hyatt Worldwide, and Eli Lilly, who are all among the top companies for diversity where inclusive leadership practices contribute to sustained growth and shareholder value. For more details on the research that demonstrates how DEI enhances financial performance within companies, check out my book, *Diversity, Equity, & Inclusion For Dummies* (John Wiley & Sons, Inc., 2022). The key takeaway is that companies with diverse leadership teams have shown that they outperform their peers financially.

A diverse and inclusive workplace culture can significantly enhance a company's reputation. This commitment resonates not only with employees but also with the broader global community, positively impacting reputation. Potential employees, customers, and business partners are more likely to be drawn to a business that is known for their DEI policies. In today's interconnected world, a company's commitment to inclusivity becomes a significant factor in shaping its image across the globe.

Boosting Employee Engagement, Productivity, and Retention

Inclusivity plays a major role in enhancing the employee experience. When emotional, social, and psychological needs are met and when workers feel connected, included, and valued, their performance, satisfaction, and retention rates increase. Moreover, when individuals perceive that their unique perspectives and backgrounds are acknowledged and respected, they are more likely to be actively engaged in their work, collaborate with colleagues, and contribute positively to the overall work environment.

Engaged and motivated employees also tend to invest more *discretionary effort* (meaning, they go above and beyond what is expected) and come up with more creative solutions that contribute to the efficiency and long-term sustainability of the company.

REMEMBER

As a woman and a person of color, I worked for companies where I experienced being overlooked and underdeveloped, as well as not receiving support from my own boss. Needless to say, I became disengaged, disenfranchised, and ultimately left the company for a better opportunity. Unfortunately, my story is the story many today. One of the most common reasons that workers report leaving their jobs is due to an ineffective leader or working in a toxic workplace culture (or both).

In fact, when my firm analyzes the data from the many organizational audits and staff surveys we conduct, we find that even higher numbers of those that leave their jobs are among the minority and underrepresented talent (10–15 percent higher on average). They report feeling undervalued, invisible, overlooked for development/advancement opportunities. Additionally, they report higher levels of pay disparities and eventually they leave. But for those who stay, they are disengaged, unproductive, and dissatisfied biding their time. And companies lose billions of dollars because they aren't maximizing the great talent that they recruited and hired.

In fact, employees who are not engaged or who are actively disengaged cost the world $8.8 trillion in lost productivity, according to Gallup's *State of the Global Workplace: 2023 Report* (https://www.gallup.com/workplace/349484/state-of-the-global-workplace.aspx). That's equal to 9 percent of global gross domestic product (GDP). In 2022, only 23 percent of the world's employees were engaged at work. This is an increase of two percentage points from 2021 and surpasses the prior high point of 22 percent recorded in 2019.

The internal steps listed under "Accessing a Larger Talent Pool" earlier this chapter also apply here. Leaders must establish core values, policies, and performance expectations that foster belonging, access to opportunities, equity, and inclusion for all employees. Having visible diversity among your leadership ranks allows them to see themselves and demonstrates your commitment to advancement and development for all staff. Establishing ERGs is a rich source of support, mentoring, and community that diverse talent finds essential for their success. Offering flexible work arrangements and open and transparent communications are also key drivers of retention and engagement.

Here are a few other simple solutions you can implement as daily practice to drive employee engagement, productivity, and retention. They are often underutilized by leaders and appear on wish lists and exit interviews from top talent:

>> **Create meaning and purpose.** Workers want to feel that the work that they do is tied to something significant and bigger than they are individually.

>> **Provide clear objectives and goals for achieving performance.** Ensure that they are aligned with your organization's core values and that you are living those values.

>> **Identify worker potential and help them to grow and develop new skills.** You can also ask them what their 1-, 2-, and 3-year goals are so that you can help them to achieve them.

>> **Recognize and appreciate good work.** Workers want to hear "thank you" more than leaders think and they like creative and fun ways of showing appreciation.

- >> **Give the "what" and "why" of tasks but leave the "how" to your staff.** They want autonomy and freedom to figure things out versus being micromanaged or prescribed that it has to be done a certain way.

- >> **Admit when you make mistakes and use them as teachable moments for the team.** Allow the team to do the same and to share their failures and how they course-corrected.

- >> **Treat each person as an individual and appreciate their uniqueness/ diversity.** No one wants to be overlooked or feel invisible to their leader.

- >> **Allow flexible work arrangements and be willing to provide reasonable accommodations as needed.** Where possible, allow people the flexibility to thrive. This could mean flexible work hours, remote work, or a hybrid work schedule.

REMEMBER

Work is not *where* you go, it's *what* you do. So find ways to make work work!

As you enhance the employee experience, the natural outcome is increased employee engagement. Leaders who prioritize inclusivity not only attract diverse talent but also retain that talent by creating a workplace where individuals feel respected, valued, and empowered. By implementing inclusive policies, celebrating diversity, providing ongoing learning opportunities, fostering inclusive leadership, offering flexible work arrangements, supporting ERGs, and ensuring regular feedback, leaders can cultivate an environment that encourages diverse talent to stay and thrive, ultimately contributing to the organization's overall success.

Driving Innovation and Creativity

Companies have come to understand that reaching and meeting the needs of a diverse customer and consumer base, with its large and important part of the total buying power, is critical to expanding market share, exceeding customers' expectations, and outpacing competitors. In addition, it promotes a culture of collaboration and open communication within teams. This collaborative atmosphere encourages cross-functional cooperation. When this takes place, leaders can leverage the collective intelligence of their workforce.

TECHNICAL
STUFF

Research consistently shows that diverse teams bring together useful perspectives, experiences, and thought processes. Deloitte postulates that diversity of thinking is a wellspring of creativity, enhancing innovation by about 20 percent (https://www2.deloitte.com/us/en/insights/deloitte-review/issue-22/diversity-and-inclusion-at-work-eight-powerful-truths.html). Additionally, the Conference

Board, a global, nonprofit think tank and business membership organization with more than 100 years of providing cutting-edge research (mostly available to members only), revealed in a recent study that inclusive cultures are four times more likely to be innovative (https://www.conference-board.org/topics/innovation-leadership/inclusion-innovation-diversity-business-growth). Formally leveraging inclusion initiatives to promote innovation also has clear bottom-line impact.

The most innovative organizations create an expectation that innovation is not the responsibility of a single function. Rather they view innovation as a priority for the whole company, supported by organizational structures, processes, and talent management. While technology companies are often touted for their innovation ability, innovation can be bred into any company's operating values. Companies such as Cerner, Procter & Gamble, 3M, Colgate, DuPont, Johnson & Johnson, U.S. Bank, JP Morgan Chase, Disney, Novo Nordisk, and Visa are known for promoting cross-functional collaboration as a source of innovation.

Here are some of the ways that companies have been recognized for driving innovation and creativity through their commitment to implementing inclusion and diversity initiatives:

>> **Salesforce:** Salesforce, consistently ranked among *Fortune*'s 100 Most Admired Companies, is renowned for its commitment to diversity and inclusion. The company has implemented various initiatives to foster inclusivity, such as the establishment of equal pay practices. Salesforce believes that a diverse and inclusive workforce fuels innovation by bringing together individuals with different perspectives and experiences. Inclusive leadership at Salesforce is also exemplified by the commitment to providing equal opportunities for career advancement. They actively support ERGs, ensuring that various voices are heard and valued. This inclusive approach has contributed to Salesforce's reputation as a hub for creativity and innovation in the highly competitive tech industry.

>> **Johnson & Johnson:** As a perennial member of DiversityInc's Top 50 list, Johnson & Johnson has embedded diversity and inclusion into its core values. They actively seek diverse talent, fostering a workplace where individuals feel empowered to contribute their unique perspectives. The impact of inclusive leadership at Johnson & Johnson is evident in the company's innovative approach to healthcare solutions. By embracing diversity in its workforce, the company is better equipped to address the diverse healthcare needs of a global population. This commitment has not only driven innovation in product development but has also enhanced decision-making processes by incorporating a broader range of insights.

>> **Microsoft:** Microsoft is also a regular on *Fortune*'s 100 Most Admired Companies list and is recognized for its efforts of creating an inclusive culture that values the diversity of thought. Microsoft actively invests in programs such as the *Diversity and Inclusion Report* and the Autism Hiring Program. Inclusive leadership at Microsoft has played a pivotal role in fostering a creative and innovative work environment. The company believes that a diverse team is essential for building products that cater to a global audience. By encouraging employees to bring their authentic selves to work, Microsoft has become a hub for creative problem solving, resulting in groundbreaking technological advancements.

>> **The Walt Disney Company:** The Walt Disney Company is renowned for creating magical experiences both on screen and within its organization and understands the power of diversity and inclusion in driving creativity and innovation in the entertainment industry. Inclusive leadership at Disney is evident in the company's commitment to diverse storytelling. By embracing narratives that reflect a variety of perspectives, Disney not only captures a broader audience but also encourages a culture of creativity and innovation among its employees. The emphasis on inclusivity has contributed to Disney's reputation as a great place to work, as recognized by the Great Place to Work Institute.

Growing Customer Loyalty and Expanding New Markets

A workplace culture that values diversity of thought, experiences, and backgrounds enhances customer loyalty and market relevance. For example, when product development teams bring together individuals with varied backgrounds, they are better equipped to anticipate and meet the diverse needs of a broader customer base. This not only enhances customer satisfaction but also positions the company as one that listens closely and responds to their customers' needs.

Inclusive leaders who are adept at navigating the complexities of diverse markets and who understand the nuances of different cultures, demographics, and societal norms allow companies to tailor their approach and offerings to meet the specific needs of each market. This cultural intelligence not only facilitates market expansion but also helps companies avoid pitfalls associated with cultural insensitivity.

Building on what I shared earlier in this chapter about Microsoft, who has driven innovation and creativity through their inclusion initiatives, it was also able to tailor its strategies to effectively navigate cultural differences. For instance, the company localized its products and marketing campaigns, ensuring that they resonate with the specific characteristics of diverse regions. As a result, the company's innovative products and services has created a positive brand image — one that has driven customer loyalty and facilitated market expansion. Another company that has successfully leveraged inclusive leadership for customer loyalty and market expansion is Unilever. Unilever's commitment to diversity and inclusion is embedded in its corporate culture. The company has strategically aligned its products with the values and preferences of diverse global markets, earning it widespread customer loyalty. By promoting inclusive leadership, Unilever has not only strengthened its brand but has also expanded its market presence, showcasing the tangible impact of inclusive practices on both customer relationships and global market reach.

REMEMBER

When marketing, sales, or promotional materials authentically represent a variety of backgrounds, cultures, and experiences, customers feel seen and valued. Done properly, it helps to really connect with and welcome a diverse audience.

Digging into Examples of Inclusive Leadership in Action

The following sections look at how some of my *Fortune* 50 and *Fortune* 10 business clients are leading by example, where their inclusive practices are seeing impactful results.

Biases and lack of visible diversity

According to Microsoft's 2023 *Diversity & Inclusion* report (https://www.microsoft.com/en-us/diversity/inside-microsoft/annual-report), the company made significant progress in diversifying its workforce, with an increase in the representation of women and underrepresented minorities. Their commitment to inclusion has not only created a positive work culture but has also been helped by innovations such as the Xbox Adaptive Controller, designed for gamers with limited mobility.

One of my global tech clients was facing criticism for the lack of diversity in its leadership team and on its board, with employees sharing that much of the problem occurred due to biased hiring, lack of a diversity in the interviewer pool, and showing favoritism After implementing some of my recommended best practices (all of which are included throughout this book), the leaders first acknowledged the issue and took proactive steps to minimize unconscious bias in the hiring and promotion processes. The steps that they took were to:

- » Implement blind recruitment practices where identifying information were removed from resumes during the initial screening.

- » Ensure that decisions were based solely on qualifications.

- » Educate those involved in the recruiting process on behavioral interviewing and how unconscious biases affect the selection process.

- » Integrate inclusive behaviors into their performance goals and their bonus payouts at the end of each year.

Another client, who is a global financial institution, lacked diversity in their leadership ranks, leading to feelings of isolation, lack of belonging, and lack of trust among minority team members. After implementing a 5-year strategic plan for DEI, the first actions that the leaders took was to identify high-potential individuals from underrepresented groups starting with their ERGs. They created mentorship programs and learning opportunities that prepared them for anticipated leadership roles that were identified through their succession planning process. Participants were educated on the specific skills and competencies that were needed for these roles and leaders were intentional about providing coaching and feedback in addition to their mentors. By being this intentional and focused on promoting diversity in leadership, they sent a strong message about the value placed on increasing representation and inclusion. Within two years, the client had increased its representation of women and people of color in leadership roles by 12 percent. These mainly came from within the organization.

Microaggressions and a hostile work environment

After conducting an employee inclusion and engagement survey for a healthcare organization, employees from minority backgrounds reported experiencing microaggressions (find out more about these in Chapter 6) in their day-to-day interactions from their supervisors and colleagues. They stated that it made them feel isolated, singled out, and fearful to report it to Human Resources (HR). As a result, we conducted cultural sensitivity, harassment, and awareness training. Employees were encouraged to share their experiences anonymously, and we openly revealed them. Leaders actively listened and validated the employee concerns and in small groups they brainstormed ways that all staff could contribute to a culture of trust, respect, and inclusion. To ensure ongoing support, the leaders established a confidential reporting system for incidents of microaggressions, demonstrating a commitment to addressing and rectifying such behavior promptly. Additionally, we developed a resource guide for every people-leader in the organization. This guide included skill building on having open conversations about microaggressions, taboo topics, and how to manage conflict.

THINKING THROUGH WORKPLACE SCENARIOS

Now it's your turn! Read the two real workplace scenarios in this sidebar and write down your response of what actions you would take to demonstrate inclusivity as a leader. Then compare them with my recommended response.

Scenario 1: Some of the workers on your team who are from various cultural backgrounds feel that their cultural holidays are not acknowledged nor celebrated within the organization. This makes them feel minimized and fosters a sense of exclusion.

My recommended response: Make a commitment to DEI and acknowledge that all cultural holidays are important and implement a cultural awareness calendar, highlighting important holidays and events from various backgrounds. Sponsor events or activities that allow team members to share and celebrate their cultural heritage. This not only fosters a sense of belonging but also educates the entire team about the richness of diverse cultures. Acknowledge the importance of fostering an inclusive workplace where every team member feels valued, respected, and celebrated. Stress that diversity is one of our greatest strengths, and it is crucial that our organizational culture reflects the richness of our team's various cultural backgrounds. If you don't currently have one, you can explore the possibility of establishing an ERG focused on cultural diversity. This group can serve as a platform for team members to collaborate, share experiences, and contribute ideas for promoting inclusivity. Find out more about ERGs in Chapter 17.

Scenario 2: A tech company realizes that its office spaces and digital tools are not adequately accessible, creating challenges for team members with disabilities.

My recommended response: Conduct a thorough accessibility audit of physical spaces and digital platforms, identifying areas for improvement. Accommodation such as adjustable desks, accessible restrooms, and screen reader-friendly software should be implemented to ensure that the workplace is inclusive for individuals with diverse abilities. Establish a feedback mechanism to continually assess and address accessibility needs. Initiate language-inclusive practices, such as providing meeting agendas in advance, encouraging written communication for complex topics, and implementing language training programs. Be sure to exercise and encourage patience and understanding, ensuring that team members feel comfortable expressing themselves in their preferred language.

IN THIS CHAPTER

» **Discovering your passion for being a great leader**

» **Taking an inventory of your unique leadership skills and talents**

» **Assessing your leadership style**

» **Recognizing your personal brand, reputation, and credibility**

» **Analyzing how inclusive you really are**

Chapter **4**

How Inclusive Are You? Assessing Your Effectiveness as a Leader

L eaders play an instrumental role in creating an inclusive and equitable workplace environment. Those who are most effective are aware of their strengths and they work to enhance them.

Inclusive leaders possess the unique abilities to recognize and highlight each team member's individual strengths. They provide psychological safety for employees to share their thoughts and ideas freely. In addition, inclusive leaders ensure underrepresented voices are heard and amplified. They encourage diverse thinking, have diverse boards, and lead on the handling of cultural issues.

However, not all leaders provide inclusive workplaces, and many are unsure of how effectively their inclusive practices are stacking up.

Understanding Why Assessing Yourself is Important

TIP

As part of your own personal development, honestly assessing this effectiveness as a leader is a key component to growing. One part of that assessment should include identifying your strengths and challenges when it comes to leading inclusively and valuing diversity. Since this is an ongoing journey that demands constant effort, having DEI (diversity, equity, and inclusion) objectives and key results (OKRs) or key performance indicators (KPIs) in place helps maintain focus and momentum. Using OKRs is an effective goal-setting and leadership tool for communicating what you want to accomplish and what milestones you'll need to meet in order to accomplish it.

Studies have repeatedly demonstrated the advantages of diversity and inclusion for business. But in order to reap its rewards, businesses require leaders with inclusivity skills. Becoming an inclusive leader takes dedication, courage, and an acute awareness of one's own biases, along with vulnerability and humility. Leaders should demonstrate this commitment by acting upon and verbalizing it clearly in actions or conversations. Additionally, they should create and foster an atmosphere in which all team members feel free to express their ideas and opinions without fear of reprisals from any team member. They should take into account each member's distinct thinking styles, tailoring communication approaches accordingly so as to gain as many insights possible from valuable perspectives. Inclusive leaders must identify their passion and abilities, and inventory their unique skills, talents, and styles of leadership. Top leaders build their personal brand and focus on having an impeccable reputation.

By following these and other practices, you can strengthen your personal leadership brand, continue to grow both personally and professionally, maintain a successful career, and lead teams to a more productive and rewarding future. This chapter guides you through what you need to know.

ASSESSING YOURSELF

Ready to see how you are doing?

Take my leadership self-assessment shown in this sidebar and rate yourself according to your answers and total points.

Please rate your response to each statement on a scale of 1 to 5, with 1 being "Strongly Disagree" and 5 being "Strongly Agree." Be honest in your self-assessment.

- I have a clear understanding of what top talent in my industry values and expects from their employers.

1	2	3	4	5
(Strongly Disagree)				(Strongly Agree)

- I regularly gather feedback from top talent within my organization to understand their needs and preferences.

1	2	3	4	5
(Strongly Disagree)				(Strongly Agree)

- My organization's compensation packages are competitive and attractive to top talent.

1	2	3	4	5
(Strongly Disagree)				(Strongly Agree)

- I actively promote a culture of diversity, equity, and inclusion within my organization

1	2	3	4	5
(Strongly Disagree)				(Strongly Agree)

- My organization offers professional development opportunities that align with the growth and learning needs of top talent.

1	2	3	4	5
(Strongly Disagree)				(Strongly Agree)

- My organization values work/life balance and provides flexibility to accommodate the needs of top talent.

1	2	3	4	5
(Strongly Disagree)				(Strongly Agree)

(continued)

(continued)

- I am committed to transparency and open communication within my organization regarding our values, mission, and environmental, social, and governance (ESG) initiatives.

1	2	3	4	5
(Strongly Disagree)				(Strongly Agree)

- My company actively supports ESG practices that align with top talent's values.

1	2	3	4	5
(Strongly Disagree)				(Strongly Agree)

- My company regularly assesses and updates our benefits and perks to meet the evolving needs and preferences of top talent.

1	2	3	4	5
(Strongly Disagree)				(Strongly Agree)

- I actively seek feedback from my HR and talent acquisition teams to ensure we are employing best practices in attracting and retaining top talent.

1	2	3	4	5
(Strongly Disagree)				(Strongly Agree)

Scoring

40–50: You are excelling in understanding and meeting the expectations of top talent.

30–39: You have a good grasp of what top talent expects, but there is room for improvement in some areas.

20–29: You have work to do in aligning your practices with the expectations of top talent.

10–19: Significant improvements are needed to attract and retain top talent effectively.

Hopefully this assessment helps you discover the degree to which you are meeting the needs of top talent. In most cases, there is room for improvement that can be addressed. Take a deeper look at each of your practices, determine which can use immediate improvement, and track your progress. Lastly, continue to assess and address how you approach leading the team while adopting best practices.

Identifying Your Passion and Ability to be an Inclusive Leader

In order to make a positive impact in your workplace, you must first take a deep look at your passion and ability to lead an inclusive group. In fact, this can prove to be one of the most important steps to take as a leader.

Why is passion so important as a leader? Here are just a few reasons:

>> When you are passionate about your leadership role, you are more likely to be motivated and driven to excel.

>> Passion can drive you to continually seek knowledge, develop new skills, and grow in your role.

>> Working in an area that aligns with your passion is rewarding.

>> Passion can make you more resilient in the face of obstacles and adversity.

>> Passionate leaders often bring fresh perspectives and innovative ideas to their roles.

But how do you go about identifying your abilities and determining that passion? Here are a few ideas:

>> Start with a bit of self-reflection. Examine your values, beliefs, and experiences. Reflect on your own journey and consider moments where you felt strongly about inclusivity or witnessed exclusion. Identify what aspects of inclusivity resonate with you personally.

>> Expand your knowledge about aspects of DEI, social justice, and cultural competence. This will equip you to advocate for inclusivity and manage it effectively. To read more about the fundamentals, terminology, and history of DEI check out my book *Diversity, Equity, & Inclusion For Dummies* book (John Wiley & Sons, Inc., 2022).

>> Open conversations with people from diverse backgrounds. Listening to their experiences and perspectives can deepen your understanding of the challenges they face and how you can contribute. By setting a positive example and embracing inclusivity in your daily life, you lead by example and positively influence others.

>> Get involved in organizations or initiatives that focus on inclusivity and diversity. Collaborating with like-minded individuals can help you discover your passion and leadership potential in this area. You can also seek out mentors and ask for guidance.

>> Create your own initiatives or projects related to inclusivity. This can include organizing workshops, awareness campaigns, or events that promote diversity.

>> Connect with like-minded individuals who share your passion for inclusivity. Building a network of allies can help you gain momentum and support for your leadership endeavors.

>> Measure the progress and impact of your efforts regularly. Gather data, seek feedback, and measure the outcomes of your inclusivity initiatives to refine your leadership approach. To learn more about measuring DEI, refer to Chapter 16.

>> Stay current on the latest trends and developments in the field of inclusivity and leadership. Continuous learning and adaptation are essential.

Inclusive leadership often starts with a personal commitment to making the world a more equitable and inclusive place. Your passion and dedication will inspire others to follow. By following these tips over time, you can have a significant impact on yourself and the workplace.

Assessing Your Unique Leadership Skills and Talents

Understanding your unique skills and talents as a leader is essential for adapting and growing. This process starts with introspection. Reflect on your professional experiences and personal journey. Consider moments where you excelled, received positive feedback, or felt particularly engaged. These instances often highlight your unique leadership qualities.

For example, you may recall a project where you demonstrated exceptional problem-solving skills, a presentation where your communication skills stood out, or a situation where your ability to motivate and inspire others shone through.

TIP

Gather feedback from colleagues, mentors, or team members. Ask for their insights on your leadership strengths. These external perspectives can provide valuable insights into what sets you apart as a leader. They might highlight your empathetic nature, your ability to bring out the best in others, or your strategic thinking.

Consider the various roles and responsibilities you've held throughout your career. What tasks did you excel at? Did you lead projects, teams, or initiatives? Consider the skills and qualities that allowed you to thrive in those roles. Perhaps you always did well with delegation, conflict resolution, decision-making, or fostering collaboration.

Reflect on your personal values and passions. What causes or issues align with your core values? Leadership often stems from a strong connection between personal values and one's desire to make a difference. Your passion for a particular cause, whether it's sustainability, social justice, or innovation, can be a unique talent as a leader. Understanding these values and the causes you're passionate about helps you recognize the skills and qualities that drive your leadership in those areas.

Also, consider the feedback and recognition you've received in your leadership roles. Have you received awards, promotions, or acknowledgments for your contributions? These accolades can shed light on your standout leadership talents. They often indicate that others have recognized your exceptional skills in specific areas.

Identifying Your Leadership Style

It's important to be aware of the many different styles that leaders use. By understanding the traits and characteristics of each, you can better identify the style, or styles, that most fit your personality at work and refine accordingly. With that said, let's take a look at a few of those common leadership styles.

TIP

Learning more about these and other forms of leadership styles proves useful to any aspiring business leader who wishes to grow on a professional level.

Selfless leadership style

Selfless leadership is an approach to management in which leaders prioritize the needs and relationships of their team members before themselves. This is done in an attempt to increase employee engagement and build trust, which in turn increases performance and productivity.

Although some leadership styles rely on fear, anger, and micromanagement to move their teams forward, selfless leaders employ different methods. Instead of using fear, anger, and micromanagement for motivation purposes, selfless leaders use some common leadership traits. These include:

>> Listening

>> Serving others

>> Empathizing

>> Healing

>> Foresight

>> Stewardship

>> Commitment

REMEMBER

Selfless leadership can be challenging to implement as it requires changing how managers think about their work. Its implementation can slow the decision-making process due to its collaborative nature, but can be an effective style for some.

Transformational leadership style

Transformational leadership focuses on setting an uplifting tone at the top and helping team members find meaning in their work. It can be an effective strategy for business leaders seeking to motivate their teams towards reaching a common vision.

Leaders who take this approach must keep their ego under control while encouraging followers to become more self-reliant. Also, they seek feedback from followers before making decisions based on what information is received.

Transformational leadership differs from transactional leadership by encouraging employees to go beyond expectations and work toward an overall common goal, to improve motivation, and to boost productivity.

Transactional leadership style

Transactional leadership emphasizes procedures, rules, and a formal manager/subordinate hierarchy. It uses clear goals and instructions to motivate employees. Rewards can be offered as an incentive to work hard while punishments are used to ensure expected work gets completed on time.

Transactional leadership favors stability over innovation and can be particularly effective when applied to result-driven industries such as manufacturing or shipping companies, with set deadlines for reaching certain goals or customer demands.

WARNING

Business leaders should use transactional leadership styles strategically. Although they're effective in certain situations and with specific types of employees, these styles are less flexible than other approaches. As such, they shouldn't be relied upon too heavily as a solution in times of crisis or team formation. When used properly though, transactional leadership styles can help business leaders become better leaders while creating the ideal team dynamic for their organization.

"Laissez Faire" leadership style

Laissez faire means to "leave alone," and managers who employ this style allow their team members to manage their work without direct supervision. This form of leadership allows greater accountability among team members and can increase retention rates. In addition to that, this style helps create a more relaxing company culture.

REMEMBER

Laissez faire leadership usually works best with highly experienced teams that can set their own deadlines and oversee projects independently. However, it is not as suitable for lesser experienced groups or when tasks require greater oversight.

Democratic leadership style

Under a *democratic leadership* style, a business leader seeks input from all team members. This allows each one of them to feel valued as members of the company, contributing their decisions and working hard towards its success. Also, this approach encourages creativity and inclusivity, as various viewpoints help find unique solutions to problems.

Collaboration on ideas can enhance discussions in meetings. Brainstorm sessions and workplace communication often leads to more innovative problem solving, higher-quality projects, and strengthened team dynamics between management and employees.

REMEMBER

While implementing democratic leadership can be challenging, it is nonetheless an excellent choice for numerous reasons. A democratic leadership style teaches employees how to think through problems independently and make their own decisions, helping them grow as leaders themselves. Plus, this style fosters collaboration and respect between employees that enhances employee morale.

Providing coaching sessions to your leadership teams may be one way of further encouraging this form of management.

Situational leadership style

Situational leaders are aware of their team's needs, and adjust their style to get the most from all members. This type of approach to management is particularly effective in business as it caters specifically for each employee and their unique circumstances.

TECHNICAL STUFF

Situational leadership has proven itself highly effective in improving productivity levels. According to an article published by *Frontier Psychology* (https://www. frontiersin.org/articles/10.3389/fpsyg.2022.896539), this style has a positive effect of 50.9 percent on job satisfaction and employee performance.

As an example, new employees may benefit from being guided by an engaging leader who inspires confidence and facilitates understanding of work processes. Conversely, more experienced workers might only require support from leaders who allow them to make their own decisions with greater autonomy.

Situational leadership models provide business leaders with an effective method for becoming better leaders. This can help management identify suitable management styles for every person and situation.

Building Your Personal Brand and Reputation

Leadership refers to an individual's ability to influence and inspire others toward action that will produce desired outcomes. And part of that ability is tied directly to your own reputation and personal brand.

Personal brands are what people think about you based on how you act, what you accomplish, how you look, how you talk, or anything else that makes you who you are. Leaders must understand how their personal brand impacts them in their careers and how to build it to get ahead and to grow.

REMEMBER

An effective personal brand is vitally important for leaders, as it allows them to distinguish themselves and stand out in the workplace. A strong personal brand can also enhance performance under high-pressure situations.

Personal brands are formed through deliberate actions that showcase who a person is and their core beliefs. These actions could stem from professional experiences or personal motivations in life. Establishing a personal brand online also can increase visibility within an organization and increase chances of being considered for higher-level roles.

Why building a strong personal brand matters

Personal branding can be a powerful asset in leadership. It enables you to build stronger relationships with colleagues, deepen conversations, and project an authentic persona. It also allows you to strengthen networks, attract top talent, and ultimately meet career goals.

WARNING

Personal branding should not be seen as a means to "sell yourself," nor boast excessively about yourself. Instead, it should focus on highlighting what sets you apart from other professionals in your field and showcases your unique value proposition.

As an example, if you are known for being an innovative thinker who always finds solutions for complex problems, then making that one of your key personal brand attributes may help establish you as a thought leader and expert in your field. This can help with furthering career advancement and providing greater opportunities.

An effective personal brand can also help build trust between you and your audience, which is the cornerstone of leadership and sales. This is particularly relevant if you are an influential leader with large audiences at conferences or networking meetings.

Notably, all levels of an organization can benefit from having a powerful personal brand. Some of the world's most successful leaders — such as Elon Musk (Tesla, SpaceX, and SolarCity), Arianna Huffington (Thrive Global), and Gary Vaynerchuck (VaynerMedia) — have established an effective personal brand they use to expand their businesses and achieve success. These individuals did not magically become successful overnight with strong branding strategies in place. Rather they established them over time by following some basic tips that any entrepreneur or professional can put into action today (see later in this chapter).

Why your reputation as a leader matters

As a leader, you are expected to set the right strategic direction, execute efficiently, and foster an atmosphere that encourages others to work hard. This can be quite a challenge for any individual and requires them to be confident while also open to constructive feedback from those working under them.

REMEMBER

Personal branding helps people see your strengths, giving them confidence to follow you. It also highlights areas for improvement so you can concentrate on strengthening your leadership abilities. In order to successfully lead teams, motivating those under your leadership may also be essential. Your reputation is key to managing an entire team or just a few people successfully, whether or not it involves leadership positions. People will be less inclined to collaborate if they form negative opinions of your professional integrity or values. Negative associations could damage your career in ways you may never even anticipate.

WARNING

Poor professional reputations can also have serious repercussions for both individuals and companies alike. A bad name can drive away potential customers and investors, which in turn decreases business value significantly, leading to bankruptcies or other major business failures.

The best leaders have an outstanding professional track record that makes them valuable assets to any team. Their ability to inspire and motivate followers, helping achieve business goals is paramount. Furthermore, they know how to convey their vision convincingly. Supporting teams while aiding individual professional growth is something these leaders excel at as well.

Strengthening your personal leadership brand

Building a personal leadership brand involves taking an introspective approach. You must assess yourself honestly and consider all that you offer as a leader; this can be accomplished through self-evaluation and peer reviews.

TIP

By defining your leadership strengths, these can become tools for emphasizing unique value while increasing impact as leaders:

>> Identify your unique leadership traits, passions, and values (the ones that set you apart from other leaders). Then find ways to live them consistently and authentically at work.

>> Gain insight into how others perceive you as a leader. Ask for feedback from your manager, co-workers, and family members about your communication and decision-making styles as well as any strengths and weaknesses they see in you. Once you have this insight into how others see you, compare this against your desired leadership brand (discussed earlier in this chapter).

>> Identify your unique leadership traits, and then consider how best to apply them in your role. For instance, if one of your defining characteristics is technical proficiency, perhaps using that strength in a coaching capacity would benefit other team members.

>> Step back and assess what impact you want your leadership to have on others. This can be accomplished with a vision statement or goal that can be shared with your team; for instance, if one of your core leadership traits involves serving others, consider creating an employee engagement program or volunteer initiative to demonstrate this trait.

THE THREE PS OF PERSONAL BRANDING

Need an easier system to learn and implement important personal branding steps? The three Ps might be a useful tool for you.

If you want to create your own personal brand effectively, the first P you have to do is Prepare; the second P is all about Packaging; and the third P is Presentation. Let's take a deeper look at each.

Preparation

Preparation is about understanding and assessing your skills: What are your strengths? What are your weaknesses? What new opportunities do you bring and what threats do you need to address? This is what we coin as a SWOT (Strengths, Weaknesses, Opportunities, and Threats) analysis.

Preparation is about putting all the pieces together. This could include dusting off your resume, getting a coach or a mentor to help you close development gaps, going back to school, or taking a certificate course. Preparation may be learning new things or gaining new knowledge (which in itself is an important piece of preparation).

Packaging

The second P is packaging, and this really is an important component because you have to be sure about how you present yourself. You must be transparent and present yourself in a way that people really do see your value, your worth, and your skills. Packaging may come in the form of your attitude, how you dress, the aura that you portray when you enter a room, your body language, your energy level, and your smile. What first impressions do others have of you? Do you reflect professionalism, approachability, relatability, knowledge?

Packaging is about how you position yourself inside and outside of the organization, or the way you introduce yourself at different events. These are all a part of Packaging and they lead into the next component . . . Presentation.

Presentation

Presentation is what you say and what you do, and how you do it when you have the opportunity to present yourself.

Presentation is how you communicate, how you engage your audience/listeners, and how you move people (whether inspirational, motivational, or educational). Presentation is also the way you follow up and in the way you talk to others one on one. So how are you presenting yourself in the organization, with your team, and among your peers?

Diagnosing Your Level of Inclusiveness

REMEMBER

An inclusive leader possesses characteristics such as a growth mindset, objective decision making, and the ability to elicit diverse opinions from team members. These characteristics not only help attract talent from underrepresented groups but are also more capable of innovating and delivering results.

Inclusivity is an attribute that can be defined, assessed, coached, and developed as part of business leader's development. Start by finding an inclusive mentor whose behaviors and skills you admire. Closely watch how they lead, what practices they use on a daily basis, and how they educate themselves for continual growth.

TIP

Solicit feedback from team members or use an inclusion and engagement survey and leadership assessments such as the one included near the start of this chapter (see the sidebar, "Assessing Yourself"). These can give measurable metrics on how inclusive you are and what areas may need improvement. Be sure to analyze your leadership decisions, such as your hiring practices, promotions, and development. Take a close look at your communication with your team to see if you are using inclusive language and that you listen to all voices (check out Chapter 13 for more on this subject).

Other important diagnostic tools include collecting and analyzing data related to your team's diversity (covered in Chapter 16), using employee surveys to collect feedback (covered in Chapter 15), researching industry best practices, investing in diversity and inclusion training, and lastly staying informed on the latest developments.

2

Developing the Skills to Lead Yourself

Get clear on the most basic questions in life: your who, your why, and your what. Determine ways to become the best version of yourself so that you can bring out the best in others.

Explore the many ways that our biases show up and apply strategies for making less biased leadership decisions.

Distinguish between authenticity and transparency and discover why both have become key leadership competencies that must be developed.

Understand the major components of empathy and emotional intelligence and evaluate how well you demonstrate them both. Discover ways to harness these skills to build greater trust among your team members.

Recognize the importance of working across cultural differences and borders, and explore how to become a more culturally competent leader.

Chapter **5**

Getting Clear on Your Purpose, Vision, and Values

W ho am I? Why do I exist? What is my purpose? These are the most basic questions in life. But the problem with these questions is that far too many people are not clear on their "why" and as a result, they spend years in search of significance, meaning, and fulfillment.

How do I know? Because for almost 20 years, I've been asking audiences all over the world whom I keynote to, including those whom I coach, if they know their "why" in life. Ninety percent of them say no. Are you part of that 90 percent club?

REMEMBER

You might be wondering, what does this line of questioning have to do with leading today's workforce inclusively? Everything! Knowing your "why" is key to your success because it affects how you show up every day, how you make decisions, how you treat others, and how you respond to life's challenges.

In this chapter, I will get personal. That's because understanding your purpose extends beyond the workplace; it starts inside. I share my journey to finding my own "why" and provide tips for how you can identify yours using a list of reflection questions. I also walk you through the importance of being clear about your vision and living by your personal values.

Knowing the Importance of Your Purpose

Purpose is the driving force behind our actions, the reason we wake up each day with a sense of direction and meaning. It encompasses our goals, values, and aspirations, reflecting our innermost desires and intentions. Knowing one's purpose is akin to discovering a compass that guides us through life's intricate maze.

Knowing your purpose is about understanding what unique talents, experiences, skills, and perspectives you bring to the table and how it contributes to your team and the organization.

I believe that effective leadership starts with leading yourself — knowing your "why" and your purpose and by knowing this, it brings a degree of fulfillment, meaning, and resolve. Additionally, it guides life decisions, influences behavior, shapes goals, offers a sense of direction, and fuels passion.

TIP

This is the kind of leader people want to follow (find out more about this in Chapter 2). Nobody wants to follow a parked car. They want to work for leaders with vision, passion, self-confidence, and who are *self-actualized* (in other words, they who know who they are what they stand for), and who have the capacity and skill to develop them and take them to the next level.

REMEMBER

I remember when I didn't know my purpose or my value and I was leading others. It wasn't good. I was inconsistent, ineffective, and unfulfilled. But when I got clear on both, I showed up differently and my team felt it. It enhanced my self-esteem and confidence. It kept me focused on what was important and enabled me to make better decisions and foster a fun and collaborative environment. My employees felt more secure as a result, and I was able to build a high-performing team. And this is what the new generation of talent expects from their leader.

Research consistently shows that individuals who have a strong sense of purpose lead more fulfilling and happier lives. They tend to be more productive, are better problem solvers, and enjoy better health. When we understand why we do what we do, even mundane tasks take on greater meaning. Knowing your purpose also provides resilience in the face of adversity. When challenges arise, a clear sense of purpose can help us overcome obstacles and persevere. And it simplifies decision making. When you have to make choices, you can align them with your purpose and reduce ambiguity.

When you truly know your purpose and your value, it makes you a more authentic and impactful leader and this combination means that you can achieve anything. And that attitude transfers to others whom you lead and work with.

Asking the Right Questions to Uncover Your "Why"

As a certified leadership coach, I am often asked "How do I find my purpose if I'm not clear on it?" I believe that your purpose has been there all along — from your early childhood it was likely revealing itself. It follows you throughout your life and speaks in a still, small voice from within. The question is: "Do we listen and do we adhere to that voice?"

For me, my purpose spoke to me in times of reflection, goal setting, when dealing with challenges, when I failed, and every New Year's Eve when I would make new resolutions (I no longer set them; when I discovered my purpose, I created a life plan that I live by rather than making changes at the turn of every year). My purpose also showed up in the hobbies, interests, volunteer work, and the type of jobs that I was attracted to. You can read more about my personal story in the nearby sidebar, "How I Discovered My Purpose."

HOW I DISCOVERED MY PURPOSE

I knew at a young age that I was gifted at speaking, to be a leader, a teacher, and that I had a passion to help and to teach others. I remember playing with my three brothers where I was the teacher and they were my students in school. My mom told me that my kindergarten teacher saw that gift of speaking and asked her for permission for me to be a speaker at my kindergarten graduation ceremony. She recalled that when I did speak, I wasn't nervous and I enjoyed it.

Through a series of events during my adolescent years, I was constantly being put in front of groups to speak, mostly by teachers who recognized that I had that kind of a gift. Although I received good grades in school, on my progress reports I'd have mostly As and Bs, but under the section where it listed "opportunities for improvement," my

(continued)

(continued)

teachers would write, "Shirley is a great student, and very smart, but she needs to focus on being less talkative in class." This pattern of evaluations followed me throughout grade school and high school. At times, it made me more self-conscious about sharing my opinion — sometimes I found myself holding back ideas that I knew were good ones, because I didn't want the teachers to label me negatively and overlook all of my other great qualities. But I remember having a knack for connecting with people, was never short on words, and sought out leadership roles such as student government, debate club, and was captain of my sports teams.

Then in my career, I was attracted to certain roles that tapped into my love for interacting with people, interpersonal communications (written, verbal, and in-person), and leading projects and teams. Over the years as I became more serious about living my life with purpose, I found that asking and being able to answer specific questions enabled me to become very clear about it. They are listed later in this chapter.

Additionally, I reflected on the many life experiences and the lessons gleaned from them, as well as talking to my supervisors, attending leadership courses, earning my Ph.D. in Leadership and Organizational Behavior, and taking skills inventories.

My purpose is "to empower individuals and organizational leaders with the tools and strategies for finding meaning, fulfillment and success in their careers, workplaces, and personal lives." I accomplish this through training, coaching, consulting, writing books, and producing products and services. In fact, I published my memoir detailing my journey to reinvention in my first book, *Reinvent Yourself: Strategies for Achieving Success in Every Area of Your Life* (self-published in 2014, with a new edition in 2020). Not only did my 30+ years in corporate America prepare me, but so did my life experiences. And when I coach others and share the things that I've been through and survived, they can better relate to me and receive my advice.

TIP

Here's a list of those questions I asked myself that helped me to define and refine my purpose. As you review them, I encourage you to answer them for yourself if you are not clear about your own. If you are clear, use them to reaffirm your purpose. Ask yourself:

>> What am I most passionate about?

>> What activities or hobbies bring me the most joy and fulfillment?

>> What are my strengths and talents?

>> What did I enjoy doing as a child?

>> What would I do even if I didn't get paid for it?

>> What am I naturally good at?

>> What do others often compliment me on?

>> What are my values and principles?

>> What are the core values that I hold dear in life?

>> What causes or issues do I deeply care about?

>> What subjects or topics can I spend hours exploring without getting bored?

>> What impact do I want to make on the world?

>> What positive change or contribution do I want to see in the world?

>> What do I want people to say about me at my celebration of life (eulogy)?

>> Are there any significant life events or experiences that have had a profound impact on me?

>> What have I learned from my challenges and successes?

>> What roles and responsibilities resonate with me?

>> What roles do I naturally gravitate toward in my personal and professional life?

>> What responsibilities do I willingly take on without feeling burdened?

>> What inspires me in others?

>> Who are the people I look up to, and what qualities or actions do I admire in them?

>> What role models have influenced my values and aspirations?

>> What dreams have I put on pause?

>> What do I keep procrastinating on but wish I could get it done?

>> What would I achieve if I weren't so fearful?

>> What skills or competencies do I want to develop further?

>> To what extent am I fulfilled right now? What would make me feel more fulfilled?

>> If I had all the money I needed and knew that I wouldn't fail, what would I be doing in business and in my personal life?

REMEMBER

Finding your purpose will not happen overnight; it will evolve over time. Reflecting on these questions regularly, journaling, seeking feedback from trusted friends or mentors, and exploring new experiences can all contribute to a deeper understanding of your purpose. Be patient with yourself and allow the journey of self-discovery to unfold organically.

Getting Grounded on Your Personal Vision Statement

A *personal vision statement* is a concise declaration of your aspirations that reflects your desired future state. It acts as a North Star for directing your actions, establishing clear objectives, making strategic decisions, and setting priorities towards achieving a purposeful and fulfilling life.

A number of other benefits can be realized as a leader when you are grounded on your personal vision. By sharing it with your team, it serves as a source of inspiration and can ignite passion and commitment among team members. It aligns the goals and efforts of team members with your overarching vision and fosters greater synergy and collaboration within the team. Additionally, when team members understand their leader's personal vision it provides clarity for them to make more informed choices. Lastly, leaders with well-defined personal vision are often perceived as more credible and trustworthy by their teams.

TIP

Identifying and getting clear on your personal vision is a process that involves introspection and reflection. Here are some to consider when crafting yours:

>> **Self-reflection/assessment:** Take time to engage in deep self-reflection about your purpose. Write down your strengths, passions, and your goals. Identify the values that are important to you (which I discuss in the next section of this chapter). Write down what truly matters to you in both your personal and professional life.

>> **Dream big:** Don't limit yourself when crafting your vision. Imagine your ideal future without constraints, allowing your imagination to soar.

>> **Be specific:** Your vision should be clear and specific. Use concrete language to describe what you want to achieve.

>> **Align with values:** Ensure that your vision aligns with your core values and principles. This alignment provides a strong foundation for your journey.

>> **Think long term:** Focus on the long-term impact you want to make. What legacy do you want to leave behind?

>> **Seek feedback:** Reach out to your trusted mentors, advisors, and friends to refine and validate your personal vision. They often see things in you that you may not see and they can also act as *accountability partners* (a colleague who will agree to hold you to your word, who will follow up, ask you the tough questions, and help to keep you on track).

>> **Revise as needed:** Your personal vision may evolve over time, so be open to revising it to reflect your changing aspirations and circumstances.

EXAMPLES OF WELL-WRITTEN PERSONAL VISION STATEMENTS

Using the steps described in this chapter, here is my personal vision statement:

"To be a world-renowned and highly sought-after global thought leader and keynote speaker that delivers transformational value in the areas of organizational leadership, high performance, and personal reinvention."

After I refined and internalized my purpose, my vision statement complemented it by laying out what I wanted the future state to look like. It guided my actions and decisions.

Today, I have the pleasure of coaching leaders on crafting their own vision statements. Here is a list of some of those that leaders have created:

- "To lead with integrity, empathy, and innovation, shaping a future where sustainability and social responsibility are at the forefront of organizational success."

- "To create a world where every child has access to quality education, and no one is left behind, by championing educational equity and inclusivity."

- "To leave a legacy of kindness, compassion, and positive change by building strong, diverse communities that thrive together."

Now it's your turn! Walk through the process using the steps I've just outlined and begin to get clear on your personal vision statement.

REMEMBER

A personal vision statement is the cornerstone of effective leadership. It provides direction, and ignites inspiration and communication, among your team. Ultimately, personal vision is not just a leadership tool but a life philosophy that empowers individuals to lead with purpose and make a meaningful impact in their organizations.

Establishing and Living Your Personal Values

Personal values are the fundamental beliefs and principles that guide an individual's behavior, decisions, and actions. For leaders, having well-defined personal values is of utmost importance and leaders must walk the talk and live their values in such a way that their behaviors and values match.

Honesty, faith, commitment, excellence, peace, and authenticity are my core values. These drive my behaviors and my decisions and shape the way that I approach all of life's challenges.

Here are some other reasons I have found that matter to workers and to the workplace culture:

>> **Ethical leadership:** Personal values provide leaders with a framework for ethical decision making. When leaders align their actions with their values, they set a positive example for their team and organization, fostering a culture of integrity.

>> **Consistency and trust:** Leaders who consistently demonstrate their values build trust and credibility with their team members and stakeholders. Trust is a crucial element of effective leadership.

>> **Goal alignment:** The act of crafting personal values helps leaders see whether their individual goals are aligned with the goals of their organization. This alignment ensures that leaders are working toward objectives that resonate with their beliefs and passions. Conversely, it might reveal that a leader is not a good fit with their current organization.

>> **Decision making:** When leaders are clear about their values, they can make decisions more efficiently and confidently. Values serve as a filter through which leaders evaluate choices.

So what are your personal values? Can you clearly articulate them now? In *Diversity, Equity, & Inclusion For Dummies* (John Wiley & Sons, Inc., 2022) I list some common values to live by. I've included them here for your reference (see Figure 5-1). Spend a moment perusing this list and place a check by those that motivate you the most. If a value has little or no meaning to you, cross it out. For instance, if "humility" is a value that resonates for you, then "boldness" may have less value. Pare that list down to the five values that you believe should guide most of your decisions every day. They may be a mixture of values that are very meaningful to you and those that are essential to success in your role or industry right now. And don't hesitate to come back to this list when life changes — you become a parent, get a promotion, get married or divorced, and so on — to see whether your values have shifted somewhat.

REMEMBER

Aligning your goals with your values creates a roadmap for personal and professional growth. When your actions are congruent with your values, you are more likely to stay true to them. I believe that you have to be true to who you are, continually strive to become a better version of yourself, and put your very best forward when you commit to something.

☐ Abundance	☐ Daring	☐ Intelligence	☐ Preparedness
☐ Acceptance	☐ Decisiveness	☐ Intuition	☐ Proactivity
☐ Accountability	☐ Dedication	☐ Joy	☐ Professionalism
☐ Achievement	☐ Dependability	☐ Kindness	☐ Punctuality
☐ Advancement	☐ Diversity	☐ Knowledge	☐ Recognition
☐ Adventure	☐ Empathy	☐ Leadership	☐ Relationships
☐ Advocacy	☐ Encouragement	☐ Learning	☐ Reliability
☐ Ambition	☐ Enthusiasm	☐ Love	☐ Resilience
☐ Appreciation	☐ Ethics	☐ Loyalty	☐ Resourcefulness
☐ Attractiveness	☐ Excellence	☐ Making a Difference	☐ Respect
☐ Autonomy	☐ Fairness	☐ Mindfulness	☐ Responsibility
☐ Balance	☐ Family	☐ Motivation	☐ Security
☐ Being the Best	☐ Friendships	☐ Optimism	☐ Self-Control
☐ Boldness	☐ Flexibility	☐ Open-Mindedness	☐ Selflessness
☐ Brilliance	☐ Freedom	☐ Passion	☐ Simplicity
☐ Calm	☐ Fun	☐ Performance	☐ Stability
☐ Caring	☐ Generosity	☐ Personal Development	☐ Success
☐ Charity	☐ Grace	☐ Professionalism	☐ Teamwork
☐ Cheerfulness	☐ Gratitude	☐ Quality	☐ Thoughtfulness
☐ Cleverness	☐ Growth	☐ Recognition	☐ Traditionalism
☐ Community	☐ Happiness	☐ Risk Taking	☐ Trustworthiness
☐ Commitment	☐ Health	☐ Security	☐ Understanding
☐ Compassion	☐ Honesty	☐ Service	☐ Usefulness
☐ Cooperation	☐ Humility	☐ Spirituality	☐ Versatility
☐ Collaboration	☐ Humor	☐ Stability	☐ Vision
☐ Consistency	☐ Inclusiveness	☐ Peace	☐ Warmth
☐ Creativity	☐ Independence	☐ Perfection	☐ Wealth
☐ Credibility	☐ Innovation	☐ Popularity	☐ Well-Being
☐ Curiosity	☐ Inspiration	☐ Power	☐ Wisdom

FIGURE 5-1: What values motivate you the most?

In the pursuit of meaning and fulfillment, knowing your purpose and crafting a personal vision statement are essential steps. Understanding your purpose not only leads to personal satisfaction but also empowers you to make choices that align with your values and aspirations. Common personal values, such as integrity, empathy, resilience, gratitude, and continuous learning, provide a moral compass for navigating life's complexities. Staying true to these values requires mindfulness, a supportive community, goal alignment, and ongoing inspiration. As you embark on the quest to find your "why" and create a personal vision, remember the words of my mentor and friend, the renowned motivational speaker, Les Brown:

You have something special. You have greatness within you.

Embrace your purpose, define your vision, and let your greatness shine.

Chapter **6**

Minimizing Your Own Biases and Microaggressions

"Wow, you speak English really well."

"Tall black men make the best basketball players."

"You must be really good at math or science."

"Gen Y and Gen Z are so entitled."

"You don't act like the others who are [fill in the blank]."

Ever heard these statements, or ones like them?

While often intended as compliments, they are actually biases and microaggressions. Not only have I heard them said to me, but I too have been guilty of saying them to others. And all of us have likely been guilty of both of these at some point.

This chapter covers what are biases and microaggressions, and how they play out in the workplace in our everyday interactions and in our decision making as leaders. More importantly, I detail some specific ways that you can minimize (or interrupt) them.

Defining Unconscious Bias

Unconscious bias refers to your brain's ability to make decisions on your behalf without your permission. Oftentimes, bias happens so quickly that you're not even aware that a decision has been made. It's part of the human makeup and everyone has it. We need bias to protect us from danger.

TECHNICAL STUFF

Biologically, people are hard-wired to prefer people who look like them, sound like them, and share their interests. Biases are taught and developed early in life and they strengthen over time via life experiences, messages that are reinforced by the media, TV shows, in our schools and communities. Ultimately this shapes our worldview, informs how we treat others, and how we make decisions.

Consider the following example: In a team meeting, a manager is assigning new projects to team members. Despite having a diverse team with members of different backgrounds, skills, and experiences, the manager consistently chooses individuals who share similar characteristics as themself for high-profile assignments.

Here's another example: It's human nature to take the same route to and from work each day. Having done it for so long, you have actually trained your brain to take you to and from work/home without thought. As you're leaving home heading to the office, you are completely consumed with thoughts about the project meeting you are leading, the lunch appointment with a client, and the afternoon interview with a top candidate for a position on your team. By the time you complete your mental checklist of tasks for the day, you snap out of it and realize that you have arrived at the corner of the parking lot at work. You don't recall much of the drive, nor the drivers around you, nor the pedestrians that crossed your path. Ever experienced this? Scary, huh? This is how bias works. It happens below the level of conscious thought, which is why it's often referred to as *unconscious* or *implicit bias.* So how does this happen?

REMEMBER

Your brain has two thinking systems: two separate and distinct mechanisms for observing, interpreting, and acting on data. These two systems are often referred to as your Fast Brain and your Slow Brain. It's your *Fast Brain* that makes decisions on your behalf without your permission. In the two examples I shared, the manager was likely using their Fast Brain when they kept selecting people who were most like them versus using their Slow Brain to be more conscientious about how their decisions might affect other qualified team members who did not look like them. And when driving the same way to work and back home each day, we are training our brain to be on auto-pilot using our Fast Brain. Read more about how the two systems — System One and System Two — work in Table 6-1.

TABLE 6-1   **Fast Brain versus Slow Brain**

System One: Fast Brain	System Two: Slow Brain
Automatic thinking, below the level of consciousness	Deliberate, conscious thinking
Based primarily on emotion and memory	Based primarily on logical, analytical thought
Incredibly fast and efficient	Fast, but certainly slower than System One; requires more glucose and oxygen to function
Driven to keep you safe, healthy, and alive	Drives other core values (equity, respect, integrity)
Where bias originates	Where the ability to disrupt or mitigate bias is found

TECHNICAL STUFF

This concept of System One and System Two thinking was detailed in *Thinking, Fast & Slow* by Daniel Kahneman (Farrar, Straus, and Giroux, 2011) and I also delve into this in further detail in *Diversity, Equity, & Inclusion For Dummies* (John Wiley & Sons, Inc., 2022).

Our brains make hundreds of decisions like this every day. Some of them, like the examples shown earlier in this chapter, are designed to keep us safe. Others are based on reliable patterns and make life much more efficient, allowing our brains to concentrate on more important matters that need our attention.

WARNING

Sometimes, however, these decisions are based on *heuristics*, or mental shortcuts, and can range from benign to harmful or even dangerous. One such heuristic is *egocentrism*, or the tendency to rely too heavily on one's own perception. This might explain why a leader believes that everyone on their team shares their definitions of inclusion, belonging, work/life balance, or success, even if they've never asked the individual members of their team these important questions.

Figuring Out Microaggressions

Oftentimes, people are unaware of their own biases. After all, these are decisions that sometimes happen in less than a second, below the level of conscious thought. Many times, however, these same biases are very apparent to those around them, particularly if the perpetrator of a bias is a leader.

REMEMBER

One way that biases reveal themselves is through *microaggressions*. These are often experienced in day-to-day interactions by people of color, women, LGBTQ populations, older workers, people with disabilities, and others who are from underrepresented and/or marginalized groups. The name might suggest that microaggressions don't mean much — being *micro* — but while each behavior might be viewed as a small thing, the cumulative impact of many microaggressions over time can be very damaging.

This is especially true when the microaggression is being exhibited by a leader and targets one or more people under their leadership. When these behaviors are repeated, they can easily create a workplace that feels toxic, especially to those who belong to underrepresented and/or marginalized groups.

Here are some examples of common microaggressions in the workplace:

>> Constantly offering to help a person with a disability, even when they haven't asked for assistance.

>> Talking loud or very slow to someone who is blind.

>> Answering a phone call in the middle of a conversation.

>> "Oh my gosh, that's so gay."

>> Complimenting forceful white male leaders, while complaining about the same behaviors and assessing them as negative when demonstrated by women or people of color.

>> Pronouncing a person's name incorrectly, after being informed how to pronounce it.

>> Continuing to refer to someone as "she" or "her" when that person told you that their pronouns are "they" and "them."

>> "You speak very good English" (to a person of Asian descent).

>> "You are so articulate" (to an African American or person of African descent).

>> Clutching your handbag or backpack when a Black colleague steps into the elevator.

>> "Can I feel your hair?" (to a Black woman).

>> "I never would have known you were gay."

>> "Where are you from?" (to a person of a different race/ethnicity/color).

>> "Wow, you really get around in that thing" (to a person in a wheelchair).

>> Following someone around a store because of their color, saying nothing but watching their every move.

>> "Alright girls. . ." (said by a male supervisor).

>> "I can't be racist; I have Black friends."

>> Assuming a married man has a wife, or a married woman a husband.

>> "You're so brave" (to a person with a disability).

>> Assuming that a person who is Jewish must be a great business dealer or conversely, that they are shrewd and dishonest.

>> "Okay guys, let's get this meeting started" (to a room with both men and women).

>> "What was your name before?" (to a transgender person).

As you reviewed this list, did any of these points seem odd to you? Have you said or done some of these things before? How might you feel if you were the recipient of these words or behaviors? Now imagine that these phrases or actions are pervasive and frequently repeated; consider what the impact might be. If you're still challenged, this points to the thing that makes both bias and microaggressions difficult to manage — it's hard to fix a problem that you can't see.

Understanding Intent versus Impact

The reason why so many people who exhibit microaggressions fail to recognize them is because they are usually acted on without any malicious intent. And remember, all of us have likely said or thought something about an individual or a group that was ill-informed. As leaders, most of us who say or do these things do not set out to make people feel diminished, targeted, or "othered." And yet, the impact of their words and actions may still be negative.

It is entirely possible for a person to have good intentions and nonetheless cause harm. Even when the direct report who is experiencing harm can see that their leader meant well, it doesn't necessarily diminish the harm done.

For this reason, good intentions can never be an excuse or rationalization for a microaggression that does harm. When confronted with their own microaggressions, many people believe that a simple, "but I didn't mean it that way," will suffice. This is inexcusable for anyone, but especially for a leader, who should serve as a role model for appropriate behavior.

Returning to the list of microaggressions I introduced in the previous section, I'll unpack a few of the likely intents and impacts in Table 6-2.

Some of the impacts listed might seem hyperbolic to you. But if you feel yourself getting defensive, take the perspective of someone who has been on the receiving end of this statement or behavior many, many times.

Having read through Table 6-2, does the earlier list seem a little less "micro" now?

If you've read through the list and are now worried about saying anything that might be meant as a compliment but could be misconstrued, take heart. If your intentions don't match the impacts shown in the right-hand column, it's not very likely you'll make those particular mistakes in the future. Of course, this is only a partial list of microaggressions; there are many others. And yes, you might make some mistakes in the future.

TABLE 6-2 Intent versus impact

Microaggression	What You Likely Meant (Intent)	What Was Heard or Felt (Impact)
Constantly offering to help a person with a disability, even when they haven't asked for assistance.	"I'm a caring, compassionate person."	"I don't expect there's anything you can do on your own."
Answering a phone call in the middle of a conversation.	"I'm a busy, important person."	"Almost anyone calling me right now for any reason would be more important than this conversation."
"Oh my gosh, that's so gay."	"That's odd."	"Gay people are abnormal."
Complimenting forceful white male leaders, while complaining about the same behaviors and assessing them as negative when demonstrated by women or people of color.	"These are my individual reactions to different individuals' leadership styles, and they have nothing to do with race or gender."	"I make allowances for white men who do things that I find unacceptable coming from women and people of color."
Pronouncing a person's name incorrectly, after being informed how to pronounce it.	"This name is hard for me to pronounce."	"Your culture and humanity are a nuisance to me; I can decide what your name is."
Continuing to refer to someone as "she" or "her" when that person told you that their pronouns are "they" and "them."	"I am new at using pronouns or not sure how to respond."	"You don't agree with or choose to ignore my preference for how to be acknowledged."
"You speak very good English" (to a person of Asian descent).	"I assume that English is your second language, and I admire your fluency."	"When I look at you, I see a foreigner."
"You are so articulate" (to an African American or person of African descent).	"That was a great presentation."	"I didn't expect you to be able to speak so professionally or profoundly."
Clutching your handbag or backpack when a Black colleague steps into the elevator.	"You're a stranger, I don't know you."	"I assume you are both criminal and violent because of your race."
"Can I feel your hair?" (to a Black woman).	"I'm naturally curious and would like to get to know you better."	"My curiosity is more important than your personal autonomy."
"I never would have known you were gay."	"You don't fit a lot of the negative stereotypes about the gay community."	"I really don't like gay people, but I'll make an exception for you so long as you never make me uncomfortable."

(continued)

TABLE 6-2 *(continued)*

Microaggression	What You Likely Meant (Intent)	What Was Heard or Felt (Impact)
"Where are you from?" (to a person of a different race/ethnicity/color).	"I'm just trying to get to know you."	"You don't belong here."
Assuming that a person who is Jewish must be a great business dealer or conversely, that they are shrewd and dishonest.	"I have a lot of respect for your culture."	"I don't trust Jews; they're sneaky."
"What was your name before?" (to a transgender person).	"I'm really interested in your journey."	"Please revisit a possibly painful experience for the benefit of my curiosity. Also, I'm potentially unwilling to accept you for who you say you are."

REMEMBER

The journey toward becoming an inclusive leader is not about never making a mistake; it's about learning. The more you learn about groups that are not your own, the easier it is to take their perspective and the less likely you are to offend. Microaggressions are not fostered in malice, but in ignorance. Therefore, the answer is not found in good intentions, but knowledge.

Identifying the Effects of Bias in the Workplace

The first and most obvious impact of bias is faulty decision making. The decisions made by our Fast Brain (explained earlier in this chapter) are only as good as the patterns that it employs. Some patterns (for example, traffic lights and road signs) are usually reliable, while others (such as broad stereotypes about marginalized groups) are not. Being able to make important decisions about work, especially when they involve evaluating people who are different from us or marginalized in some way, with our Slow Brain leads to better decisions that allow us to evaluate others more objectively and fairly, to critique their work more accurately, and to recognize talent whenever we see it and not just when it comes in a very particular package.

WARNING

But bias (and by extension, microaggressions) also have a negative effect on workplace culture. Members of marginalized groups, often having lived with these identities their entire lives, have learned how to detect when they're being treated differently or unfairly. Some might say that marginalized folks are too sensitive when it comes to bias and microaggressions, but I think a better argument is that people from dominant groups are often insensitive around these topics, only because they've never been negatively impacted by bias or microaggressions and have not been forced to learn how to navigate the world from a targeted vantage point.

Working in an environment rife with bias and microaggressions means always monitoring what you say and do, being afraid to ask questions or to disagree with the majority, or even being afraid to add valuable input to your team's work, for fear that it will be used against you somehow. Toxic workplace environments like these encourage quiet quitting of employees, causes them to withdraw from sharing ideas or solutions, and to start looking for a new and better job. They make it difficult to foster creativity and innovation, and to hire or retain talented people. I further discuss quiet quitting later in this chapter and also in Chapter 11.

The following sections feature a series of real stories and examples that detail the ways that your decisions as a leader could be negatively affected by bias and microaggressions. These examples all involve Arrow Company, a fictional employer marked by homogeneity and toxic leadership. As you read, substitute the name of your company and see if it doesn't worry you.

Sourcing and selecting new talent

In the past, job applicants mostly approached the sourcing and recruiting process with a feeling of powerlessness. After all, they wanted (or likely needed) a job, and those sorting through résumés, conducting phone screens, and interviewing potential employees had the power to either hire them or deny them employment. However, a new generation of job seekers has emerged. They realize, of course, that they are being evaluated during an interview, but what many employers don't realize is that they, in turn, are being interviewed by the job seekers. Consider this first scenario:

>> Arrow Company has low ratings on websites such as Glassdoor.com and elsewhere on social media. The scores are even worse when you isolate what women, people of color, and LGBTQ professionals say about the company. To counter this, Arrow Company offers higher starting salaries than their competitors, but the people who apply for jobs there are still predominantly white and male.

>> When applying for a job at Arrow Company, Janice wears her wedding ring, as she always does. Her interviewer, Sandra, notices the ring and compliments her on it. "How long have you been married?" Sandra asks. Janice doesn't want to begin her interview on a sad note, so answers "five years," while not mentioning that her wife recently died after a short illness. She hopes that

there will be no more questions, as she would rather focus on her qualifications than her identity as a lesbian. It occurs to her that such a question is probably illegal, and she begins to wonder if she even wants this job.

>> Kendrick, on the other hand, had a mostly good experience with his round of interviews, until he met with Craig, a senior leader, in the final round of interviews. As the interview ended, Craig congratulated Kendrick on his stellar résumé and for being so "professional and articulate" during the interview process. Kendrick leaves the interview thinking, "What did they expect? That I wouldn't be able to form complete sentences? Now I know why my cousin warned me about this place."

This new generation views workplace culture as just as important or more important than competitive pay when deciding where they want to work, and those priorities are only reinforced where the job seeker is part of a historically marginalized group. When they are the targets of bias and microaggressions before they've even agreed to work for Arrow Company, it's no wonder that the workforce isn't nearly as diverse as the CEO would like it to be.

Onboarding and orienting new talent

The onboarding and orientation process is another opportunity to make a first impression (your initial first impression occurred in the recruitment process), as you welcome new staff and make them glad they decided to join your company:

>> On his first day on the job, Tyrone receives a copy of the employee handbook, outlining many important policies and procedures at Arrow Company. Having had several experiences with biased leaders in the past, he thumbs through the document, looking for information on how Arrow Company handles employee complaints, but there's nothing there.

>> Walter is a new hire at Arrow Company in his sixties. Even though he's only a few years younger than he was when his father retired, Walter enjoys working and plans to do so for as long as he's able. As part of his new hire orientation program, he watches a video that includes a welcome message from the CEO, stating how happy they are to welcome "new, young, and energetic talent" to Arrow Company, and how he hopes they look forward to "working hard and playing hard" in their new role. Looking around, Walter notices one other older person in the room, who is rolling her eyes in reaction to the video.

It's safe to say that the leaders at Arrow Company missed their opportunity.

While it's understandable that leaders don't want to dwell on eventual conflicts, the lack of information provided to Tyrone (whose life experience warrants his concern) has already made him feel vulnerable. Meanwhile, the ageism in the CEO's welcome video was very apparent to Walter, even if it wasn't obvious to anyone else in the room, and now he wonders if he's made the best choice.

REMEMBER

Leaders should ensure that the onboarding and orientation process sets all employees, especially their new hires from historically marginalized groups, up for success.

Developing, promoting, and engaging talent

All employees want to be recognized for their individual contributions, the value and results they bring to their work, and be appropriately rewarded. The employees of Arrow Company are no exception:

>> The leaders of sales teams at Arrow Company are predominantly white, male, and were all promoted to leadership because they routinely made high sales year over year. There was no accounting for repeat customers, customer ratings, or any other quality metrics. Therefore, they approach their teams with a similar mindset. Those that make the highest sales numbers are rewarded and promoted, and those with lower numbers are not. Women and people of color have a difficult time succeeding at Arrow Company, and the customers who buy their products are homogenous as well. Whenever the economy goes into recession, Arrow's revenues are hit hard and they usually begin a large layoff of staff. Their competitors, who have a more diverse and loyal customer base, can usually weather the storm.

>> During a recent calibration meeting, Janet starts to notice that all the young men who are up for promotion are described with aspirational phrases like, "I think he'd be really good at that" or general descriptors like "very bright" or "solid work ethic." However, when evaluating a young woman's performance, questions arise, such as "Has she done this kind of work before?" or "Can she handle the travel demands with three children?" Often, their promotions are put off until they can prove themselves worthy. As a result, many more men at Arrow Company are recommended for promotion.

>> Chet is finishing up Alejandra's performance appraisal for her past 12 months at Arrow Company. Alejandra's projects throughout the year were consistently on time, well under budget, and executed with high quality. But Chet can't stop thinking about her poor choice of words when speaking to a journalist six months ago, that earned the company some bad press in an industry journal. Under the category of "Excellence," Chet rates Alejandra as "Fair."

Bias can cloud a leader's judgment, causing them to focus more on the negatives than the positives (in Alejandra's case) or holding different kinds of people to different standards (as Janet noticed in the calibration meeting).

Communicating with talent

Whether your communication takes the form of company-wide memos, staff meetings, or informal communications, it's important to take the time to ensure that the message received is the message you intended. Consider these scenarios:

>> Peter is a mid-level manager at Arrow Company who leads a small team. A father of two young children, Peter finds it easy to make small talk in the break room with Glenda, a member of his team who has children close to the same age as his. He finds it much more difficult to connect with new team member Erich, a single gay man with no kids who just moved to a hip neighborhood downtown.

>> Max, the chief human resources officer at Arrow Company, has noticed that the company has difficulty retaining and promoting women and people of color. He has decided that it's time to invest some of his budget into Diversity, Equity, and Inclusion (DEI) activities, perhaps focused on hiring more diverse employees. He drafts a memo to all staff announcing his newfound focus on DEI and assures them that this in no way means lowering standards of quality at Arrow Company. The next morning, he is made aware that Arrow Company is trending on social media. Most of the angry posts contain screenshots of his memo.

REMEMBER

Communication is both a matter of what you say (as shown in Max's disastrous memo to all staff) and what you don't say (for example, Peter giving Erich the cold shoulder in the break room because they seemingly have nothing in common). Either way, if your biases are left unchecked, they will affect how, when, and if you communicate to anyone on your team or in your organization. Even if your biases are not obvious to you, they soon will be to those on the receiving end of your words (and silences).

Retaining top talent

Of course, it's not enough to simply hire top talent. A company also needs to create an inclusive culture that encourages staff to stay and contribute. Here's the situation at Arrow Company:

>> Meiwen is the only woman in her team of five. Whenever her boss, Bart, asks for a volunteer to take notes during meetings, all eyes turn to Meiwen. She's aware that men at Arrow Company expect women (especially Asian women)

to be supportive, nurturing, and conciliatory as opposed to strong, dynamic, or assertive. Because of this, she doesn't want to be pigeonholed as the note-taker and, like the others, remains silent. But when Bart asks her directly to take notes yet again, she fears that refusing will cause him to have another one of his outbursts. After a long silence, Meiwen says, "Sure, no problem." She applies for three jobs in her city later that day.

>> Keiwon, Angela, and Majeedah are the only Black people on their large sales team at Arrow Company. On Thursdays, they typically slip out of the office and eat lunch together. These weekly lunches allow them to vent their frustrations and gain support from each other in a safe space. At a recent lunch, Keiwon and Angela are especially defeated, both having been denied a promotion for the second time, despite rave reviews from their customers. Majeedah finally says out loud what the other two are thinking. "If you were white, you'd have been promoted last year. After seeing that memo last week about 'not lowering our standards,' I think it's about time I move on." Keiwon and Angela nod their heads in agreement.

TECHNICAL STUFF

Quiet quitting is a term that refers to employees who purposefully do the bare minimum required of them. They aren't invested in the company's success, they don't go the extra mile, and they remain silent even when they have good ideas. In other words, they have quit their jobs in every way, but haven't vacated their office and still collect a paycheck.

For every Meiwen, Keiwon, Angela, and Majeedah, there are just as many employees at Arrow Company who have quit their jobs quietly. And between the costs associated with paying employees who don't contribute to Arrow Company's goals and recruiting costs associated with replacing employees who actually leave the organization, the toxicity and bad leadership at Arrow Company comes with a fairly hefty price tag.

Interrupting Biased Behaviors

The best reason to mitigate your biases and thereby prevent microaggressions is to improve the quality of your decisions. Mitigating your biases allows you to see talent more clearly, especially when it arrives in a package you didn't expect.

But the negative impact of bias and microaggressions on an organization's culture should not be minimized. In many of the examples given earlier in this chapter, you can see how bias and poor decision making has made the organization less diverse, less inclusive, less safe, and ultimately less successful because of the way these microaggressions impact people, particularly people who are different from the leaders of the organization. As a result, Arrow Company is battling a negative brand, bleeding talent, and I'd be willing to bet that the employees that are staying are generally withdrawn and dissatisfied with the climate and culture.

TIP

Fortunately, there is a way to interrupt your biases and prevent microaggressions from occurring. The three-step process includes:

1. **Recognize when a bias has occurred.**

2. **Validate or invalidate your bias.**

3. **Chart your path forward.**

To see this process in action, let's look at a few examples from BoardTech, a fictional organization and direct competitor of Arrow Company. This workplace isn't perfect — it's filled with human beings who all have a tendency toward bias and can make mistakes. But unlike Arrow, it's a company that prioritizes its culture, pays attention to the tenets of inclusive leadership, encourages its leaders to lead inclusively, and holds them accountable when they don't live up to those standards.

Step 1: Recognize when a bias has occurred

Because bias happens below the level of conscious thought, it can be difficult to spot. How then, can you manage something that you don't even see? It's not easy, but it's possible. Let's look at how three leaders at BoardTech do it:

>> **Scenario 1:** Valerie was one of the first leaders at BoardTech to sign up for the unconscious bias training course that was offered. She learned a lot, but one of the most useful lessons was about her own emotional responses. Since that training, she constantly brings her awareness to her feelings about her staff. Whether she's happy or frustrated or nervous or annoyed, she can almost always link that emotional response to a story she's created. For instance, in a recent meeting with her team, she found herself seeking out the input of one member of her team, Diego. She tracked how often she looked his way, hoping he'd add his opinion, hoping she wasn't doing so at the expense of others on her team.

>> **Scenario 2:** Four years ago, Steve had to fire a member of his team who had been caught stealing from the company. He had noticed some irregularities on the team's balance sheets, and after prompting an investigation, one of his employees was led out of the building by security. It was an emotionally charged day that Steve won't likely ever forget. What made it particularly difficult for Steve was that he had placed a lot of trust in Michelle, the employee responsible for the theft. In fact, when she was first suspected of stealing

company funds, he was hesitant to believe she was capable of such an act. Today, Steve welcomed a new member to his team. Sylvia is also a hard worker and can often be seen laughing and smiling with others on the team. She seems like a welcome addition to the team, but Steve remembers how he was duped before, and doesn't want to place his trust in someone who doesn't deserve it.

>> **Scenario 3:** Marsha knows that feedback is an important part of her role as a leader, so always takes a lot of time in preparing her team's performance appraisals each quarter. Before she begins work, she checks for signs of bias. The two appraisals in front of her are for Carlos and Jane. She has worked closely with Jane on several projects this year and looks forward to relaying specific examples about her excellent work. She notices she isn't as enthusiastic about Carlos, who tends to keep to himself, works from home whenever possible, and isn't as forthcoming as others on the team with input or ideas.

Valerie, Steve, and Marsha are all currently being affected by bias. However, they haven't acted upon that bias yet, and what's most important, they all recognize that bias is taking place. How did they do it? In Valerie's case, she remembered a key learning from her unconscious bias training course, which is that bias is often paired with an emotional response. Steve leans on his own life experience, remembering a painful episode when he felt betrayed by someone he trusted. Marsha is proactive in her search for bias. She knows that how she assesses her staff each quarter has a profound impact on their careers, and so checks herself for bias before she even begins the work.

Recognizing that a bias has occurred moves the decision from your Fast Brain to your Slow Brain, and makes you capable of making a deliberate and more objective decision.

Step 2: Validate or invalidate your bias

In this next step, it's important to remember that noticing a bias isn't the same is finding a flaw in your decision making. Therefore, rather than simply ignoring your biases, you need to validate or invalidate them. Once you notice that a bias is occurring, ask yourself, "What story, if any, am I creating here?" Then, once that story is raised to your consciousness, it's often fairly easy to deduce whether or not the story should be immediately discarded or warrants a closer look. Let's again look at those scenarios:

>> **Scenario 1:** Valerie wonders why she's so keen to hear from Diego during this meeting, and why she seems to value his input more than others on her team. While on a break, she takes a moment to piece it together. Diego has a background in marketing and branding. And while Valerie's team has a great deal

of expertise in communications, most of their efforts are internal. This project, however, involves some external communications. Diego often mentions how messages tend to play out in social media, or how the local media might put a particular spin on a press release at BoardTech's expense. These are valuable insights that Valerie herself had not considered. When she returns to the meeting, she notices that she's not the only one paying attention to Diego's input.

>> **Scenario 2:** At home that evening, Steve's wife asks about his day. She seems to notice that he's quieter than usual. He immediately tells her about his new employee, and how much Sylvia reminds him of Michelle. When he wonders aloud if she can trust her, his wife is incredulous. "You mean you plan to hold it against her that she's friendly and a hard worker? Not every happy person is a thief, you know." As soon as she speaks, Steve knows she is correct. It would be wrong of him to keep a team member at arm's length because of someone else's bad behavior.

>> **Scenario 3:** Marsha reflects on her lack of enthusiasm for Carlos, especially as it compares to Jane. When he's in the office, he keeps to himself, and is usually the first person out of the door at 5 p.m. He often works from home. When he dials in, he rarely turns his camera on or unmutes his line. Marsha wishes he were a bit more extroverted like herself. She knows through conversations with Carlos that he has two young children who spend the day in a daycare facility when he comes to the office. So, he's quiet and he has work/life challenges that he manages. Marsha knows that this isn't sufficient to warrant a negative assessment. She opens Carlos's self-assessment and begins to read.

REMEMBER

Sometimes our biases are valuable to us. In Valerie's case, it appears her unconscious wish to hear more from Diego had everything to do with an expertise that outweighed everyone else's in the room, including her own. She was right to question it, however. If this pattern continued unchecked, she could find herself playing favorites, at the expense of others on her team. Steve required the help of an objective viewpoint to talk through his bias. His quickly reminded him that he cannot disadvantage a new team member for exhibiting positive behaviors. Marsha invalidated her biases on her own, by detailing the "evidence" of her story in neutral, factual terms. And so, she turns to a much more reliable (and let's hope, instructive) piece of data: Carlos's own self-assessment of his work.

Step 3: Chart your path forward

Once a bias has been validated or invalidated, you can use your Slow Brain to make a deliberate and objective decision. Let's see how the leaders of BoardTech moved forward:

>> **Scenario 1 (conclusion):** For the remainder of the project, Valerie was impressed by the knowledge that Diego brought to the team. However, not wanting to ignore other team members, she tasked Diego with crafting a social media strategy for the project and asked two other team members to assist him. In this way, they could learn more about external communications, and he could gain some valuable leadership experience under her guidance. The project was a big success, and when the CEO of BoardTech called Marsha personally to congratulate her, she informed her that much of the credit should go to Diego, who received an award for his input.

>> **Scenario 2 (conclusion):** The next day, Steve invited Sylvia to a one-on-one meeting, designed to learn from her what she wanted to achieve in her new role and how, as her leader, Steve could assist her in her goals. During their conversation, Sylvia expressed an interest in working with some of BoardTech's global clients and a willingness to do a lot of travel if necessary. This was very different from Michelle, who had expressed different goals four years ago. Getting to know Sylvia as an individual helped Steve disassociate her from a powerful story from his past, and he mentioned a project involving vendors from Southeast Asia that could benefit from her skills.

>> **Scenario 3 (conclusion):** Upon reading Carlos's self-assessment, Marsha was deeply impressed by how much Carlos had accomplished in the past year, and how highly his clients spoke of him. He also indicated in his self-assessment that he appreciated the opportunity to work from home, as it afforded him the opportunity to pick up his children from school, and he could get so much more done away from the hubbub of the office. He was very pleased a month later, when he received a rating of "Excellent" from Marsha, and the option of more work-from-home days.

The decisions that the leaders at BoardTech made could have been very different had they not taken the effort to interrupt and manage their biased thinking. It's clear that these leaders put effort into leading inclusively and reap the rewards. It's a safe bet that valuable employees like Diego, Sylvia, and Carlos won't be actively seeking work elsewhere anytime soon.

Is your organization more like Arrow Company or BoardTech? In other words, does your organization value inclusive leadership? Do they teach leaders how to identify their biases (blind spots) and microaggressions and the impact that they have on their followers? Are they educated and held accountable for being inclusive, or do they see it as a nice "extra" and ultimately not that important? Where would you rather work, and what kind of leader would you rather be?

Chapter **7**

Leading with Authenticity and Transparency

I n an increasingly diverse, and ever-evolving workforce, two key competencies have emerged from the new generation of talent as essential for leaders: transparency and authenticity. Both of these not only contribute to stronger leadership but also foster healthier organizational cultures.

This chapter explains each of these competencies, why they matter more now than ever before, and why leaders tend to retreat from them. It guides you through an assessment of your effectiveness in demonstrating these two competencies and offers some steps to become a more authentic and transparent leader.

Defining Authenticity and Transparency and Seeing How They Relate

In an era characterized by rapid information flow, polarization, and heightened sensitivity, the need for more authentic and transparent leadership cannot be overstated. And while these words are often used interchangeably, they do have distinct concepts and outcomes. *Authentic leaders* inspire trust and loyalty among their teams, creating a workplace culture that values sincerity over pretense. *Transparent leaders* contribute to an atmosphere of accountability and openness, mitigating the risks associated with misinformation and fostering an environment conducive to collaboration. The following sections define each with more examples of what they look like.

Authenticity

REMEMBER

I define *authenticity* as being true to your best self and genuine in your actions and your words; speaking and behaving in alignment with your values and the freedom to be your best self. Authenticity has also been defined as the genuine and unfiltered expression of your thoughts, emotions, and values. Authentic leaders are true to themselves and their principles. They don't feel the need to put on a facade or act differently in various situations. This quality makes them relatable, trustworthy, and able to form deeper connections with their teams.

All of these attributes reveal what research shows that top talent is seeking and expecting from their leaders. In fact, *Harvard Business Review* found that 75 percent of employees want to experience more authenticity at work. Here are five examples of what authenticity looks like:

>> Remaining accessible and approachable.

>> Seeking out feedback from employees and making it easy for them to relay their ideas.

>> Being honest in relaying information with staff — in emails, calls, texts, or other internal messaging platforms — no matter how difficult the news.

>> Owning up to mistakes when they are made and telling stories of your lessons learned.

>> Admitting when you don't know the answer to something rather than making it up. This example is really important because it shows vulnerability.

Take a moment to reflect on the degree to which you demonstrate these five behaviors effectively and consistently. Identify where you need to improve.

Transparency

I define *transparency* as a proactive commitment to being appropriately honest, open, and vulnerable with your followers. Just as authenticity is not doing whatever feels good to you at the time, neither is transparency saying everything that pops into your mind as it occurs to you. After all, sharing everything you know about any given situation with your team is unwise, and in some cases, illegal.

Here's what I mean: I worked with a leader who would say and do things that were harsh, insulting, and borderline harassment such as berating people in meetings, calling people "dumb and stupid," and asking if they had a brain. When she was given feedback about the impact, she would respond with "I tell it like it is and I keep it real. If they can't handle it, well, they just need to grow thicker skin." She had it all wrong. This is not the kind of "realness" and "truth-telling" I'm describing relative to transparency (or authenticity for that matter). Nor is it what workers want. Additionally, you should be aware of the laws that govern your region, country, and industry in terms of what you can and cannot say at work. For instance, in many places, disclosing an employee's health status without their consent is illegal. And even if you are not bound by law, it still might be inappropriate to share privileged information about your team or about the company at large.

Leaders who fail to practice transparency include those who are not honest with their team. If there's a compelling reason why you cannot or should not disclose something or be truthful, simply state that you're unable to share. Transparent leaders will say this when necessary but will also not use it as an excuse to avoid conflict or because it might put the leader in a bad light. Like authenticity, transparency requires courage — often in the form of vulnerability.

Transparent leaders can answer the following questions:

>> Will I be in violation of a law or pertinent company policy by imparting a piece of knowledge?

>> Does my team have the right to know this information?

>> What are likely to be the short-term and long-term effects of sharing (or not sharing) at this time?

Understanding Why Some Leaders Shy Away from Authenticity and Transparency

While transparency and authenticity offer numerous benefits, not all leaders actively embrace or practice these competencies. Here are some common reasons that I've heard from leaders who shy away from authenticity and transparency:

>> **Fear of vulnerability:** Some leaders perceive transparency and authenticity as a sign of vulnerability. They fear that sharing personal thoughts or doubts might be seen as a weakness, which could undermine their authority. Consequently, they opt for a more guarded and distant leadership style.

>> **Cultural and organizational norms:** Organizational and cultural norms can influence leadership behaviors. In some corporate cultures, leaders are expected to maintain a certain level of distance and formality. In such environments, authenticity may be perceived as unprofessional.

>> **Short-term focus:** Leaders under intense pressure to deliver short-term results may prioritize immediate gains over long-term trust-building. They may resort to less transparent or authentic practices to achieve quick wins, even if it erodes trust in the long run.

>> **Lack of awareness:** Some leaders may not fully grasp the significance of transparency and authenticity in today's diverse and global workforce. They may not be aware of the positive impact these competencies can have on their leadership and their organization's success.

Understanding these reasons is essential for recognizing the barriers that exist and for addressing them in the pursuit of more effective leadership practices.

Analyzing Your Effectiveness as an Authentic and Transparent Leader

So, how authentic and transparent are you? Consider the following workplace scenarios from the Goode Company, a fictitious workplace (but reflective of real company issues) where people make mistakes, but organizational culture is a priority, and leaders are both educated and held accountable for how they lead inclusively.

>> **Scenario 1:** A year ago, Rhonda placed one of her team members, Sam, on a Performance Improvement Plan. Sam wasn't meeting his goals, and his work was often shoddy and riddled with errors. Rhonda made it clear that Sam's performance was going to have to improve if he wanted to remain with the company. For a while, it seemed to be working, but Sam's performance soon sank bank to previous levels. He just didn't seem capable of the kind of quality and output than his role required. A week ago, Rhonda made the difficult decision to let Sam go, and Sam accepted the opportunity to resign from Goode Company himself. In a team-wide email message, he framed his departure as his decision. Many of the people on Rhonda's team were surprised. They liked Sam, and clearly were not aware of his performance issues. In a team-wide meeting, one team member noted that Sam was clearly fired in a way that seemed very sudden, making her feel less safe on the team.

>> **Scenario 2:** Herman attended a senior leadership team meeting last month, and the news was not good. Profits were down across the entire industry, and there was no way Goode Company could meet its financial goals this year. Herman proposed several ways to streamline costs that he believed would save money while protecting the people on his team, but most of his colleagues were swayed by the CFO's suggestion to implement a 10 percent layoff across the board. Today, the planned layoff was announced, and several members of Herman's team are understandably upset. When four of his team members stop by his office to discuss the announcement, their first question is, "Did you know about this?"

>> **Scenario 3:** Lisa grew up in the Midwestern United States. She was the first person in her family to attend college and has always taken pride in her work ethic and determination, both of which led — she believes — to her success. She was one of the very first female vice presidents at Goode Company, and enjoys helping her team members locate their passions and create plans to achieve their goals. Goode Company had recently adopted a 360-degree performance appraisal process, which means that in her latest performance assessment, some members of her team gave anonymous input about the quality of her leadership. She was dismayed to learn that some members of her team feel ignored or even disrespected by Lisa. Many of the comments were positive, but some reported that she dismisses concerns about work/life balance and plays favorites within the team. Lisa has always believed that she treated everyone on the team equally, offering to be a mentor or a sponsor to anyone with aspirational goals who requested those things.

In the above scenarios, our leaders (Rhonda, Herman, and Lisa) have a lot of options. Before reading the conclusions to the scenarios, take a moment to think through the following questions:

>> Who should speak up? Who should remain silent?

>> Is there anything they could do in the moment that would immediately satisfy their followers? Is that the best course of action?

>> Is there a difference between what their followers want in the short term and what would serve them best in the long term?

>> What's the best outcome for Goode Company and its organizational goals?

>> If you were in their shoes, what would *you* do?

Now, let's look at how these leaders reacted to their situations:

>> **Scenario 1 (conclusion):** Rhonda was disappointed to witness the emotional upheaval caused by Sam's departure. After the first person shared her reaction, Rhonda asked if anyone else would like to respond or share their own experience. Several hands went up. As people spoke, Rhonda was struck by how sudden Sam's departure seemed to everyone in the room. She, of course, knew different. She had been discussing Sam's performance gap with him for an entire year, and had given him many chances to improve. Indeed, when the time came to let Sam go, he wasn't surprised in the least. He knew exactly what was expected of him, and how he had fallen short of those expectations. But it's clear now that her team liked Sam, and felt a little defensive on his behalf. Rhonda wished she could correct the record somehow. But she also felt sure that she had made the right decision to let him go, and her followers neither needed nor wanted her to say a word against him. Rather, they were clearly feeling insecure about their own jobs in the wake of his "sudden" departure. When the team finished sharing, she said, "I know that you miss Sam, and it's clear that you valued him as a colleague. And, when Sam came to speak to me before he resigned, it was mutually understood that our conversation would be confidential, so I'm going to ask everyone to respect that. I'm also hearing people perceiving some uncertainty about their own roles, so I'd like to address that. As your leader, I'm a big believer in frequent and immediate feedback. If I'm doing my job correctly, everyone on this team should always know whether they are meeting or exceeding my expectations or falling short. If you have any questions about how you're doing, please meet with me one-on-one. I'm always available to speak with you."

>> **Scenario 2 (conclusion):** Herman had been dreading this moment ever since the senior leadership team voted to proceed with a layoff. Herman was one of only two people in the room to vote "no," but the decision had been made, and the CEO was convinced that a layoff was inevitable in any case, and acting now

would be better for the long-term sustainability of Goode Company. Looking at the slightly panicked faces in his office, he selfishly wished that he could tell them how hard he fought to prevent this. But votes were confidential, and he knew why. While 10 percent of the company would soon be laid off, 90 percent of staff would remain, and it would not serve them to separate the senior leaders into camps of "good ones" and "bad ones." This was a leadership decision, and Herman must support it to the best of his ability. "I did know," Herman said. "The possibility of a layoff has been underway for about a month, and the decision was made a week ago. I'm not at liberty to discuss the conversations that took place, and for legal reasons, I couldn't say anything to the team until the official announcement was made today. I know the news is shocking and disappointing for you. I'm going to suspend the agenda for this afternoon's team meeting so that we can have a conversation about the layoff and what you can expect going forward. There, I will answer any questions I can."

» **Scenario 3 (conclusion):** Days after receiving the results of her performance appraisal, Lisa met with a trusted mentor to discuss the comments she received. Years earlier, she had worked with her mentor to identify her core values, and ambition was one of them. She thought that leading this way was a natural extension of her authentic self. During the conversation, she wondered aloud if it was a bad thing to encourage her team to dream big and to make plans to achieve those dreams. "I wouldn't say that," her mentor said. "I'm an ambitious person too, and when I think back to all the bosses I've had, I would have loved a leader like you. But success looks a little different to everyone. You know what it means for you, but what if there's someone on your team who works to support their family and dreams of being the best parent to their children they can possibly be? What if someone's passion revolves around the volunteer work they do on evenings and weekends? So long as everyone is doing their job and doing it well, can you also support those dreams?" The feedback was a little difficult to absorb at first, but the more she thought about it, the more Lisa saw the wisdom in her mentor's words. She could still be committed to her core values and help people succeed, but she needed to make room for lots of different ways to define success. The next week, she requested one-on-one meetings with each of her staff, and told them about the feedback she had received. "When you first came to the team," she said to each of them, "I asked you what you wanted out of your career. Now I'm interested in what you want out of life, and if there's a way I can help you achieve that. Think about it, and let me know."

How did your responses compare with the choices that Rhonda, Herman, and Lisa made? Is there anything you might have said or done that they didn't? Did they say too little or too much? Were they appropriately authentic and transparent throughout? In the nearby sidebar, "The Credibility Paradox," I provide some food for thought, targeted responses, and learnings to keep in mind when dealing with such situations.

THE CREDIBILITY PARADOX

So why don't leaders always behave with authenticity and transparency? Well, besides misunderstanding the terminology to mean doing anything you feel and telling the absolute truth at all times, the other reason has to do with what I call the Credibility Paradox.

Some leaders can be defensive, or don't like saying things that might cast them in a negative light. Let's look again at our scenarios:

- Rhonda did not tell her team that she and Sam had been discussing his performance issues for a year. To do so might have assuaged their immediate fears but might have led to other problems. For instance, if Rhonda is willing to reveal confidential information about a former colleague's performance, who else does she talk about when they're not in the room? Instead, Rhonda urges everyone on her team to respect Sam's privacy and ends by offering their own one-on-one conversation if they need more clarity.

- Herman wishes he could bolster his credibility among his followers by assuring them that he was against the idea of a layoff from the beginning. But he also knows that disparaging his colleagues on the senior leadership team will not help his those who keep their jobs adjust to work after the layoff occurs. It also wouldn't help his working relationships with other senior leaders! Most importantly, Herman knows that what his followers need is not someone to blame for the current situation, but guidance in how to navigate it, which he promises to provide in the team meeting.

- In Lisa's case, she makes the brave choice to tell her team about the feedback that she received, even though she's under no obligation to do so. She might have worried that divulging the feedback would tarnish her credibility in some way, but by sharing her imperfections and immediately following it up with corrective measures, she is showing her team that she's only human, and she's capable of learning from her mistakes. There's a good chance that her credibility will increase because of her transparency.

This is the heart of the Credibility Paradox. When a leader is thinking first and foremost about their reputation, they can often make choices that will boost their credibility in the short term, and damage it in the long term. By taking the long view and focusing on the needs of their followers, even if it means exposing their vulnerabilities or letting people know that they are less than perfect, they will likely increase their credibility over time.

Mastering Authentic and Transparent Leadership

Leaders who understand the significance of transparency and authenticity and actively work to cultivate these competencies are better equipped to lead their organizations to success amidst a more diverse and interconnected global workforce. Of course, the biggest benefit to being an authentic and transparent leader is that it allows your followers the freedom to be their best selves, and you get to hear from them what they're truly thinking and feeling.

TIP

To develop these competencies, leaders can engage in self-reflection, practice active listening, build a culture of transparency, embrace vulnerability as a strength, develop cross-cultural competency, and seek education and training. Let's expound on each of these:

>> **Engage in self-reflection:** Leaders should engage in self-reflection to gain a better understanding of their personal values, strengths, and weaknesses. This self-awareness can help them become more authentic by aligning their actions with their core values and principles.

>> **Practice active listening:** Leaders should actively listen to their team members, taking the time to understand their perspectives and concerns. This not only fosters trust but also enables leaders to adapt their communication and decision-making processes to better meet the needs of their teams.

>> **Build a culture of transparency:** Leaders can encourage transparency by setting an example and making it clear that open communication is not only accepted but expected. They should create channels for team members to ask questions, provide feedback, and express their ideas and concerns.

>> **Embrace vulnerability as a strength:** Leaders should recognize that vulnerability is not a weakness but a strength. Being willing to admit mistakes and express uncertainty can make leaders more relatable and trustworthy. It also sets a precedent for openness and learning within the organization.

>> **Develop cross-cultural competency:** In global workforces, leaders must be aware of and respect cultural differences (see Chapter 9 for more on this). Understanding the communication norms and values of diverse team members is crucial for practicing transparent and authentic leadership.

>> **Seek education and training:** Organizations can provide leadership development programs that focus on transparency and authenticity. These programs can help leaders recognize the importance of these competencies and provide tools to develop and enhance them.

REMEMBER

Practicing these behaviors of authenticity and transparency are not signs of weakness as many leaders believe; they are signs of strength and maturity. And they lead to increased employee productivity, engagement, loyalty, and satisfaction.

TIP

Keep these questions in mind as you strive to be your most authentic and transparent self:

>> What are the core values that drive you? Are you driven by achievement and advancement, or compassion and cooperation? Do you strive for harmony and stability, or innovation and risk taking? Would you rather be known for your optimism, your competence, or because you made a difference in peoples' lives? The first step toward authenticity is locating who you are, beyond what you've been taught to be or what your organization rewards. Then you can decide how to make your authentic self work for you, your followers, and your organization's success.

>> How will you ensure that those values show up in your everyday leadership behaviors? How can you adapt those behaviors when your followers have a different perspective on work and life?

>> When there's something you'd like to share with your team, ask yourself:

- Will I be in violation of the law or company policy if I disclose?

- What will be the short-term and long-term impacts of disclosure?

>> When there's something you'd rather not share with your followers, ask yourself:

- Do they have a right to know this information?

- What's the source of your hesitancy? Are you worried about revealing your own imperfections — in other words, showing up as a human being?

- Will speaking up require courage? If so, what's the fear you must first overcome?

- Even if you lose credibility in the short term, might you gain credibility over time by being transparent?

>> Are your followers serving you (traditional leadership) or are you serving them (servant leadership)? In the next 30 days, think about how you could show up in service to the people on your team. This could be in the form of securing necessary resources, removing obstacles that hamper their work, or even injecting a little fun into the working week (so long as you're committed to what's fun for *them*, not just what's fun for *you*).

>> Is your leadership helping the individuals on your team grow and evolve professionally? Think about the past year, and identify the ways that each of your direct reports (or closest followers) have experienced some upward

movement. Did you have a hand in their development, or did they have to do everything themselves? Now, think about what each of these people could achieve if you were fully committed to their growth and evolution. What are some plans you could put in action now?

>> Is your leadership helping the organization to experience a change? A transformational leader creates positive change in social systems. This could be your company, your client organization, or the communities you serve (or some combination of the three).

>> How well do you listen to your followers? Do you know what they need to do their best work? Are you aware of ways that you could intercede to make them feel more included and give them a sense of belonging?

>> When was the last time you challenged your followers in a way that sparked creativity, innovation, or problem solving?

- Does your team exhibit a sense of pride in their work? Are they happy to come to work each day? Are they exhibiting observable behaviors (smiles, laughter, sharing their accomplishments) that communicate this, or is this a guess on your part? How can you find out how they really feel? Keep in mind that a direct question from their leader is likely to prompt what they think the leader wants to hear.

- Are you proud of your team? Can you name two or three accomplishments for each of your direct reports (or closest followers) over the past year? Can you name one or two unique skills, talents, or knowledge areas for each of these people? If not, why not?

- Can you think of a time when your team disagreed with your preferred path forward, and you changed direction based on this consensus? If not, what would it take for your followers to convince you to proceed differently?

As you work to gain the trust of your followers, strengthening your authenticity and transparency is important. Because these two qualities require courage and vulnerability, they can be difficult for some leaders. Keep going! The rewards are well worth the effort.

IN THIS CHAPTER

» Understanding empathy and its role in leadership

» Applying empathy to workplace scenarios

» Breaking down emotional intelligence

» Taking a personal assessment of where you are

» Making the business case for greater empathy and emotional intelligence

» Applying empathy and emotional intelligence as a leader

Chapter **8**

Demonstrating Empathy and Emotional Intelligence

know what you're thinking. This is where we talk about the mushy stuff — right? Well . . . sort of.

Empathy and emotional intelligence are often considered soft skills and that language alone makes them sound minor, or less important than expertise or the technical aspects of your job. *Soft skills* encompass a set of interpersonal, communication, and emotional abilities that are rather intangible and relate to how individuals interact with others. These skills have become increasingly crucial for leaders due to the evolving nature of the workplace and the recognition of the importance of effective human interactions. Conversely, *hard skills* are specific, teachable abilities or knowledge that can be quantified and measured. These skills are often job-specific and can be acquired through education, training, or experience. Examples of hard skills include proficiency in a programming language, data analysis, project management, foreign language proficiency, or technical expertise in a particular field. If you felt a little nervous when you read the title of this chapter, then you already know that soft skills aren't always easy — and leaders who tend to believe that emotions should be suppressed at work whenever possible might find this work to be the most difficult. And yet, it's incredibly necessary.

This chapter is where I'm going to write about understanding people, forging deep connections, and yes: feelings. And sure, I'm going to make the case for leaders increasing their empathy and emotional intelligence at work because it makes people happier — both those who report to a leader and the leaders themselves. But I'm also going to show how more empathy and emotional intelligence leads to a better worker experience which contributes to better results such as higher sales, more innovative ideas, increased revenue, and greater impact in the marketplace.

Let's get started!

Understanding Empathy and its Role in Leadership

It is integral for decision-making processes to acknowledge people's feelings, behaviors, and concerns from different perspectives. Only by embracing empathy can today's leadership be effective in creating an environment that strives for innovation, collaboration and connection in the workplace.

Empathy is a valuable human quality that has gained significant recognition as a critical leadership skill for today's workforce. Research continues to reveal that empathy enables leaders to better comprehend their team members' experiences, maximize collaboration, enhance trust and employee morale, and drive productivity.

REMEMBER

There are many definitions floating around about *empathy*, but the most common one used is "understanding or being able to relate to the feelings of others." The one that I prefer is "recognizing emotions in others; avoiding judgment; feeling with others when appropriate; conveying your understanding of another's emotions; and responding appropriately."

MOST COMMON REASONS FOR THE GROWING RECOGNITION OF EMPATHY

This book tackles the difficulties that are inherent when you lead across difference, and leading with empathy is no exception. Relating to and understanding someone who is very similar to you is easy (whether that's race, gender, background, socio-economic status or social hierarchy [caste system], education, religion, sexual orientation, or culture). But developing a deep understanding across multiple differences and intersections is much more difficult. Yet the business case is compelling as to why we see a growing recognition of empathy as a critical leadership competency in the workplace. Here are the most common that I've observed in my HR and leadership consulting work:

- **Complex work environments:** Today's workplace is characterized by increased diversity, remote work, accelerated paces of change, external social, economic, and geopolitical issues, and rapid technological advancements. In responding to such complex realities, leaders need empathy to navigate the varying needs and challenges of their teams.

- **Changing worker expectations:** Employees today seek more than just a paycheck; they desire a sense of belonging, respect, equitable treatment, and purpose at work. They are also demanding that their leaders be inclusive, authentic, and fair. Empathy from leaders fosters these elements, contributing to higher job satisfaction, engagement, and retention.

- **Globalization:** With organizations spanning international borders, leaders must be able to navigate diverse cultural norms and expectations. Empathy aids leaders in understanding and respecting these differences, fostering collaboration and trust among global teams.

- **Mental health awareness:** Awareness of mental health issues in the workplace is growing. With workplace stress, burnout, and anxiety at record highs, leaders must be better equipped to support employees' emotional, psychological, and mental well-being, if they want to cultivate a healthier work environment.

In this way, empathy isn't just a feeling, it's also an action. Feeling with or understanding how someone else might feel is an important first step, but entirely internal. If your followers don't in turn feel that you understand them and are taking their emotions into account as you make decisions, all that internal work doesn't add up to much.

An idiom that is often used to describe empathy is "walking in someone else's shoes." Expanding on that phrase a bit, it's obvious that it's a lot easier to walk in someone else's shoes if the shoes fit. When you slip into a pair of shoes that feel like they were made for you, it doesn't feel strange or foreign. Before long, you could even forget that the shoes aren't yours. This isn't the case when the shoes are way too big or way too small, or with platforms and heels a lot higher than you're used to. Then, walking in someone else's shoes is likely to be uncomfortable and awkward.

Digging into the Three Types of Workplace Empathy

Leadership empathy cannot be underscored enough. A leader who exhibits this skill plays a critical role in creating an environment of trust and respect. Examples include the ability to be understanding when employees are struggling with personal issues or life challenges, responding to requests and feedback with empathy and patience, and valuing feedback that provides insights into how the work environment is seen by those on the ground.

Let's take a look at a useful framework that identifies three types of empathy: cognitive, emotional, and compassionate. It was created by Positive Psychology in Action (PPIA), an organization that focuses on spreading knowledge about the science of happiness and helps people bring out the best in themselves and others (https://ppinaction.com).

TIP

To illustrate each type, I've crafted a scenario about leaders at the fictitious company BoardTech to illustrate them. As you read each one, consider your immediate reaction and then reflect on how you would respond with empathy before reading my commentary underneath them.

Cognitive empathy

Cognitive empathy is perspective-taking on a purely intellectual level. Sandra, a leader at BoardTech, has just learned that Adrian, one of her direct reports, spent the weekend moving his mother into an assisted-living facility for people who suffer from dementia. Adrian spoke openly about what it's like when his mother doesn't recognize him and how her long-term memory seems to go in and out. Sandra's mother is in her 80s, but still very healthy, both physically and mentally. As Adrian tells his story, Sandra listens intently. At one point, Adrian wipes a tear from his eye, but quickly composes himself. Sandra doesn't attempt to encourage or dissuade Adrian from showing emotion during their conversation, but finally says, "Thank you so much for telling me. I can't imagine what that's like for you. If there's anything I can do to support you right now, I'll hope you'll let me know."

In this example, Sandra couldn't immediately relate to Adrian's story. Her own mother doesn't have those same struggles. Importantly, she didn't pretend that she understood on an emotional level. She even says, "I can't imagine what that's like for you." Nonetheless, Adrian felt supported by Sandra. He now knows that when he's dealing with important issues in his personal life, he can feel safe telling Sandra about it, knowing that he won't be judged, and that Sandra will react well.

Cognitive empathy means that you might not be feeling what another person is feeling, you can still respect those feelings as real and valid. Despite having a healthy mother herself, Adrian's emotions made sense to her. Nor did she try to control Adrian's emotions in any way. When Adrian shed a quick tear during the conversation, Sandra did not immediately grab a tissue from her desk and wave it in front of him, which could have felt as though Sandra wanted Adrian to stop crying, immediately. Rather, Sandra accepted Adrian's display of emotions in a way that engendered comfort and trust. Finally, she ended the conversation by asking Adrian to let her know if he needed any additional support.

Emotional empathy

Emotional empathy is physically feeling what someone else is feeling. Althea has been working at BoardTech for a little over two years. Two months ago, she approached her manager, Ronald, about a program at BoardTech which sends junior staff to an overseas office for an 18-month rotation. The program is designed for exceptional talent, and Ronald believed that Althea was an excellent candidate, despite her short tenure. He not only helped her apply for the program, but wrote a recommendation for her, detailing all the reasons why Althea was a good choice. Ronald has just received word that Althea had been accepted into the program and would be sent to BoardTech's Berlin location, her first choice. When Althea showed up for their scheduled one-on-one meeting that afternoon, he exclaimed, "Glückwunsch! Du gehst nach Deutschland!" Upon hearing this, Althea screamed in delight and began hopping up and down. Ronald joined in her laughter until they could both catch their breath. "Really?" she said. "Ja," Ronald answered, and the two of them began to laugh once more.

Sometimes, it's entirely appropriate for a leader to feel with an employee. In this example, Althea's emotional response was one of joy, and Ronald — who had also put in some work to get Althea the global assignment she wanted — was nearly as excited as she was at her success. By joining in with her exuberant display of relief and excitement, he was able to quickly communicate that her emotions were welcome, this is indeed a very big deal, and that he cared about her career. Emotional empathy means that you're feeling exactly what the other person is feeling. Most people seek out friends or family members if they need this kind of emotional validation, but under the right circumstances, it can be not only appropriate from your leaders, but also wonderful.

Compassionate empathy

Compassionate empathy is feeling with someone and taking supportive action, if needed and wanted. Renee was happy to invite Malcolm to join her team as an IT specialist. He came with many skills that BoardTech sorely needed, and during his interview displayed a real willingness to learn and grow. He was exactly the kind of person Renee enjoyed working with. However, his first few months haven't been easy. BoardTech recently acquired a small start-up, and Malcolm has been tasked with integrating the acquisition's financial data and intellectual property into BoardTech's existing IT set-up, and it's been a challenge. Malcolm has repeatedly apologized for missing key deadlines and several errors in his work, explaining that the start-up's system was a real mess, and has caused far more problems than anyone anticipated. In their latest meeting, Renee said to Malcolm, "I recall a challenge I had on a similar project when I was new here. So, I know how you feel. I appreciate the fact that you hold yourself to a high standard of quality; it's one of the reasons I hired you. Let's sit down together and look at the project plan and see where we might need to make some adjustments."

In this example, Malcolm is displaying some frustration, mostly aimed at himself. It would likely not help matters if Renee were to match Malcolm's frustration by mirroring it. Instead, she taps into a memory she had of being in a similar situation. In a calm, supportive way, she lets Malcolm know that she can relate to his frustration but goes a step further and connects his frustration to his underlying desire to do well in his new role. Finally, she offers what Malcolm really needs in this situation — a way forward. She suggests that they sit down together and change some of the deadlines so that Malcolm has the time he needs to produce high-quality work. This plan will allow Malcolm to approach the work with the same kind of calm assurance that Renee is modeling.

Being an empathetic leader

There is no one right way to be an empathetic leader. Sometimes, it's enough to simply let the members of your team know that you understand how they feel, as Sandra did. Sometimes, it's appropriate and valuable to share in their emotional journey, as Ronald did. At other times, the most empathetic thing you can do is mirror the kind of emotion that you'd like your follower to emulate as Renee did when she met Malcolm's irritation with a more relaxed style.

TIP

A skilled empathic leader makes the decision that best meets the moment, but — and this is important — is always sincere in their response. If you cannot express true emotional empathy, for example, don't fake it. Rather, be gracious enough to realize that different people will react to the same situation differently, and the emotional reaction that your followers experience are likely real and valid for them. Not being able to immediately relate should not prevent you from being supportive or kind.

Figuring Out the Four Domains of Emotional Intelligence

Of course, the most important thing for an inclusive leader is not experiencing the correct emotion at the correct time. Rather, inclusive leadership shows up in a leader's observable behaviors: what they say to their followers, and the actions they take. Understanding the emotions of others is just one aspect of this.

REMEMBER

Emotional intelligence, sometimes called EQ or emotional quotient, is the ability to recognize, regulate, and convey your own emotions and to conduct interpersonal dynamics with an awareness of others' feelings and motivations.

TECHNICAL STUFF

According to Daniel Goleman, an American psychologist who helped popularize the term, emotional intelligence has four domains. They are:

>> **Self-awareness.** Being conscious of your own feelings and your thoughts about them.

>> **Self-control.** Being able to mitigate your reactions to triggers, even during a crisis.

>> **Social awareness.** Being aware of the ways an emotionally fraught situation could impact the people, organization, and systems involved in correcting the problem.

>> **Relationship management.** Being able to manage conflict, inspire others, foster teamwork, and move people toward a common desired goal.

Consider the following scenario: Nora was promoted to the role of VP of accounting three years ago and is widely considered to be a fair and compassionate leader. She has good relationships with his direct reports, characterized by openness and trust. However, two of her direct reports, both of whom have worked at BoardTech for decades, have never worked well with each other. Jay and Adriana are both team leaders with strong personalities but disparate work styles. Jay is widely recognized for expert crisis management, but Adriana feels as though a more methodical approach to his work would prevent many of the fires he so success-fully puts out. Furthermore, she says that greater discipline on his part would make her work and the work of her team much easier. In a recent team meeting with ten of her direct reports, another team leader congratulated Jay on success-fully navigating yet another potential disaster, and Adriana, who was normally cool and collected, exploded in anger. She called Jay unprofessional and noted that if she, a woman of color, dealt with as many potential disasters as Jay, she would have been fired long ago. Jay fired back with some harsh words of his own, insinu-ating that Adriana was simply jealous of his success. Nora stood, and the room became silent, as everyone waited for her to speak.

If you were Nora, how would you handle this situation? What would you say in the moment to manage the conflict in the room, and what might you say privately to Jay, Adriana, or other team members later? What actions might you take over the long term? This is a conflict that has the potential to roil an entire department, and Nora's actions could very well have long-term consequences. The next sec-tions look at how each domain can help Nora make the wisest choices.

Self-awareness

The first domain of emotional intelligence is self-awareness. Leaders who are self-aware not only understand what they're feeling at any given moment, but also understand how emotions work. As I discuss in Chapter 6, your emotions are generated in a part of your brain that fundamentally outside your control. There-fore, you cannot dictate to yourself what you should be feeling; you can only rec-ognize your emotions for what they are and accept them with humility.

REMEMBER

Leaders who are self-aware know themselves well enough to know what's likely to trigger negative emotions such as anger, fear, or sadness. While it's not possi-ble to control how you feel, recognizing what is likely to activate a negative response makes it easier to correctly name your emotions, allowing you to prepare for situations in advance.

In Nora's case, her first action is to recognize and name her own emotions. Hav-ing done the necessary inner work long before this meeting, she knows that growing up in a peaceful and tranquil home, with parents who rarely raised their voices, has made her very uncomfortable with the kind of open conflict being displayed by Adriana and Jay. She also recognizes within herself an annoyance with their long-standing feud, which pre-dates her leadership of this team. For years, she has wondered why they continue to nurse their grievances toward each other, rather than communicating openly. While she appreciates them both for their hard work and excellent results, she finds this aspect of their personalities a little childish. Nora won't (and probably shouldn't) say any of this to Jay or Adriana, but being able to precisely name how she feels about this situation places her in control of her behavior, rather than cede control to emotions she doesn't fully understand. Finally, she admits to herself that she has always admired Jay's ability to manage high-pressure situations and is aware (based on many conversations with him) that not all the crises he deals with are of his own making. At the same time, she can also recognize a grain of truth in what Adriana says about the double standards often applied to women of color in the workplace, and she wonders if she herself would be as universally praised as Jay for exhibiting some of the same behaviors.

TIP

Are you a self-aware leader? Ask yourself the following questions:

>> Do you have difficulty naming your emotions?

>> Do you have a trusted person or people with whom you can openly discuss how you feel?

>> What are triggers, pet peeves, or situations that may cause an emotional reaction for you?

Self-control

While an emotionally intelligent leader cannot decide what to feel, self-awareness allows them to separate how they feel from how they behave. The second domain of emotional intelligence is self-control. A self-controlled leader can mitigate their behaviors, even during a crisis.

REMEMBER

Importantly, a self-controlled leader is not inauthentic. I am always careful to define authenticity not as the freedom to be yourself, but rather "the freedom to be your best self." Behaving in complete alignment with your emotions is not authenticity; it's immaturity. An emotionally intelligent leader behaves in alignment with their values.

For Nora, self-control will require her to manage both emotional reactions she accurately perceived in herself. While her discomfort with raised voices might prompt her to simply put a lid on the conflict and restore peace as soon as possible, she knows that her desire to simply avoid the conflict won't address the root of the discord on her team. Likewise, she can recognize that she's irritated by what she perceives as childishness without treating her team as though they were children, which tends to provoke even more child-like behavior. Additionally, she knows that there is something about both Jay and Adriana that she can admire or relate to, and it might be beneficial for her in this moment to lean into those feelings as she articulates a response. Finally, she can tap into her own core values as a leader. She knows that one of her core strengths is an ability to make each member of her team feel valued and appreciated, which will now require her to validate the strong feelings present in two of her direct reports, while encouraging them both to approach their differences constructively.

TIP

Do you possess the self-control that is necessary for emotional intelligence? Ask yourself:

>> Are you able to separate how you feel from how you want to behave when emotions run high?

>> Do you have difficulty remaining calm when you're annoyed or frustrated?

>> Can you articulate why you do the work you do and why it's important?

Social awareness

The third domain of emotional intelligence is social awareness. This refers to the ability to recognize all the ways that your actions will have an emotional impact on the individual people involved, the entire team, or perhaps even the organization. Social awareness requires a leader to look at a problem or situation through multiple lenses at once, and often requires a leader to choose the best option from a list of less-than-perfect responses.

To practice social awareness well, Nora must recognize that the altercation between Adriana and Jay has taken place in a public setting in the presence of their peers. As a result, this conflict is not a private matter between two colleagues, but something that involves her entire team. While she might prefer to quickly table the conflict until she can meet with her two quarreling team members separately, doing so might cause others on her team to take sides or project their individual pet peeves, fears, or insecurities onto the situation. Therefore, her initial response should address the entire team in a way that will engender their trust. She also reminds herself that she doesn't need to solve the acrimony between Adriana and Jay today. This will likely involve several conversations over time, but what she can accomplish in this moment is to let the entire team know that she can be trusted to deal with the situation fairly.

TIP

Do you possess a keen sense of social awareness? Ask yourself:

>> Can I view a single situation from multiple lenses when necessary (individual, interpersonal, team, organizational, societal)?

>> Can I accurately predict how individuals and groups will react, both emotionally and behaviorally, to my words and actions (or to my silence and inactions)?

Relationship management

The fourth domain of emotional intelligence is relationship management. Daniel Goleman defines this as "the ability, through inspiring others, managing conflicts, fostering teamwork, and other competencies, to moving people in the direction you desire." In other words, this domain requires leaders to adopt and hone a vast array of social skills. These include, but are not limited to:

>> **Vulnerability.** The ability to discuss either your strengths or weaknesses with followers when appropriate.

>> **Communication skills.** The ability to deliver a message that is understood as you intended it, but also the capacity to listen and understand rather than respond.

>> **A willingness to praise.** Both individually and collectively, in public and in private.

>> **Conflict mediation.** Performed in a fair and equitable way that values and respects all involved parties.

As she responds to the argument between Adriana and Jay that erupted during a team meeting, Nora has both the empathy and the discernment to recognize that they both possess valuable strengths, valid arguments, and development areas. She believes, as do others on the team, that Jay is a wonderful leader during a crisis, and she knows that many of the high-pressure situations he's managed in the past three years have been brought on by external forces outside his control, and he's acquitted himself well. She also believes that he often leans on these skills and that his highly reactive style does sometimes keep him from preventing minor mistakes from becoming emergencies. And so, she sees some validity in Adriana's comment about the double standards she's held to as a woman of color, who would likely be rebuked for some of the same behaviors. Moreover, she's always been appreciative of Adriana's methodical, detail-oriented style and her commitment to quality and accuracy. However, she believes that Adriana doesn't always appreciate how Jay's role fundamentally differs from hers and how she often enjoys more autonomy than Jay, and therefore more control over outcomes in her department. Therefore, as she responds to Adriana and Jay in the moment and works with them to mediate this conflict in the coming weeks, she wants to maintain trusted relationships with them both while hopefully helping them to gain more appreciation for each other.

TIP

How adept are you at managing relationships in an emotionally intelligent way? Ask yourself:

>> Are you able to be vulnerable with your direct reports, peers, and leaders?

>> When communicating emotionally precarious messages, are your messages generally understood as you intended them?

>> Do you listen to understand, or to respond?

>> Do you frequently and sincerely praise your team (and individuals on your team) for a job well done?

>> Can you resolve conflicts on your team in a way that doesn't threaten their sense of value or belonging?

Discovering Your Level of Empathy and Emotional Intelligence

With the thousands of leaders that my firm coaches, trains, and consults with, I can unequivocally state that most leaders overestimate their skills and abilities and their effectiveness as a leader. The evidence comes when we conduct surveys, focus groups, and/or listening sessions with their direct reports and the general staff. There is often a disconnect and gaping hole between the leaders' self-ratings and those from the staff. I find that leaders tend to rest their laurels on the results that they get (or I should say that their team produces), or the lack of feedback from their staff, and their confidence in their technical and functional skills.

That's why it is critical to assess and seek out feedback on your skills and their effectiveness (not just in getting results, but how you lead the team as a whole and individually), and to develop in the areas where you are lacking.

TIP

Why not take a personal assessment on your level of emotional intelligence, as shown in the "Assessing Yourself" sidebar?

ASSESSING YOURSELF

When it comes to emotional intelligence, react to the following statements by giving yourself a score between 1 and 5. A "1" indicates that you either strongly disagree with the statement or never exhibit the behavior described. A "5" indicates that you strongly agree with the statement or almost always exhibit the behavior described. After you respond to each statement, add up your scores.

- In very stressful or emotional moments, I can easily name or process how I'm feeling.

1		2	3	4	5
(Strongly Disagree)					(Strongly Agree)

- There is someone (or more than one person) in my life with whom I can openly discuss how I feel.

1		2	3	4	5
(Strongly Disagree)					(Strongly Agree)

- I know about my triggers, pet peeves, and situations that cause me to have an emotional reaction.

1		2	3	4	5
(Strongly Disagree)					(Strongly Agree)

- When emotions run high, I can separate how I feel from how I wish to behave at that moment.

1		2	3	4	5
(Strongly Disagree)					(Strongly Agree)

- I have difficulty remaining calm when I am annoyed or frustrated.

1		2	3	4	5
(Strongly Disagree)					(Strongly Agree)

(continued)

(continued)

- I can resist the impulse to blame others for my behaviors, even if they provoked an emotional response.

1	2	3	4	5
(Strongly Disagree)				(Strongly Agree)

- I can name my own personal core values that I strive to live by every day.

1	2	3	4	5
(Strongly Disagree)				(Strongly Agree)

- My work is important to me, for reasons I can easily articulate.

1	2	3	4	5
(Strongly Disagree)				(Strongly Agree)

- I can project a feeling of optimism with colleagues, direct reports, and clients, even when I'm nervous or agitated.

1	2	3	4	5
(Strongly Disagree)				(Strongly Agree)

- I can typically predict how colleagues, direct reports, and clients will react to changes or increased demands.

1	2	3	4	5
(Strongly Disagree)				(Strongly Agree)

- I can listen to others' perspectives without showing judgment.

1	2	3	4	5
(Strongly Disagree)				(Strongly Agree)

- I often take time to imagine another person's perspective to better understand their emotional state.

1	2	3	4	5
(Strongly Disagree)				(Strongly Agree)

- I can communicate my understanding of another's feelings, even if I don't feel the same.

1	2	3	4	5
(Strongly Disagree)				(Strongly Agree)

- I can discuss my strengths and weaknesses, when appropriate, to leaders, peers, clients, and/or direct reports.

1	2	3	4	5
(Strongly Disagree)				(Strongly Agree)

- I frequently and sincerely praise colleagues, clients, and direct reports for a job well done.

1	2	3	4	5
(Strongly Disagree)				(Strongly Agree)

- I can mediate conflicts between people in a way that does not threaten their sense of value and belonging.

1	2	3	4	5
(Strongly Disagree)				(Strongly Agree)

Scoring

71–80: You have a high degree of emotional intelligence. Not only are you able to name and regulate your own emotions, but you can help others manage their emotional states as well. Just remember not to get frustrated when others don't share your EQ; not everyone will.

(continued)

(continued)

56–70: You have some strengths associated with EQ, but also some developmental opportunities. It's possible that you view an inability to manage your emotions as a form of authenticity or transparency. Remember that the ability to govern your behaviors does not inhibit you from naming your emotions and being honest about how you feel.

16–55: You are being led by your emotions more than you are able to lead them. To be truly effective in the workplace, especially as a leader, you'll need to uncover some strategies to improve self-awareness and self-control.

How well did you do? Remember that your scores are only as valid as how honest you were with yourself when filling out the survey.

Realizing the Need for Greater Empathy and Emotional Intelligence

Although the benefits are abundant, many leaders lack empathy and emotional intelligence due to a variety of reasons. Two of the most common explanations are insufficient training or education, and perceiving these skills as soft, non-tangible, or less important than hard skills.

WARNING

Even if these skills are strongly emphasized during business courses, it often takes real world experience and practice to fully understand how they can benefit your leadership style. Being empathetic and/or emotionally intelligent can be difficult if a person's life experiences haven't prepared them to recognize and understand their own emotions or the emotions of those around them. Some people are naturally resistant or even closed off to emotional understanding which can greatly reduce their effectiveness. Time constraints due to stressful working environments can lead leaders to forget or have the wrong priorities. As a result, paying attention and taking time out of their day to practice mindfulness, understand their own emotions, listen to their team members' individual needs, and make effective decisions is often forgotten.

The gap between what is required and what many leaders possess can be complicated by the way the human brain works. As discussed in Chapter 6, your Fast Brain is designed to take control of your behaviors during life-threatening emergencies. This is called an *amygdala hijack,* and is often experienced by a fight, flight, or freeze response. It's impossible to exhibit any self-control over your emotions when your Fast Brain (which mostly processes emotional data) is in control. Leaders who wish to behave in an emotionally intelligent way must remind themselves that work emergencies are rarely (if ever) life or death, and must consistently choose to override their Fast Brain with the more values-driven Slow Brain.

Empathy involves the mirror neuron system of the brain, a structure which allows humans to connect with others and often prompts them to imitate, or *mirror,* the emotional responses they observe. Unfortunately for leaders who wish to be empathetic, the mirror neuron system has an inverse relationship to power. In other words, the more powerless a person feels, the more activated their mirror neuron system is. This is surely an evolutionary trigger, allowing people who are vulnerable to establish safety through social connections. Inversely, the more powerful a person feels, the less likely their mirror neuron system is to unconsciously connect with others. This neurological phenomenon does not mean that it is impossible for leaders to be empathic. It does mean, however, that for anyone in a position of power, empathy must be a conscious choice, rather than an implicit response. Often, leaders who are new to their roles will greatly overestimate their levels of empathy because they are not aware of the effect their new position has had on their mirror neuron system.

By using empathy and emotional intelligence as business levers, leaders can make decisions based on intuition as well as rational analysis, bringing a more holistic approach to their business strategy. At its core, business leaders who embrace empathy and emotional intelligence will create environments where people feel valued, appreciated, and inspired to achieve their full potential. With the ability to look beyond surface level understanding, leaders who possess these traits will foster deep connections and meaningful relationships while simultaneously elevating their businesses bottom-line. Ultimately, empathy and emotional intelligence are vital for fostering meaningful relationships between leaders and followers and promoting success from within an organization.

TECHNICAL STUFF

DETAILING RESEARCH ON THE BENEFITS OF EMPATHY AND EMOTIONAL INTELLIGENCE

A myriad of studies has established a compelling business case for why leaders should demonstrate empathy and emotional intelligence with their teams:

- According to the Businessolver 2023 *State of Workplace Empathy Report* (https://www.businessolver.com/workplace-empathy/), 93 percent of employees are more likely to stay with an empathic employer.

- A study published in the *Harvard Business Review* (https://hbr.org/) found that companies with a strong empathic culture experienced a 20 percent increase in productivity.

(continued)

(continued)

- A study conducted by the NeuroLeadership Institute (https://neuroleadership.com/) revealed that 45 percent of employees working under high-empathy leaders reported a strong sense of trust in their organizations, compared to only 15 percent in low-empathy environments.

- According to a Society for Human Resource Management (https://shrm.org/) survey, 72 percent of employees considered respectful treatment of all employees a significant factor contributing to their job satisfaction. Empathic leadership fosters a respectful and positive work environment, leading to higher morale.

- In research by global consulting firm Catalyst (https://www.catalyst.org/reports/empathy-work-strategy-crisis/), 889 workers were surveyed about empathy in the workplace, and the results are startling. Some key findings of the research include:

  - Empathy is a force for productivity, life-work integration, and positive work experiences.

  - Employees with empathic managers and leaders are more innovative and engaged in their work than employees with less empathic managers and leaders.

  - Empathic leaders foster inclusion.

  - Women of color in particular experience less burnout when they have more empathic senior leaders.

  - Senior leader empathy is linked to reduced intent to leave.

- Research from the Center for Creative Leadership shows that leaders with higher EQ are better at building and maintaining positive relationships, fostering collaboration among team members.

- A study published in the *Harvard Business Review* found that teams led by emotionally intelligent leaders are more likely to collaborate effectively and achieve higher levels of performance.

- In a study by Hay Group, it was discovered that leaders with high EQ are more likely to be successful, with 90 percent of top-performing leaders displaying high EQ.

- According to a study conducted by TalentSmart, 90 percent of top performers in the workplace possess high emotional intelligence, which correlates with increased productivity.

Applying Empathy and Emotional Intelligence in the Workplace

Knowing how others are or might be feeling, recognizing and naming your own emotions, and seeing an issue from multiple lenses doesn't do much good unless the people around you can see it in action!

TIP

Here are some simple things that you can do to not only inhabit these traits but exhibit them too:

>> **Active listening.** To demonstrate this trait, leaders need to seek out the needs and concerns of their teams. Ask questions and try to understand the other person's point of view. What makes this kind of listening "active" is showing the person that you are listening. This means:

   • Giving them you full an undivided attention (eye contact where culturally appropriate, putting your smartphone away).

   • Non-verbal communications (nods, smiles, facial expression) in response to what they're saying.

   • Clarifying questions to aid in your understanding ("How did that make you feel?" rather than "Don't you think you could have tried . . .?").

   • Restating what you've heard for validation ("What I'm hearing you say is . . .").

>> **Reiterating shared values and goals between leader and staff.** This is exactly why organizations create core values, so that leaders and teams can use them to help make decisions and guide behavior. Reminding a common goal prevents in-fighting or working at cross-purposes and demonstrates that leaders and staff must collaborate to achieve success.

>> **Praise and rewards for outstanding work.** Showing recognition for good work helps build morale amongst the group which enhances empathy for all involved. Most people enjoy being praised in public, but some do not. Learn the unique preferences of everyone on your team. After all, if your goal is to bolster a person's drive, embarrassing them in public is probably not going to get you far. However, it's almost always appropriate to praise an entire team at once in public settings.

>> **Performance feedback tailored to the individual.** For example, focusing on small wins and promoting achievement even when success isn't guaranteed.

Showing empathy throughout the team strengthens relationships within the workplace not only between team leads but also between colleagues which promotes a more successful work environment.

» **The Platinum Rule.** Many of us learned the Golden Rule growing up, which is "treat others as you'd like to be treated." This maxim is surely well-intentioned, but it presumes that everyone likes what you like and wants what you want. It requires both empathy and emotional intelligence to learn about others and see the world from their perspective so that you can instead "treat others as *they'd* like to be treated."

IN THIS CHAPTER

» Exploring culture as a foundational concept

» Understanding cultural competence and cultural intelligence

» Uncovering why these competencies are important to leaders

» Charting the path of monocultural and intercultural mindsets

» Exploring the five orientations of cultural competence

» Making progress in the realm of cultural competence and cultural intelligence

Chapter **9**

Developing Cross-Cultural Competence and Cultural Intelligence

Cultural competence and cultural intelligence have become important to many organizations who are seeking to transform their cultures to be more welcoming and reflective of a multicultural workforce. They have embraced the reality that these competencies better prepare their leaders to foster a more inclusive, innovative, and respectful workplace.

In this chapter, I explore these concepts by defining what they mean, detailing their importance in today's workplace, and laying out a roadmap for developing the skills and mindset needed when becoming a more culturally competent leader with a high degree of cultural intelligence.

Defining Culture

In order to fully understand cultural competence and cultural intelligence, you must first understand "culture" because it is at the root of these two terms and the behaviors that encompass them. For something we talk about as often as we do, it can be difficult to pin down exactly what we mean by "culture." Is it just the feeling of a particular place or people, or is it something deeper? Is it a word we can apply to countries, regions, communities, companies, industries, cities, or all of the above?

Lots of definitions of culture are out there, but here are a few that I find most applicable:

>> Culture is a set of predictable beliefs and behaviors shared by a defined group of people. It can also be illusive and invisible, yet its effect can be seen and felt. In other words, culture is like the wind in that you can't see it but you do experience it (feel it).

>> "That complex whole which includes relation, belief, art, law, morals, custom, and any other capabilities and habits acquired by man as a member of society." These are the words of Edward Burnett Tylor, who wrote them in *Primitive Culture* (1871). He was an English anthropologist and considered by many to be the founder of cultural anthropology.

>> "The cumulative deposit of knowledge, experience, beliefs, values, attitudes, meanings, hierarchies, religion, notions of time, roles, spatial relations, concepts of the universe, and material objects and possessions acquired by a group of people in the course of generations through individual and group striving." This definition was coined by Larry A. Samovar and Richard E. Porter in their textbook *Intercultural Communication* (Wadsworth, 1994), which is studied in many colleges and universities throughout the world.

A culture can belong to any defined group, including ethnicities, nations, industries, or workplaces. For instance:

>> It is typical for many East Asian cultures to value emotional restraint, particularly in times of conflict.

>> France and Spain are neighbors, but it is very common for the work week to end at 3:00 p.m. on Fridays in Spain, whereas the French generally work their usual hours on Fridays and do not have the afternoon off.

>> In most hospitals, you'll notice doctors and nurses employing different uniforms so that the roles are easily distinguished.

>> In some workplaces, it's expected that employees will write self-assessments entirely based on their strengths and successes; in other organizations, the self-assessments commonly point out knowledge or skill gaps to make a case for further professional development opportunities.

REMEMBER

Culture can be a complex and expansive concept, and much of it is not directly observable with the five senses. To simplify things a bit, I'm going to define culture in this way for the purposes of this book: *Culture* consists of the norms, values, attitudes, and predictable behaviors supported by structure and strategies that an organization rewards or highly regards.

Let's examine culture more closely with these considerations:

>> A *defined group of people* in this sense, could be any defined group (large or small). It could refer to Hispanics or Latinos, the residents of Amsterdam, the citizens of Japan, those who are hearing impaired, Jewish people, LGBTQ people, scientists, actors, Gen Z, or people who work for Apple, LinkedIn, Deloitte, Walmart, or Amnesty International. For this reason, a leader need not work in a global organization for cultural competence to matter.

>> Culture shows up in both beliefs and behaviors. This boundary makes culture a bit easier to understand, since behaviors are often observable.

>> Moreover, beliefs and behaviors are often linked. For instance, military organizations depend on a strict hierarchy during combat; therefore, even during peacetime, military uniforms display a person's rank in a way that is highly visible. Contrast this with most tech companies, which believe that good ideas can come from anywhere, and the employees' position on the organization chart is not nearly as visible. Most of the time, behaviors stem from beliefs — but sometimes, a behavior, repeated over time, can impact the beliefs of a group of people. The Deaf, for instance, communicate visually rather than verbally. As a result, they have come to believe that eye contact as a form of respect. Within the Deaf community, it is extremely rude to look away from a Deaf person during a conversation, even for a moment. Moreover, when hearing people look at sign language interpreters more than the people with whom they're conversing, this is incredibly offensive.

WARNING

>> When discussing workplace cultures, a leader can espouse beliefs, but can only enforce behaviors. However, a leader without much cultural competence might be coercing their followers to behave in a way that does not align with their deeply held beliefs, leading to a culture that feels toxic and unwelcoming.

>> Culture is predictable because beliefs and behaviors are widely shared within a group. Cultural outliers can and do exist, in any nationality, identity group, industry, or company. But for a belief or behavior to be considered part of a group's culture, it must be shared and repeated by enough people within the group, so that insiders and outsiders alike can accurately predict how people will feel and respond in any given situation.

REMEMBER

Culture may be difficult to pin down, but it matters, even if your organization is only located in one country, or even one town. Differences are everywhere, which means culture is everywhere. If people with differing identity groups (such as race, ethnicity, religion, or sexual orientation) or different roles (for example, research, marketing, human resources, or finance) exist in your organization, you need to learn to work with all those differences.

Knowing the Difference between Cultural Competence and Cultural Intelligence

Working effectively among people with different beliefs, values, and behaviors is important. But a great leader needs more than just knowledge about different groups.

REMEMBER

Cultural competence is "the capability to shift cultural perspective and appropriately adapt behavior to cultural difference and commonalities," according to Mitchell R. Hammer, PhD, the founder of the Intercultural Development Inventory (IDI; https://idiinventory.com). The IDI is a theory-based, developmental psychometric instrument that measures cultural competence.

I often use the IDI when working with clients, particularly boards and senior/ executive leadership teams when they want to transform their culture to be more inclusive, welcoming, and less-biased. I start with assessing the leaders' level of cultural competence in the company's top ranks because I believe that like a thermostat, they set the temperature in the work environment in which the staff have to work. I appreciate the tool because it's based on an easy-to-understand model of cultural competence and is developmental in nature, meaning that it doesn't just diagnose a leader's degree of cultural competence, but offers strategies to become more competent in the future. There is no right or wrong response and there is no pass or fail. And most of all, it is valid and reliable and has been vetted on a large global scale.

The IDI positions cultural competence (or, as they prefer, intercultural competence) not as knowledge, skills, or abilities — but rather as a mindset. The Intercultural Mindset (find out more about this later in the chapter) can lead to behaviors that create a more equitable and inclusive work environments for those you lead. But while new behaviors can be exhibited immediately, mindsets are not immediately changeable, and becoming more culturally competent takes time and effort. In this way, both culture and cultural competence are a combination of beliefs and behaviors.

Cultural intelligence, or CQ, is a more recent concept that comes in to play while on the journey towards developing cultural competence. It goes beyond knowledge and understanding to encompass the capability to adapt and excel in culturally diverse settings. To be culturally intelligent does not imply an encyclopedic knowledge of all the world's cultures. But at the very least, an inclusive leader should have a baseline awareness of the different cultures represented on their team, within their organization, or among their customers (and potential customers). Most importantly, however, a culturally intelligent manager has a deep sense of their own cultural beliefs and behaviors.

This sounds like an obvious piece of knowledge to obtain; after all, you might expect to be aware of your own unshakeable beliefs. However, when you have mostly lived within a cultural group, some of these cultural beliefs might feel so obvious to you that they've never merited much thought. Some people use the analogy of a fish in water to illustrate this concept. If a fish has lived its entire life in the ocean, is it possible that it isn't even aware of the concept of water? It's all around the fish, but invisible. It could be something that it completely takes for granted, unless it's unlucky enough to ever be taken out of the water.

In the same way, it's possible to not know your own culture at all, but simply to assume that everyone is alike and shares your core beliefs. This is indicative of the "Denial" mindset in the IDI, described later in this chapter, that misses difference.

Cultural intelligence consists of four components: CQ Drive (motivation), CQ Knowledge (cultural understanding), CQ Strategy (adaptive thinking), and CQ Action (behavioral flexibility). Together, these components allow leaders to navigate unfamiliar cultural territories effectively.

Even if you don't know much about any other culture besides your own, a deep knowledge of self, combined with accepting that other cultures exist in the world, is a good place to start.

How much do you know about your own culture? Consider the following examples, and as you read, monitor how you feel and how this might contrast with the organization you work for:

>> **Power distance:** This refers to the belief that some people are naturally deserving of power over others. Behaviors associated with high power index would be soldiers addressing their leaders according to their rank (whereas many civilian organizations, particularly in Western countries, prefer leaders and followers to all be on a first-name basis).

>> **Emotional expression:** This refers to the extent that a culture values the expression of emotion. In very expressive cultures, displaying how you feel is a sign of integrity, that you truly mean what you say. In more restrained cultures, too much emotional expression (or expressing the wrong emotions) might be seen as unprofessional and reckless.

>> **Uncertainty avoidance:** This refers to the extent to which people and societies are threatened by ambiguity or imprecision.

>> **Individualism versus collectivism:** This refers to how much a culture values the rights of the individual as opposed to the needs of the group. In an individualist society, members are expected to be self-reliant and provide for themselves and their immediate families only. A collectivist society is one where members have a wider safety net, wherein relatives, clans, and organizations collectively provide for them in exchange for fierce loyalty to the group.

>> **Achievement versus relationship:** This refers to the extent to which the dominant values are assertiveness and wealth (achievement) or caring for others and quality of life (relationship).

TIP

Most cultures fall somewhere in the middle on most of these scales, but with definite preferences toward one end or the other. Ask yourself the following questions:

>> Where do you fall?

>> Where is your organization?

>> What kind of culture would best enable your organization to fulfill its specific mission?

Discovering Why these Competencies Matter to Leaders

Cultural competence and cultural intelligence are indispensable leadership competencies in today's diverse workforce. Quite simply, it's easy to be an inclusive leader if you're followers are just like you. In that case, "treating others the way *you* want to be treated" is sufficient, because all your followers want exactly what you want. The obvious problems that arise from this are:

>> Your followers are never exactly like you.

>> You wouldn't want them to be, anyway.

REMEMBER

Countless research studies in the field of organization development prove that well-managed, diverse teams outperform homogeneous teams. But a diverse team under the guidance of a leader who does not possess the cultural competence to value and bridge those differences will often be mired in conflict and misunderstandings and cannot possibly realize the benefits of being more culturally competent and intelligent. Companies are focusing on developing these competencies among their leadership ranks, and even their general staff, for a number of reasons. Here's a summary of the most common reasons:

>> **Enhanced communication:** Effective communication is the foundation of any successful organization. Leaders with cultural competence and intelligence can bridge communication gaps that often arise in diverse teams. They are more likely to understand subtle nuances in language, nonverbal cues, and cultural norms, facilitating clearer and more meaningful interactions.

>> **Improved team dynamics:** Diverse teams can be powerful sources of innovation and creativity, but they can also experience conflict and misunderstandings due to cultural differences. Leaders with cultural competence and intelligence can foster cohesion by promoting understanding and respect among team members, leading to improved collaboration and productivity.

>> **Increased employee engagement:** Employees who feel valued and understood are more likely to be engaged and committed to their work. Leaders who demonstrate cultural competence and intelligence create inclusive environments where employees from diverse backgrounds can thrive, leading to higher job satisfaction and retention rates.

>> **Effective global leadership:** In today's interconnected world, many organizations operate on a global scale. Leaders with cultural competence and intelligence are better equipped to lead international teams, navigate cross-cultural negotiations, and adapt to varying business practices, ultimately driving the organization's global success.

>> **Higher innovation:** Diverse teams are known to generate a wider range of ideas and perspectives. Cultural competence and intelligence enable leaders to harness this diversity by creating an environment where all voices are heard and valued, resulting in innovative solutions to complex problems.

>> **Ethical leadership:** Cultural competence and intelligence are closely linked to ethical leadership. Leaders who are culturally competent are more likely to make fair and just decisions, avoiding biases and discrimination. This not only benefits the organization but also upholds its reputation as a socially responsible entity.

Mapping the Two Mindsets of Intercultural Competence

While the IDI is built on the model of a continuum of five separate orientations, described later in this chapter, the continuum is framed against the journey of moving from a monocultural mindset to an intercultural mindset.

Monocultural mindset

The *Monocultural Mindset* is one that centers on one's own culture and views any other cultural differences that may exist in the world through that cultural lens.

As a result of this limited perspective, people who possess a Monocultural Mindset will often use broad stereotypes to identify cultural difference and will have simpler, less nuanced perceptions and experiences of both cultural difference and commonality.

Intercultural mindset

The *Intercultural Mindset* makes sense of cultural differences and commonalities based on the values and practices of one's own and other cultures.

As a result of this broader perspective, people who possess an Intercultural Mindset use cultural generalizations (with room for variance and outliers) to recognize cultural difference and have more complex perceptions and experiences of cultural difference and commonality.

THE TWO MINDSETS AT WORK

Consider an advertising agency that is implementing a new time-reporting process, asking all employees to track the hours spent for each project and each client. In the first few weeks, the project management staff have acclimated to the new system fairly well, while the creative staff (writers, graphic artists, and similar roles) are struggling to adapt.

Laura, a project manager with a Monocultural Mindset, cannot understand why her creatives are finding the task of time reporting so difficult, as she is able to consult her calendar at the end of each day and assign her hours in a matter of minutes.

Keith, a project manager with an Intercultural Mindset, can view the task from multiple points of view. He quickly realizes that his creative staff doesn't keep regular hours the way he does, and that they often work on a number of different projects within the same hour, making their time much more difficult to calculate. Perhaps most importantly, his creative staff aren't involved in invoicing their clients, and so don't know how valuable the tracking of hours can be.

While Laura and Keith are experiencing similar struggles with their creative partners, Keith is much better equipped to devise solutions, beginning with explaining to his creatives how these numbers are used to collect payment, and providing tips for tracking hours while multitasking.

Exploring the Five Orientations of Cultural Competence

The IDI is further categorized into five different orientations on the Intercultural Development Continuum (see Figure 9-1). From left to right, they are: Denial, Polarization, Minimization, Acceptance, and Adaptation.

The orientations move from the Monocultural Mindset on the left to the Intercultural Mindset on the right, and each conveys a higher level of cultural competence, an important trait for anyone who wants to be an inclusive leader.

WARNING

Cultural competence should not be conflated with "goodness" in the moral sense. It's possible to be a morally good person at any point on the continuum, just as it's possible that someone at any point on the continuum might also be a jerk.

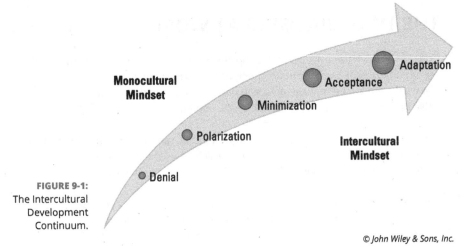

FIGURE 9-1:
The Intercultural
Development
Continuum.

The continuum is drawn as an arrow, as people are born on the left-hand side and through our life experiences, many of us move to the right. Where we end up has a lot to do with the life experiences we allow ourselves to have, so those who choose a sheltered existence where they don't come in contact with people of different cultures might be naturally to the left of someone who adventurously travels the world and engages with a culturally diverse group of people.

And a person's environment can also have an influence on their cultural orientation. Sometimes, a person is rewarded for a particular mindset, and disincentivized for moving further to the right toward a more intercultural perspective.

TIP

In short, there's no point in judging people for where they are on the continuum. Yes, there are bad people in the world, but it bears repeating that there are good people who inhabit each of these orientations.

The next sections look at each of the orientations in more detail.

Denial

The orientation furthest to the left is *Denial.* People who inhabit this orientation tend to miss difference. Because of their monocultural mindset, they tend to see the world through their own cultural lens, often without the knowledge that another perspective might exist. Someone in Denial might therefore say or do things that seem insensitive at best, and malicious at worst. But the underlying cause of these words and actions isn't malice, but ignorance.

For instance, an American in the Denial orientation who visits Japan would surely notice that the Japanese tend to bow rather than shake hands, and that many use chopsticks to eat their food. But beyond these surface differences, they might assume that the Japanese in every other way are just like Americans. If they witnessed an interaction between a young professional and their manager, for instance, they might quickly wonder why the young person is so deferential. They wouldn't know that the Japanese culture has deep-seated beliefs about respecting authority. Furthermore, the American in Denial might insist that they would never behave in such a way — when, if they had been born and raised in Japan, they might behave exactly that way.

People are born into the Denial orientation, and most people are exposed to cultural differences which prompt them to change their mindsets. But people in Denial generally live their lives in fairly closed cultures and don't have the exposure to difference to need to leave this orientation.

Polarization

The next step in the Intercultural Development Continuum is *Polarization*. People who inhabit this orientation tend to judge differences. Unlike those in Denial, they recognize that some people are culturally different, and not only behave differently but hold different beliefs. But they tend to have negative judgments about some cultures and see the world as an "us versus them" dynamic. Because they are still in a monocultural mindset, they place their own culture in the center of their thinking, and generally do not have the ability to see the world from another culture's perspective. In other words, they tend to lack empathy (see Chapter 8 for more on empathy).

In the workplace, Polarization might show up when staff are asked to state their pronouns when introducing themselves in a meeting. They might feel like their pronouns are "obvious" to everyone else and might not understand why some members of the team use they/them pronouns and how the practice of everyone stating their pronouns feels far more inclusive than only asking the nonbinary individuals to do so.

REMEMBER

The Polarization orientation can show up in one of two ways, called Defense and Reversal:

>> Those with a *Polarization-Defense* orientation tend to prefer their own culture over any other and tend to have negative judgments about any culture that isn't theirs.

>> Those with a *Polarization-Reversal* orientation tend to negatively judge their own culture, while preferring cultures that are not theirs.

In both cases, the tendency to negatively judge a culture (either their own or someone else's) places people in the realm of judging difference.

Those with a Polarization-Reversal orientation tend to believe that they're much further along the continuum than they are. After all, the realization that our own culture isn't perfect and that it's worth our time to learn what other cultures have to offer is a sign of growth that all culturally competent people must work through. But if other cultures are still viewed through the prism of how they compare to one's own home culture, there's still some growth that needs to happen.

WARNING

The Polarization orientation can sound awful, as though everyone with this perspective is closed-minded and bigoted. And certainly, there are many closed-minded and bigoted people who view the world in this way. But Polarization can also include people who are simply much more comfortable in certain cultural settings, and less comfortable in others. For them, their "judgment" isn't about harsh words or harmful stereotypes, but simply a longing to return to a place of comfort, usually because they don't know how to behave, succeed, or thrive in a multicultural environment. This is one example where a person's environment might have a profound impact on their orientation; if a person is the recipient of pervasive microaggressions in a particular setting, the desire to return to a different cultural space is perhaps both relatable and understandable (more on microaggressions in Chapter 6).

Minimization

In between the Monocultural Mindset and the Intercultural Mindset is a transitional orientation, called *Minimization*. People who inhabit this orientation tend to de-emphasize difference. Unlike those in the Denial or Polarization orientations, they can recognize cultural difference and will typically refrain from sweeping negative judgments about their own or other cultures, but when working or leading across difference, will tend to focus instead on what people have in common, avoiding talking about or dealing with difference.

Usually, people who inhabit this orientation are very well intentioned. They honestly don't view different cultural experiences as a threat to their own cultural practices. They usually don't mean to minimize anyone else's experience; in fact, they frequently assume that people have so much in common that navigating differences simply isn't necessary. However, by not discussing — or at times even acknowledging — what makes people different, non-dominant groups can sometimes feel as though they're not being fully included but are instead being merely tolerated.

Minimization can show up at work when communicating feedback to others. While the dominant culture might value direct and specific feedback, there may be some people on the team who would benefit from hearing the feedback more gently. However, a manager with a Minimization mindset believes that giving everyone feedback in the same way ensures a more common understanding. When feedback is given bluntly to those from different cultures, the message is certainly received, but it could foster resentment or cause those employees to avoid seeking feedback in the future.

Almost 80 percent of people who take the IDI are sorted into the Minimization orientation, so it's a very common mindset to have. Like all stops on the continuum, people tend to be sorted into an orientation because it works for them. It's possible for a person's friends, family, community, or employer to gently incentivize them to adopt the Minimization mindset, to avoid any conversations that may be uncomfortable or cause conflict. Often, members of non-dominant groups will adopt this orientation as a coping mechanism for working in an unfriendly environment. They might find that adopting an intercultural mindset might present challenges that can be sidestepped by avoiding discussions of difference.

Acceptance

The first orientation in the Intercultural Mindset is *Acceptance*. People who inhabit this orientation tend to embrace difference. They view diversity as a positive trait for an organization, and welcome opportunities to discuss both commonalities and differences with leaders, followers, and peers.

The "both/and" approach is important here. Minimization, to focus on commonalities as explained in the previous section, isn't wrong but it is limited. People with an Intercultural Mindset will still pay attention to what people have in common, and they will eagerly invite a conversation about differences as well.

People who inhabit the Acceptance orientation don't necessarily know everything about every other cultural group, but they are happy to learn more. In this way, one doesn't have to understand everything about another person in order to immediately accept or respect them.

Think about the feedback example from the last section. A manager with an Acceptance mindset might, when getting to know a new employee, ask how they'd like to receive feedback, and what else they might need from a manager in order to thrive in their role. In this way, not only understanding but valuing personal and cultural differences can make it possible for all team members to benefit from the kind of feedback that works for them.

Adaptation

The last orientation on the continuum is *Adaptation*. People who inhabit this mindset can bridge differences by shifting cultural perspectives and changing their behavior in appropriate and authentic ways. Like those in Acceptance, people in Adaptation don't necessarily have an encyclopedic knowledge of all cultures; however, they usually do possess a deep understanding of at least one cultural group other than their own. They also possess a high level of cultural intelligence and can articulate how their own worldview is culturally derived.

Often, people who inhabit the Adaptation orientation are bi-cultural themselves, either having been raised in a blended family or in an environment that drove them to navigate different cultures from a very early age. People who arrived at Adaptation in this way usually have a visceral knowledge of what it's like to be both a part of a dominant group and a non-dominant group.

Adaptation can be present at work when a leader has a global role that requires a great deal of travel. With each of their constituencies, they are able to quickly adapt and behave to different cultural practices and worldviews. This not only makes it easier to create trusting relationships across difference, but gives them a window into how these different groups see problems and work toward solutions.

WARNING

Just because people in Adaptation are at the far end of the continuum does not mean that they are necessarily nicer or more virtuous than anyone else. In fact, a key development focus for many in this orientation is to develop more patience with people who are not as adept at managing culture as they are.

WHERE DO YOU FALL?

Most people who hear about the five orientations of the IDI place themselves a little further to the right than where they actually fall. Oftentimes, our values are a little ahead of our mindsets, or we evaluate ourselves based on our best days rather than a more typical day. If you've not taken the IDI, consider that your perceived orientation might not be the same as the orientation you exhibit most often.

In the same way, it can be tempting to learn about the Intercultural Development Continuum and try to diagnose your co-workers and friends. Keep in mind that the instrument doesn't diagnose behavior, or even skill, but rather mindset. For instance, if you witness someone from a non-dominant group adopting the look or mannerisms of the dominant culture, are they truly taking on another cultural perspective (Adaptation) or simply avoiding criticism by assimilating (Minimization)? The difference lies in whether the adaptive behaviors feel authentic to the individual, and it can be difficult to know that by simply observing their behavior.

Becoming a Culturally Competent and Culturally Intelligent Leader

REMEMBER

Making progress in the realm of cultural competence and cultural intelligence doesn't happen overnight. It takes time to master new knowledge, skills, and behaviors — and in some ways, it takes even more effort to change your mindset. But change is possible, by opening yourself up to new life experiences that will cause growth and expansion.

Using the framework of the Intercultural Development Continuum (Figure 9-1), the challenge is not to simply reach for the Adaptation orientation, but rather to move through the process without skipping any steps. That means that a person in Denial will work toward Polarization. It might seem like a strange goal to move to a place of negatively judging other cultures, but Polarization is the natural next step, and a characteristically human reaction to seeing different cultures for the first time. A person who inhabits the Polarization orientation will aim for Minimization, where negative judgments can be replaced by an emphasis on what all human beings have in common. From that point on, the process is additive — meaning that you don't stop exploring commonality as you adopt the Acceptance and Adaptation orientations, but you add on a growing comfort with engaging around difference.

TIP

If you would like to take the IDI or introduce your work team to this engaging, proactive, and reliable tool, visit `http://idiinventory.com/qa-database`.

3

Leading Others

Find new ways to recruit and meet the needs of a diverse and hybrid team. Identify best practices for advancing through the stages of team development so you can maximize performance.

Describe ways to foster a psychologically safe work environment and identify factors that can undermine it.

Harness the power of coaching and giving feedback, and learn how to deliver it across differences and when dealing with sensitive topics.

Examine the impact of using non-inclusive language. Find ways to adjust your message and approach to communicate more inclusively.

Explore ways to make conflict less stressful and more productive.

IN THIS CHAPTER

» **Recruiting diverse talent**

» **Onboarding and orienting new team members**

» **Advancing through five stages of team development**

» **Understanding the advantages of a diverse team**

» **Cultivating trust and belonging**

» **Leading teams across differences and distances**

» **Steering clear of common pitfalls**

Chapter **10**

Assembling and Leading Diverse and Hybrid Teams

lead a diverse team as the CEO of my global consulting firm. I have a mix of work experiences, ethnicities, ages, sexual identities, personalities, cultures, and skills. And I was deliberate about selecting my team and looking for what I didn't have. As a result, I've achieved sustained success for nearly a decade because I learned how to utilize the unique and diverse gifts and talents of my team. Today I am proud to call them a team of "rockstars."

With the workforce becoming more diverse, globalized, and competitive every year, leaders must know how to build and maximize the performance of their team. This chapter details the important skills and practices needed for you to build a high-performing team that you too can call "rockstars."

Sourcing Diverse Talent

Before you can effectively lead a diverse team, you must build one! Often, this is a frustrating challenge for leaders who believe in diversity but think that they cannot find suitable qualified candidates. As a former recruiter, I can confirm that there is a lot of great diverse talent out there, but companies have to cast their net wider and employ new and creative tactics to locate them.

Assembling a diverse team isn't just about who you decide to hire. It's also about sourcing candidates in a way that allows you more of a choice. If your organization has a difficult time sourcing and hiring a diverse workforce, then doing so at team level requires intention, vision, and strategy.

TIP

Here are some best practices you can use to successfully assemble a diverse team. As you review them, consider how many are you currently exhibiting and where could you improve:

>> **Hire differently.** If you're using the process that everyone else uses, with the resources that everyone else uses, from the same places that everyone else draws from, it's no surprise that your candidate pool will be just as homogenous as everyone else's. Who recruits for you? Are they a diverse group themselves? Do they have a track record for attracting a diverse candidate pool? How might they react if they were directed to send you more women, people of color, or members of other underrepresented groups?

>> **Hire for the culture you want, not the culture you have.** Whenever I hear a story about a qualified candidate who didn't get a job because of "culture fit," I become suspicious. They were smart enough, skilled enough, and able to do the job, so what went wrong? Usually, this is someone who made the hiring manager uncomfortable in some way, someone who was different from the rest of the team. Sometimes, the same managers who bemoan the lack of diversity among their candidates are the first to turn someone away with this rationale. They want someone different, but the right kind of different, and not too different. The next time you hear the words "culture fit," ask a few questions. Which culture is being challenged here: Is it the culture you currently have? The one with not enough diversity among its workers? Or is it the culture you want? I'm all for turning someone away if, for instance, they indicate that they are stern taskmasters, and your company explicitly promotes a more compassionate brand of leadership. But all too often, "culture fit" is a bad excuse for not hiring the person who could have taken your team to the next level.

>> **Look for what's missing on your team.** When you're recruiting a new member of your team, it can be tempting to simply compare Candidate A to Candidate B and choose the one that's best. But this method doesn't always provide you with a complete picture. It's far better to compare your team with

Candidate A and compare that to your team with Candidate B. One candidate might have more experience in your industry or a degree from a more prestigious school, and still not offer anything new to your team. Let's say you lead a sales team that is mostly white. You know that your team should be doing a better job attracting and serving customers of color, but you also hear a lot of people who say, "You have to hire the best candidate, regardless of race." This is a true statement, but the "best" candidate in this case will be a salesperson who understands the needs and concerns of people of color. The best candidate might be a white person with a proven track record of selling to a diverse customer base, or they might be a person of color whose lived experience gives them access to knowledge that the rest of your team doesn't have. Either way, it would be irresponsible to choose someone with the same knowledge gap as the rest of the team.

» **Be flexible.** Review your systems and processes, as well as the unwritten norms, and be willing to make changes to create an environment where everyone can thrive. Often, norms and habits are formed without malice or ill intent; they work for the people who created them, but they may not work for the diverse team you hope to build. Some of your habits or traditions may not work for people with different faith traditions, abilities, dietary needs, or family structures. As your team becomes more diverse, check in to see if "the way we've always done things" still works for everyone involved.

» **Be willing to let go of old ideas.** Most of us have learned, often uncon- sciously, what a "successful person" looks like. We tend to be comfortable giving opportunities, including promotions, to people who conform to these archetypes. This can be especially true if your company has been around for a while and venerates its past leaders, all of whom probably looked the same. Rather than using the past as your criteria, measure people against what your company needs in the future. What are the skills, talents, and abilities that your company will need to compete 10 or 20 years from now? Those are the people you should be nurturing today.

» **Check the language and imagery you use to attract applicants.** How do (internal or external) applicants find you when you have an opening on your team? What kinds of messages are you sending about your workplace culture. Ask yourself the following questions:

- Is the language too gender-specific (for example, strong as opposed to proven, sound, or exceptional; lead as opposed to manage or guide; tackles as opposed to takes on, handles, or addresses)?

- Do the images of your company reflect the demographics of the changing workforce, or do they feature a homogeneous workforce that might discourage some people from applying?

- Do you recognize the holidays and rituals of different faiths, ethnicities, and cultures?

- What about your messaging directly appeals to people who are currently underrepresented in your organization?

WARNING

>> **Be aware of legal barriers and pitfalls.** Depending on what region you are hiring in, there might be different legal restrictions in place that must be adhered to. For instance, hiring quotas are illegal in the United States but might be allowed in other countries. Certain religious practices may have legal protections in certain countries, but no protections in other countries. Additionally, given the polarizing and changing views regarding Diversity, Equity, and Inclusion (DEI) in some regions around the world, it is important to consider the political, social, and economic effects. In any of these cases it is advised to consult your legal counsel to be sure you are complying with local, regional, and national laws.

Acclimating New Hires to the Team

I often tell business leaders that retention strategies begin as soon as an employee receives a job offer. All employees need to feel celebrated and appreciated as soon as they accept their new role.

TIP

Consider a ritual to celebrate your new employees immediately. The former CEO of one of the world's busiest airports would personally greet each new employee with a balloon bouquet, candy, and a personal message of welcome. It was a small gesture, but immediately made new employees feel appreciated, and that they were lucky to be working there. Moreover, new employees who belong to non-dominant groups (such as women, people of color, LGBTQ people, older workers, or people with disabilities) may not be aware of many unspoken norms and values that other employees take for granted.

If your organization has a difficult time retaining employees from a specific group, examine your employee engagement data, and isolate surveys based on demographic data to see if they are experiencing your culture in a vastly different way. Also, look carefully at the exit interviews that are conducted, specifically from members of that group who voluntarily left your organization. Consider asking all interviewees, "Is there anything that we could have communicated to you during onboarding and orientation that would have helped you during your time here?" The data you receive, if acted upon, can be very helpful in crafting an onboarding and orientation experience that allows all employees the chance to be successful.

Leading Your Team Through Five Stages of Development

Just as people go through different stages of their life as they grow and mature and as they go through stages of change management, the same is true for teams — they experience growing pains. The most common framework to illustrate the stages of team development was developed in the 1960s by American psychologist and researcher Bruce Tuckman. Originally, his model contained only four stages (Forming, Storming, Norming, and Performing). However, in 1977, he added a fifth stage, named Adjourning. Figure 10-1 outlines the framework.

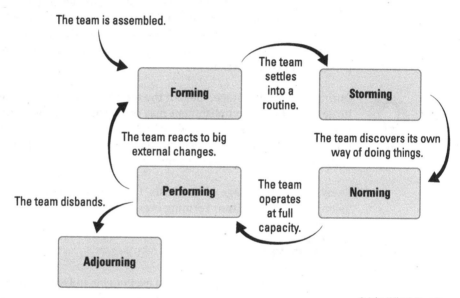

The team is assembled.

The team settles into a routine.

Forming

Storming

The team reacts to big external changes.

The team discovers its own way of doing things.

Performing

Norming

The team disbands.

The team operates at full capacity.

Adjourning

FIGURE 10-1: Tuckman's five stages of team development.

© John Wiley & Sons, Inc.

Forming

When teams first come together, there's often a lot of excitement and optimism. Team members are excited to be part of a new team, and eager to get results and feel successful. This is the *Forming* stage.

WARNING

While the overall mood is happy, there may be some team members who experience some anxiety as well. They might wonder if they'll be accepted by the rest of the team, or if their performance will meet everyone else's standards.

What a leader might observe during the Forming stage are lots of questions from team members. At first, team members might happily work on their own or in small silos. They may be highly motivated but still unsure if they understand the common purpose of the team. Generally, people in this stage strive to make a good impression on leaders and colleagues. At the same time, their concern is for themselves first (Will I fit in? What's my role? Who can I trust?) and the team second. Since bonds of trust have yet to be formed, this is natural and to be expected. Team members are typically receptive to guidance from their leaders about group norms and processes at this early stage.

What is required of a leader during the Forming stage are coordinating behaviors. Often, the leader is responsible for selecting the team. The leader's priority should be to clearly communicate the common goal or shared purpose of a team. It's also important to ensure that every member of your team feels valued and necessary to the team's success. This requires knowing their role and believing their role to be essential, but it also means that the leader is interested in each team member as a person, not just a function.

TIP

During the Forming stage, most of the team's energy is on defining the team and its goals, so task accomplishment may be low at this stage. Unless you have prepared some very easy "quick wins" for the team to complete and immediately celebrate, you can set the team up for success by allowing them to build trust without a long list of tasks to complete right away.

Enjoy the Forming stage while it lasts. It's a lovely place to be, but it's temporary! Teams will move on from Forming eventually.

Storming

During the *Storming* stage, the initial excitement and optimism of the team begins to fade as people settle into a predictable routine. However, as the name suggests, Storming can often be characterized by frustration, conflict, and anger. This is to be expected, as team members start to put more energy into their work, they naturally put less energy into gaining everyone else's approval. When people's authentic selves begin to show, there are going to be disagreements on processes, boundaries, norms, and habits. Most people (especially leaders!) don't particularly enjoy this stage, and may secretly wish for the pleasant, polite days of Forming to come back. However, seasoned leaders know that Storming is necessary for a team to establish trust and build authentic relationships.

What a leader might observe during the Storming stage are behaviors that indicate frustration. For some, this might be an outward expression, but for others, could look like stewing silently in a private corner. As the work naturally slows down and colleagues aren't responding as quickly and happily as they used to, some team members might feel that the work isn't happening fast enough. Often, the leader becomes a scapegoat, as they have "allowed" the team to devolve into bickering and constant irritation.

The first trait required of a leader during the Storming stage is patience. Leaders who have lived through this stage many times have come to expect it. They don't blame themselves when the first signs of conflict arise and are able to smile and listen to the team, even when they're not behaving quite as nicely as they were a short time ago. Moreover, leaders who are shepherding a team through Storming do a lot of coaching. They must be a trusted resource to everyone on the team (even those who place blame the decrease in civility at the leader's door!), and coach the team to place more trust in each other. When conflict arises during the Storming stage, a leader's job is not to take sides but to facilitate a way for the two parties to resolve it together.

When the team looks like it might be splintering apart, it's helpful to assist everyone in refocusing on their goals. One way to do this is to break the goals down into smaller achievable steps. While it can be wonderful for a team that is Forming to think about what they can accomplish in a year or two, a team that is Storming will be much better served by knowing what needs to happen by the end of the week.

It's especially important during the Storming stage to keep an eye on your team members from marginalized or underrepresented groups, to ensure that they're not feeling the effects of this volatile stage more so than other people on the team. While this stage should be temporary, the reality is that it tends to be a more prolonged experience for those in the minority group.

Norming

When and if the *Norming* stage is reached, team members will find a balance between their personal needs and expectations and what they team needs and expects from them. I say "if" because, unlike Storming, there's no guarantee that a team will reach this stage. However, if the team and its leader can effectively build norms that are flexible and inclusive, there should come a time when everyone on the team experiences a sense of safety in expressing their authentic selves. This includes asking questions, offering new ideas, or even challenging the team's work. (See the next chapter for more on psychological safety.)

What leaders might notice, if they're observant, is that team members are knocking on their doors less often and resolving conflicts on their own without many signs of outward conflict. This is because they trust their team members more to hear them out and are much more willing to assume positive intent when something doesn't go as planned. Often, teams in this stage will begin developing their own inside jokes, and certain team members might be given nicknames.

What is required of a leader during the Norming stage are empowering behaviors. As team builds bonds of trust among each other, they want to know that their leader trusts them as well. Check in, get feedback, and reward team members for a job well done — but resist the urge to micromanage and allow the natural leaders on your team to take ownership of their work.

Just because things seem to be going well during this stage, that's mostly due to the team trusting each other. It doesn't necessarily mean that the norms and processes the team created or agreed to during the Forming stage are the best ones for this specific team. At the very least, leaders should be open to feedback regarding different or better ways of doing things. Even better, be proactive. Ask the team what improvements they'd like to see.

Performing

When a team is making visible progress and members begin to see the effects of their hard work, it enters the *Performing* stage. Here, they are acutely aware of the strengths and weakness of all team members (including themselves). Here, the team is finally greater than the sum of its parts, and all members feel valued and included.

What a leader might notice during the Performing stage is that the role definitions, which the team worked so hard to define during the Forming stage, have become much more fluid. Team members are willing to stray from their job descriptions, and their colleagues are not threatened or territorial in response. Dissent is expected, and handled so collegially that an outside observer might not notice it.

What is required of a leader during the Performing stage is very similar to what the team needed from them during Norming. Listening and receiving feedback are still critical. However, as the team begins to self-manage regarding their tasks, the leader should set aside some time to foster continued team engagement. This might seem unnecessary, but the Performing stage should not be taken for granted, as it can change.

While it's possible for a team to remain in Performing mode for a long time, change can and will happen. Key members of the team (including leaders) may leave, they may or may not be replaced, priorities might shift, changes in the marketplace may demand new ways of working, or something like a global pandemic may have a huge impact on the way a team works together. When these things happen, it's likely that the team will cycle through the stages of team development again. If you are a new leader on an established team, you will likely be welcomed by many friendly faces who hang on your every word. This is a repeat of the Forming stage, and you will likely experience some Storming and Norming before you can lead a Performing team. However, if the bonds of the team are strong and they are used to engaging as a Performing team, the cycle should move very quickly. But much of this depends on you being the type of leader that the team needs during each phase of the cycle.

Adjourning

They say nothing lasts forever. And that's true for some teams as well. If a team has completed its work or is disbanding for some other reason (the company is restructuring, closing its doors, or there's a monumental change such as a large layoff that will necessitate a return to the Forming stage eventually), the team goes through a process of *Adjourning*. During this phase, the team either completes its task and celebrates its success or decides what will be finished and what not before all or most of the team says goodbye. Even if the team is dissolving for the very best of reasons (such as if the task was successfully completed and its success has been recognized, and the leader received a big promotion based on the team's exemplary work), there's often an air of sadness about the team breaking up or changing.

What a leader might notice during the Adjourning stage could be as varied as the team members themselves. Some might become anxious and less focused on their tasks, whereas others could find that hyper-focusing helps them deal with the impending sense of loss. There will often be a strong desire to reminisce. If the future of the individual team members is unclear (for example if many must look for their next job), they could begin to separate prematurely as a form of emotional protection.

What is needed from a leader during the Adjourning stage is to help the team to acknowledge its upcoming transition. Obviously, if there are still deliverables that are required during this time, they should be attended to. If possible, time should also be spent evaluating the team's work, allowing each member to take some lessons learned with them. Even if the reasons for the team's dissolution don't feel very celebratory (a reduction in force or a company shutting down), encourage your team to celebrate each other and whatever successes you did achieve together. Let each team member know what you valued about them, so they can take that into their next chapter.

REMEMBER

As with any transition in life, there's no one correct way to adapt or mourn. As a team prepares to break apart, allow for a range of different reactions. Obviously, if a team member seems to be in abject denial, a leader can help by gently reminding them of the upcoming closure. If a team member is acting out in ways that are having a negative impact on the entire team, some coaching may be necessary. Otherwise, allow people to grieve and separate in the ways that feel the best to them. It's entirely appropriate and predictable that individuals return to a self-focused outlook during this stage, and there's no real benefit in transitioning as an intact group.

Figuring out what stage your team is at

Teams who come together will almost certainly enter the Forming stage. The Storming stage is almost certain to follow. If the team disbands or goes through a big change, the Adjourning stage will certainly happen. But the stages of Norming and Performing aren't guaranteed. Teams that could be accurately described as toxic might be permanently stuck in the Storming stage. Other teams, that feel much more pleasant but never reach their full potential might be in the Norming stage but not able to break through into Performing. Even teams that are performing at their peak (Performing) could cycle through the process again when a significant upset forces them to regroup and create new ways of doing things.

That said, your team isn't guaranteed to be in the Performing stage just because you've been together for a while. Much of this has to do with how diverse your team is, and how inclusive of a leader you are. Diverse teams that lack inclusion typically underperform homogenous teams, but a diverse team that exhibits inclusion can almost always outperform a homogenous team (see Figure 10-2). So if your team isn't operating at full capacity, you might not have enough difference in the lived experience and thought patterns on your team. If your team is rife with bickering and unconstructive conflict, the fault may lie with the leader for not being truly inclusive.

Number of teams

FIGURE 10-2: Diversity and team performance. Based on research by J.J. DiStefano, M.L. Maznevski, and C. Kovach.

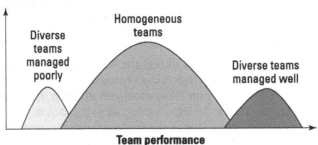

© John Wiley & Sons, Inc.

TIP

To diagnose your team's stage, ask the following questions:

» How much *negative conflict* (squabbling, territorialism, gossip) do you notice on your team?

» Is it possible that negative conflict exists but is being hidden from you?

» How much *positive conflict* (respectful dissent, collaborative problem solving) do you see?

>> Does your team perform their tasks with high quality, and within the prescribed schedule and budget?

>> Does your team take pride in their work? Do they readily recognize and celebrate the accomplishments of others?

If negative conflict can or does exist on your team, it's possible that you are still in the Storming stage. If you recently exited the Forming stage, this should not be a cause for concern; in fact, it's predictable. But if this persists, it can easily create a toxic work environment, especially for underrepresented groups. Positive conflict is a sign that you've moved on to the Norming stage, and teams that produce high-quality results and celebrate their achievements are likely at the Performing stage. If you believe your team is at the Performing stage, there is still work for you to do. As a leader, you are tasked with keeping them there, and navigating through any big changes (such as a leadership transfer, a shift in priorities, a change in scope, mergers, and so on) that could send you back to the beginning.

TIP

If your team dynamic needs to be improved, the following steps might be required:

>> Provide appropriate feedback.

>> Go through mediation.

>> Give support to team members who are struggling.

>> Be open to questions, feedback, and pushback.

>> Reinforce your common goal or purpose.

>> Manage expectations.

>> Clarify roles.

>> Establish explicit norms.

>> Help your team build relationships, particularly across difference.

Maximizing the Benefits of a Diverse Team

The business case for inclusive leadership is significant (Chapter 3 presents more detail on this), but this is especially true when you have assembled a diverse team. The combination of diversity in your team and an inclusive workplace culture can help you soar above the competition in the following ways.

Creativity and problem solving

An individual's creativity can be measured simply by examining how many ways that person can view a particular problem when crafting a solution. Likewise, a team is more creative when it contains a multitude of perspectives with which to approach challenges, problems, and obstacles.

These perspectives can include people who see the big picture and people who notice details, people who create meticulous plans and people who think more spontaneously, and people who excel at solving problems using logic and people who excel using more values-based arguments. In addition, it includes the perspectives gained from different lived experience across race, gender, sexual orientation, disability, religion, and culture.

Collaboration

WARNING

Diverse teams aren't necessarily better at collaborating, at least not at first. When a diverse team enters the Storming stage, the leader might be in for quite a storm indeed! Diverse teams arrive at the door with very different ways of gathering data, seeing the world around them, processing information, and communicating their thoughts. A lack of cultural competence on the team (see Chapter 9 for more on this) could lead people to misunderstand or even cause offense when interacting with so many kinds of people.

However, when a diverse team is led by an inclusive leader and learn to collaborate with one another, they become better at seeing all kinds of different perspectives, including customers, senior management, vendors and suppliers, and other stakeholders. They are generally open to more information and new sources of knowledge they might not have considered before. They are much better at reacting to external forces nimbly and quickly than a homogenous team who haven't developed the same skill set.

Increased business performance

People from different backgrounds, cultures, ages, and so on can be your best resource to understanding the needs to diverse customers and stakeholders. No matter how "informed" people are, they still tend to see the world through their own lenses. On a diverse team, you can implement strong marketing strategies and understand the perspectives of people from these communities instead of viewing different markets from your own single point of view. This shift helps grow your brand and increase your customer base.

TIP

When you're expanding into new markets, get feedback from a cross-section of people, and be sure to include people who represent your target market. You don't want to offend the groups whose business you seek.

Engagement and retention

People who belong to diverse and inclusive teams are happier. Therefore, they tend to be more engaged in their work and less likely to be actively looking for new opportunities elsewhere. When team members feel seen for all of who they are and see that others are too, this not only builds trust but loyalty. People who belong to diverse and inclusive teams have each other's backs and focus their competitive energies outside the team (toward market competitors in a for-profit company or toward fulfilling the mission statement in a non-profit organization).

Fostering an Environment of Trust and Belonging

Ultimately, what an inclusive leader is trying to do with a diverse team, made up of people from different cultures and backgrounds with different life experiences and skills all working together to achieve a common goal, is to create bonds between them. These bonds are trust and belonging:

>> *Trust* is defined as a reliance on someone to do the right thing or a belief that what they say/do is true. In the context of a team, it is the belief that your place on the team is secure. When trust is present, an employee can freely express their ideas, knowing that they will be heard and considered even if they are not ultimately adopted. When trust exists, an employee can ask a question without being made to feel stupid or offer criticism without being accused of not being a team player. Trust means that an employee knows that a leader won't take credit for their ideas, and that their leader wants them to succeed.

>> *Belonging* is the belief that you are accepted for your entire self, you matter, and that you are necessary for the team. Belonging doesn't necessarily mean that your weaknesses shouldn't be improved upon, or that you couldn't be replaced, but it does mean that your leaders and colleagues appreciate you despite those weaknesses, and that if you left, the team wouldn't ever be quite the same.

How do you know when trust and belonging is present on a team? Look for the following clues. When you see most or all of them on a team — especially a diverse team — you know that inclusion is also present:

>> Full participation and lots of discussion

>> Clear and accepted goals

>> Active listening and fearless sharing of ideas

>> Disagreement both common and comfortable

>> Consensus-based decisions

>> Free expression of ideas

>> Frequent, honest, and constructive feedback

>> Cooperation and caring

>> Ideas are challenged, not people

>> Clear assignments and tasks

>> Shared leadership

>> Willingness to re-examine norms and processes

As you read this list, how is your team doing? Do you see these behaviors on a regular basis? If not, what can you do to make these happen? If you're at a loss, the rest of Part 3 is full of tips and suggestions.

Leading Across Differences and Distances

Leaders play a pivotal role in fostering an inclusive atmosphere that recognizes and leverages the unique strengths of a diverse team. To effectively integrate diversity, leaders should apply some key practices and considerations.

Firstly, communication should be tailored to accommodate diverse perspectives and preferences. Recognizing that different team members may have varied communication styles, leaders should encourage open dialogue and ensure that all voices are heard, regardless of location. Leveraging technology to facilitate asynchronous communication allows team members to contribute at their own pace, accommodating diverse working styles. Leaders must also be attuned to the potential challenges faced by team members from different backgrounds. This includes acknowledging time zone differences, religious observances, and cultural nuances that may impact work schedules and expectations. Implementing flexible work arrangements and accommodating diverse needs contribute to a supportive and inclusive environment.

TIP

One example of diverse working styles especially prevalent in today's workforce is remote working. Virtual meetings often require different norms than meetings that take place around a conference table. For instance, the use of chat or anonymous polling can allow you to hear from everyone in a group, not just the most outspoken. You might want to consider requiring cameras to be turned on during a virtual meeting to increase a sense of belonging. In some cases, it's beneficial to require everyone to blur their background in order to ensure everyone's comfort in doing so. Finally, you might consider beginning all virtual meetings with a check-in, where everyone in a meeting can briefly state how they're feeling or how the group might support them.

Leaders should actively seek diversity in team assignments and projects, ensuring that opportunities are distributed equitably. Encouraging cross-functional collaboration and mentorship programs can further promote a culture where everyone feels valued and has the chance to excel.

REMEMBER

Consideration of unconscious biases is crucial. Leaders should undergo training to recognize and address biases that may affect decision-making processes. This fosters a fair and equitable workplace where talent is recognized and promoted based on merit, irrespective of demographic factors.

TIP

People are complex. Teams are even more complex. And diverse teams amp up the complexity to a greater extent! The task for a leader can be somewhat overwhelming, so to simplify matters, I've created this list of best practices for leading across difference:

>> **Provide a sense of vision and meaning.** While accounting for what makes each person on your team unique, the most effective way to get them to work as one unit is to point them all in the same direction by creating a compelling vision that matters.

>> **Align and support strategic goals.** The success of your team also means that your work benefits the whole company. So, as you craft the projects and goals for your team, make sure that they align directly with the strategic goals that your company has set for itself.

>> **Understand what motivates your people.** Are people on your team motivated by having an impact? Public recognition? Having fun at work? Being able to contribute while enjoying work/life balance? On a diverse team, the reasons will be wide and varied, and getting to know the people on your team helps you motivate them to do their best.

>> **Don't just talk the talk — walk the walk.** Nothing is more dispiriting than a leader who spouts a lot of empty platitudes but doesn't follow through. Even if you're saying all the right things, your credibility will suffer if your actions aren't aligned to your words. Don't make a lot of lofty speeches if you aren't prepared to do as you say.

>> **Implement the strategies you've learned for mitigating bias.** All humans have bias, and there are proven methodologies for managing and mitigating your personal biases as you make decisions (read more about this in Chapter 6). Your job as leader is to facilitate group decisions, so you should be using the same tools with the group. Under the guidance of an inclusive leader, your team can learn to make better decisions, individually and collectively.

>> **Recruit what you don't have.** The choice between two candidates is never just about the two candidates. It's about how each of these candidates can contribute to a team. So, even if your first choice has a more impressive résumé, your second choice might have an important skill set that the team needs more, and therefore might be the better option.

>> **Educate yourself about differences on your team.** When someone on your team represents an aspect of diversity that you have little experience with, don't place them in the role of your teacher. After all, they already have a job to do, Chances are, their job description does not include being your private tutor on their community, culture, or background. You're the leader, it's your job to know how to create an inclusive environment where they can thrive. Find reputable sources of information online or make use of your organization's Employee Resource Groups to help (find out more in Chapter 17). Obviously, you should work to get to know this individual like anyone else on your team (see the third bullet in this list), and you will pick up much from these conversations, but don't place anyone on your team in the role of educator.

>> **Practice the Platinum Rule, not the Golden Rule.** Growing up, most of us learned the Golden Rule, which is, "Treat others as you would like to be treated." The Golden Rule is certainly well-intentioned, but there's an obvious flaw, which is that not everyone wants the same things that you want. I prefer the Platinum Rule, which is, "Treat others as *they* would like to be treated." Of course, you will first have to find out what they want in a leader, but that's an integral part of the work.

>> **Integrate a mindset of inclusion into all practices and processes.** When establishing processes and group norms for your team, there's no reason to fall back on the way you've always done things, even if those practices were successful in the past. Weigh all your options against the team you have now. For instance, if you have a high number of introverts on your team, throwing out questions to the entire group and receiving "popcorn" style responses (where whoever has an idea just shouts it out) might not be as effective as

giving the group a moment to think, then going around the room and hearing from everyone in the meeting. Creating inclusive processes is much easier if your team members know they can come to you with ideas and that you will be receptive to them.

>> **Hold each other accountable.** Many teams stuck in the Storming stage are led by people who have unwittingly become disciplinarians rather than leaders. Whenever a conflict erupts on the team, one or more parties will knock on the leader's door to deliver a verdict or a judgment. This is problematic for a few reasons, but most notably, these teams are soon unable to resolve conflicts on their own. The key is to intervene only when necessary, and otherwise mediate the conflict in such a way that team members develop their own solutions until they are ready to hold each other mutually accountable without leadership intervention. This will allow the leader to focus on more strategic activities.

TIP

In addition to considering diversity, keep the following best practices in mind when leading across distance:

>> **Honesty and transparency.** Distance is a barrier, and avoiding conversations about the obstacles it presents will not erase them.

>> **Camera time.** Encourage the use of cameras during virtual meetings. If your remote workers are on camera all day, this can be exhausting, so be strategic about which meetings require the use of cameras. If workers are self-conscious about their homes, help them to create backdrops that put them at ease.

>> **Overcommunicate.** When something is important, communicate it to your team at least three times. Remote workers can easily miss verbal communication that is easily picked up by someone in the same room, so send an email.

>> **Establish new norms.** Consider making time at the beginning of each meeting for a check in. These can be short ("What are two words to describe how you're feeling today?"), but hearing from everyone will make it easier for your remote workers to speak up later.

>> **Get together once a year.** My team works all over the country, and we meet in person for a few days each December to celebrate our accomplishments and set intentions for the coming year. This meeting is something that we all look forward to, and the connections that are built or strengthened during these meetings bear fruit for the rest of the year.

>> **Have fun!** If your team celebrates birthdays or work anniversaries, set up a chat channel in addition to cutting cake in the break room. Encourage all staff to post GIFs and congratulatory messages there. Create some new traditions, too; encourage people to share photos of holiday celebrations with the team or create an annual gift exchange that is conducted virtually.

Avoiding Common Pitfalls when Leading a Diverse Team

WARNING

Just as there are many ways to lead a diverse team effectively, there are also ways that a leader can really mess up. Be wary of the following situations when you lead a diverse group:

» **Not listening to new ideas.** The reason you want a diverse team to begin with is the wealth of ideas and innovation. Sadly, a leader only needs to refuse to listen to the creative input of their team once or twice before the new ideas stop being offered.

» **Failing to provide necessary resources.** A leader is not there to do the work of the team, but to ensure that the team is able to do their best work. That includes providing them with the tools, expertise, time, and money they need to perform at their peak. Furthermore, creating a system wherein every little change or request involves multiple reviews and signatures from hard-to-reach people can dent team productivity and morale.

» **Overreacting to conflict or failure.** If every little conflict is a sign that your team is broken and therefore you are a failure, then failure is practically guaranteed. One of the reasons that Tuckman's five stages of team development (see Figure 10-1) is such a powerful model is that it explains how necessary and healthy conflict can be, and that its presence can be a sign that the team is growing in an essential way.

» **Gatekeeping information about the business.** A company that makes all its information proprietary even for employees below a certain rank can prevent a team from making strategic and inspired decisions that ultimately benefit the company. Reduce the gatekeeping, trust your people, and unleash their creativity.

» **Monitoring and micromanaging.** Unless your team has worked hard to lose your trust, don't succumb to the temptation to keep tabs on them. Believe in their ability to do their work and trust them to come to you if necessary. It's appropriate to set deadlines and check in to see how things are going, but no one does their best work if they feel as though they are constantly being watched.

» **A lack of communication.** When policies or procedures change at the company level, it's important to involve the team in the decision, or — at the very least — give them some advance warning of the impending change. While they're busy doing the work of the team, you should be doing all you can to facilitate that work. This includes passing on knowledge that is important to them.

>> **Slashing the training budget.** Part of what keeps a team engaged and productive is the ability to learn and grow. Even if someone has been in the same role for several years, it's satisfying for them to track how much they've learned over a span of time. Some learning can be done on the job, of course, by assigning team members to new and challenging tasks. But training and development, when done well, can be a vital part of an employee's learning journey.

>> **Overcriticizing and underpraising.** One form of bias that is rampant in the workforce is called *negativity bias*. This refers to the tendency to pay more attention to negative data than positive data. There's a good reason why negativity bias exists. Positive data signals that things are going well, whereas negative data points you to problems that may need your immediate attention. But as a leader, it's vital that you proactively pay attention to positive data. This will not only give you an accurate picture of your team's performance, but it also allows you an opportunity to recognize your team for a job well done. In my career, I've heard many leaders say that they are loath to thank they're employees for doing their job and will therefore reserve their praise for truly exceptional work. My thought is "Why not?" Saying thank you costs a leader very little and can be a great motivator for staff. Working for a leader who only points to what's gone wrong with no recognition of what is going well is a toxic situation.

>> **"Because I'm the leader, that's why."** You can't say yes to every new idea that comes your way. But when you do go in another direction, it's valuable if you can articulate the reasons why. This communicates to your team that their ideas were heard and considered and could help them offer better ideas the next time. If this communication is absent, your team members are likely to believe that their ideas were never taken seriously and that you believe you know best in all situations. Of course, what happens next is that the ideas dry up, and the value of your diverse team is lost.

Assembling a diverse team has benefits that extend beyond mere compliance to laws to positively impacting innovation, decision making, customer relations, employee satisfaction, and overall organizational performance. Companies that recognize and harness the power of diversity position themselves for long-term success in an increasingly dynamic and competitive business environment.

IN THIS CHAPTER

» Describing trust and psychological
  safety

» Detailing the four stages of
  psychological safety

» Highlighting the advantages of a
  trusting and psychologically safe
  workplace

» Identifying ways that psychological
  safety is undermined and how it is
  cultivated

» Building and evaluating the impact of
  psychological safety

» Celebrating what best practice
  companies do

Chapter **11**

Establishing Trust and Psychological Safety

I have some important questions for you at the start of this chapter.

Are you the kind of leader that can be trusted by your team? If so, what does that look like. If not, why not, and how do you rebuild trust when it's been broken or undermined?

Is your workplace a *safe space?* I'm not talking about being safe from physical danger, less likely to have an accident, or in compliance with your industry's safety standards. I mean a safe space where *all* staff feel free to speak up at work, they feel heard, valued as a member of the team, and have a sense of belonging, all while being the most authentic version of themselves. The kind of safety I'm talking about here is psychological safety.

This chapter expounds on both trust and psychological safety, which are relevant and timely workplace issues that continue to show up in employee expectations and in workplace surveys as two critical gaps. You'll discover what it means to have trust and to work in a psychologically safe workplace, how they are built and what to do when they are decreased, and the impact that they have on worker performance, engagement, and creativity. The chapter signs off with some examples of companies that demonstrate these skills well.

Defining Trust and Psychological Safety

REMEMBER

Trust is the foundation of effective leadership and is a fundamental element in creating and maintaining a positive and productive work environment. As such, leaders must have solid trust building skills to succeed. In simple terms, *trust* is the belief that a leader is truthful, reliable, and has the ability and competence to get the job done. Unfortunately, this skill is not something that is taught enough, nor is it demonstrated effectively or consistently enough and I have found in my work with organizations of all sizes and sectors that as a result, trust is diminished, especially among leaders and their direct reports and among senior executives and the general staff.

This lack of trust shows up in communication, the degree to which workers say they feel respected, valued, recognized, heard, developed, and in a safe space to be their authentic selves.

When a workplace isn't a safe space, or a safe to speak culture, many employees — particularly marginalized and/or underrepresented staff (for example, women, LGBTQ people, older workers, Jews, Muslims, people with disabilities, Gen Z, or people who are neurodiverse) — will show up to work in an unauthentic way, literally pretending to be someone they're not, just so they'll be accepted into the group. But when this happens, the acceptance is never genuine. There's always a fear that the acceptance is conditional on their ability to hide who they are, and that if their disguise is discovered, they'll be shunned. So work never feels safe.

REMEMBER

The concept of *team psychological safety* was first coined by Dr. Amy Edmonson of Harvard University in 1999. She defined psychological safety in the following way:

>> The shared belief, held by its members, that a team is safe for interpersonal risk-taking.

>> A sense of confidence that the team will not embarrass, reject, or punish someone for speaking up (with ideas, questions, concerns, or mistakes).

>> A team climate characterized by interpersonal trust and mutual respect, in which people are comfortable being themselves.

TIP

Because psychological safety is a shared belief, it's not enough that one person, or even most of the people on a team, feel safe. If interpersonal risk-taking is not safe for everyone, then psychological safety doesn't exist. Therefore, when judging how psychologically safe your own team is, it's not enough to report several anecdotes where team members offered suggestions, asked questions, or even challenged the group. Those few anecdotes might be exceptions to the norm. Rather, look at each member of the team and try to identify those behaviors. If there are people on your team who have never taken a risk within the team, whether it's an idea that might be rejected, or a question that might reveal a knowledge gap, or a mistake that might damage their credibility, there's good reason to believe that you have some improving to do.

WARNING

Now that you know what psychological safety is, it's just as important to know what it isn't:

>> Psychological safety is not a personality factor. Creating a psychologically safe workspace is an important skill that has much more to do with a leader's observable behaviors than their mindset.

>> Psychological safety is not being nice and agreeing with everyone. Kindness certainly helps, but simply keeping the peace does not create psychological safety.

>> Psychological safety is not about lowering performance standards. In fact, as discussed in the next section, a lack of psychological safety is much more likely to hamper your team's ability to succeed in their goals.

Outlining the Four Stages of Psychological Safety

Dr. Timothy Clark, the founder and CEO of LeaderFactor, expanded on Dr. Edmonson's work in his book *The 4 Stages of Psychological Safety: Defining the Path for Inclusion and Innovation* (National Geographic Books, 2020). In it, he defined four distinct ways that team members can feel safe in a supportive, and inclusive team. The next sections describe these four stages of safety.

Inclusion Safety

The first stage is *Inclusion Safety*, which satisfies the basic human need to connect and belong. In this stage, team members feel safe to be their authentic selves and are accepted for who their unique attributes and defining characteristics. Without inclusion safety, people engage in extensive *code-switching* (adjusting one's style of speech, appearance, behavior, and expression in ways that will optimize the comfort of others), which takes energy away from doing their job.

When Inclusion Safety is present, your Jewish colleagues can discuss their plans to celebrate the high holidays, your LGBTQ colleagues can talk about their families, introverts on the team can choose to eat lunch on their own if they wish, and a recent college grad who was just hired on your team can ask multiple questions in the meeting — all of these instances can occur without fear of judgement, gossip, or retaliation.

REMEMBER

In short, when a team exhibits Inclusion Safety, all members of the team can be who they are. The freedom to simply be is the bedrock of psychological safety, and therefore defined as the first stage; without this, none of the other stages can be achieved successfully.

Inclusion Safety is especially important during the tough times. Consider the following examples from Arrow Company, a fictional company characterized by homogeneity and toxic leadership:

- » Tristan has been working for Arrow Company for six years. When he joined the company, he heard a group of colleagues in the kitchen making fun of people with bipolar disorder, calling them "Schizos" and "Crazies." He noticed his own manager chuckling at the crude jokes. He decided that he would not share that he had the disorder as long as he worked there. He also did not confront his manager nor his colleagues and just kept his head down. He tried everything he could to cover up his condition and over time became more disengaged and distrusting of his colleagues and manager. And any time he saw them huddled together, he assumed that they were making more jokes about people with disabilities. He started missing days of work and would stay home curled up in bed as depression and anxiety overtook him. Eventually he was admitted to a health facility to get help. His colleagues all showed concerned but he didn't believe them. He asked that none of them visited him and after HR requested a doctor's note for his absence, he submitted his resignation because he did not want anyone to know about his condition. And he knew that if he went back to work for that manager and around those colleagues that he would not feel safe to be his true self.

- » Denyse is a Black woman who, while driving to work, hears the news that another unarmed Black citizen has been killed by a police officer. As she listens to the details of the story, a familiar dread and anger settle at the bottom of her stomach. She thinks about her brothers and her children and wonders how safe any of them can be in a society where this happens all too often. As she pulls into the parking garage, she remembers the last time this happened, when her feelings were minimized by white colleagues at Arrow Company who didn't understand how she could be deeply affected by the news of someone she didn't know who lived thousands of miles away. In the rear-view mirror, she practices a wide smile that she hopes will fool her colleagues, so she won't have to talk about anything other than work. She sighs, because it's going to be a long day.

Neither Tristan nor Denyse has the freedom to be themselves at Arrow Company. And when both experience a level of trauma, a mental breakdown for Tristan and a form of collective trauma for Denyse, they are forced to pretend they are something they are not to maintain an illusion they have created. Both have prioritized the comfort of those around them for an artificial sense of belonging, at the risk of their own mental health.

Learner Safety

The second stage of Clark's model is *Learner Safety*, which satisfies the basic human need to learn and grow. In this stage, team members feel safe to exchange in the learning process, by asking questions, giving and receiving feedback, experimenting, and making mistakes.

REMEMBER

When Learner Safety is present, people can be honest about their level of skill, which allows leaders and colleagues to quickly fill in the gaps. Without covering their lack of competence, employees can learn easily and far more quickly.

Consider the following example from Arrow Company:

A few months ago, Kendra was offered a role on Arrow's Global Sales Team. The position featured an increase in salary and the opportunity to travel out of the country, and she was very excited to join. Since that time, however, she has been frustrated by the lack of support offered to her by her manager and colleagues, specifically when she has questions pertaining to her customers in other countries. In fact, when she did ask specific questions about how to greet potential customers from Asia, she was made to feel incompetent because of her lack of global experience. Her manager brushed her off, saying that he valued team members who "did their homework" and counseled her to do an internet search the next time she had questions to save the team time. She is currently preparing for her first trip to Brazil, but doesn't want to further damage her credibility or annoy her teammates by asking them for assistance beforehand.

Learner Safety is clearly not a priority on Kendra's new team. Rather than answer her important questions or assist her in doing research, thereby teaching her how to effectively teach herself, they've responded with insults. Not only will these behaviors surely erode trust in general, but they will certainly prevent Kendra from asking any more questions of her manager or her team. As a result, she is likely to pretend to know more than she does, which increases the likelihood that she will make costly mistakes. Learning now becomes something she must do on her own, and likely in secret.

Contributor Safety

Contributor Safety satisfies the human need to make a difference. In this stage, employees feel safe to use their knowledge, skills and abilities to make a meaningful contribution to the work of the team.

REMEMBER

Without contributor safety, people often suffer from feelings of inadequacy and self-doubt that stifle their ability to do their best work.

These meaningful contributions can take the form of tasks that might fall outside of an employee's job description, or simply an idea about how the work could be done better. A team that doesn't exhibit Contributor Safety typically wants its employees to contribute, but to "stay in their lane," only adding value as defined by their job description or prescribed role. Employees who have previously unknown talents or knowledge of a new topic might be hesitant to bring those to the forefront in a team without Contributor Safety, for fear that they'll be seen as stepping on someone else's toes.

So, in a way, teams that do exhibit Contributor Safety are ones in which members feel secure, not only to be themselves and to ask questions, but also to let others shine. These teams might engage in some healthy competition now and then, but the overall spirit is one of collaboration, and not being threatened by each other.

Consider this example from BoardTech, a fictional company that places a high priority on inclusive leadership, and both teaches and incentivizes its leaders to lead inclusively:

Claire is new to BoardTech, having just graduated from college with a business degree. She is excited about the opportunity to join Martha's team in Client Relations. During onboarding, Martha is telling Claire about their entire portfolio of clients. Halfway through this rundown, Claire learns that one of her team's brand-new clients is the world's leading manufacturer of sailboats, and that the team has been recently tasked with learning all about sailing. Claire's eyes light up as she tells Martha that she has been sailing since she was a little girl and was the captain of her college's sailing team. Martha immediately decides that this new client should be added to Claire's portfolio, and they begin to make plans for a quick lunchtime presentation to the entire team called, "The Anatomy of a Sailboat."

If Claire wasn't excited about joining BoardTech before, she surely is now. Not only is her formal education being put to use, but she's already being asked to teach her colleagues about a subject that has nothing to do with her formal job description, but everything to do with maximizing a relationship with a brand-new client!

Challenger Safety

The fourth stage in Clark's model is *Challenger Safety*, which satisfies the human need to make things better. In this stage, team members feel safe speaking up and challenging the status quo when they think there's an opportunity to change or improve.

Challenging a leader or a group requires some courage on the part of a challenger, but leaders can still play a part in ensuring that those who do speak up with disagreements, different perspectives, or complaints are not penalized for doing so.

Consider two more examples from BoardTech:

>> Antonio is new to BoardTech, and has just joined the Public Relations Team, led by Kathy. On his third day on the job, a colleague who had been at BoardTech for years was preparing a press release celebrating the fact that BoardTech's Hispanic/Latino Employee Resource Group (ERG) had just won a national award. Before it was sent out, he looked it over, and personally found the constant use of Spanish phrases throughout to be cloying, and — on two occasions — incorrect. Being new on the team, he was nervous about raising his concerns to Kathy, but upon doing so, she agreed with his recommendations, thanked him for coming forward, and asked if he'd agree to being a resource for future press releases that address the Hispanic community.

>> Ahmad is a team leader within BoardTech's Research & Development Team. Recently, a new position opened on the team, and Ahmad wants three of his more senior team members to interview the top two candidates and advise him. After conducting his own interviews with Rachel and Ethan, he has a clear preference for Rachel. She has, to his mind, the right kind of experience for the work that Ahmad's team has been doing. But, not wanting to sway his advisors, he keeps his preference to himself when asking his three advisors for their opinions. Immediately, two of them validate Ahmad's stance, that Rachel would be a better match for the work of the team. But when Ahmad seeks the input of Rivka, she says that she'd rather the team hire Ethan. She

argues that the team already has several people with Rachel's experience, and that Ethan would bring something new to the team and could potentially help the team expand their work. Rivka makes some excellent points and seems to be swaying her teammates to reconsider Ethan, but Ahmad still prefers Rachel. Ahmad takes a deep breath, and says, "Let's talk about this. Does anyone have a reaction to what Rivka has just said?"

Even though Antonio's colleague had worked at BoardTech for a long time, Kathy took his concerns seriously, and immediately recognized that Antonio had lived experience that gave him insight into this press release that no one else on her team had. She was more concerned with issuing effective content than protecting the egos of anyone on her team.

In Ahmad's case, he wanted to increase Challenger Safety from the beginning by not immediately declaring a preference for one candidate over the other. But when two of his direct reports immediately expressed the same preference, Rivka's stated preference for her choice still put her in the role of the challenger. Although Ahmad still favored his original selection, he honored Rivka's contribution to the conversation by allowing others to react. The possibility that Rivka would sway her teammates, and even Ahmad himself, away from Rachel was certainly there. Clearly, Ahmad was more interested in choosing the best candidate than he was in having his way.

RECOGNIZING A PSYCHOLOGICALLY SAFE WORKPLACE

A psychologically safe workplace is one in which all team members can:

- Give and receive feedback
- Raise issues and concerns
- Disagree with their leader
- Disagree with each other
- Ask for clarification
- Ask difficult questions
- Ask for help
- Offer solutions to problems
- Admit errors
- Be their authentic selves

Realizing the Benefits of a Trusting and Psychologically Safe Workplace

The scenarios in the previous section demonstrate the advantages of working in a psychologically safe workplace.

The first and most obvious advantage of psychological safety is creating a humane place to work. In the previous section's examples, the Arrow Company employees (Tristan, Denyse, and Kendra) are enduring real challenges to their mental health and well-being because of a work environment that neither sees nor values them. By contrast, Claire, Antonio, and Rivka know that they can be their full authentic selves at BoardTech; in fact, they are all immediately rewarded for doing so. Therefore, any leader that claims to care about their direct reports as human beings should be striving to create a psychologically safe workplace.

REMEMBER

Better mental health and wellness comes with benefits of its own, including better team morale and more staff engagement and job satisfaction. These, in turn, can immediately be translated into higher rates of engagement, innovation, productivity, and retention. An employee doesn't have to leave their job to quit their job: some employees quit a long time ago, but they are still there. Both scenarios are a drain on the resources of your organization.

Looking at the examples in the previous section, which of the employees do you think is next to resign or to be actively seeking another job in the next six months? Which employees are the most likely to disengage, doing the bare minimum but never "going the extra mile" for their jobs. This is now called *quiet quitting*.

TECHNICAL STUFF

Gallup data suggests that a majority of workers are still quiet quitting. In fact, according to the *State of the Global Workplace: 2023 Report* (https://www.gallup.com/workplace/349484/state-of-the-global-workplace.aspx), nearly six in ten global employees are psychologically disengaged from their organization, even if they're putting in the agreed-upon hours.

Getting more specific, is it likely that Kendra will be able to navigate Brazilian culture and norms without any team support? Could Tristan have been prevented from resigning his job?

Another advantage of psychological safety is an increased ability for a team to learn, innovate, and adapt in a rapidly changing world. No matter what industry you work in, do you think you could survive in today's workplace only knowing what you knew ten years ago? If you're like most people, probably not! The world has always been constantly changing, but the rate of change seems faster than ever and shows no signs of slowing anytime soon. Therefore, a team's capacity for new knowledge, new ideas, and new ways of working is an essential competency, and a lack of psychological safety can greatly inhibit that.

Teams with higher levels of psychological safety are more productive and can solve problems more efficiently, and have a greater amount of innovation than their competitors whose workplace cultures are not trusting or safe. Let's revisit the stories of Claire and Antonio, two new employees at BoardTech. Without the enthusiastic reactions from their leaders, their added expertise might never have been used. It's entirely possible that Martha's team would have arrived at their first client meeting not knowing a mast from a rudder, or that Kathy's press release would have reflected poorly on the company and possibly even angered their own Hispanic employees.

Identifying the Factors that Drive and Undermine Psychological Safety

Leaders cannot simply order or wish that their employees feel safe and included. They must lead by example, establish trust, and create a psychologically safe workplace. Part of this is waiting for your employees to show up authentically, ask questions, contribute their knowledge and ideas, or present a challenge. At that point, a leader can ensure that these behaviors are welcomed and rewarded. If so, employees are likely to repeat the behaviors, thereby creating a healthy and high-performing work environment.

WARNING

Rewards must be both predictable and consistent. Even if you reward your employees' authentic expression, questions, contributions, and challenges nine times out of ten, just one act of perceived retaliation against speaking up can greatly undermine the psychological safety of a team, especially if the negative response is highly visible to all members of the team. Remember, someone on your team who is nervous about speaking up with an idea or suggestion will look to see how others are treated when they do the same.

Factors that undermine trust and psychological safety

Many reasons exist why an employee will refrain from speaking up. Sometimes, these have little to do with the behavior of a well-intended leader and can therefore be frustrating. However, a workplace in which people are forced to speak up is just as unsafe as a workplace where employees are punished for doing so.

Two common factors are:

>> **Fear.** Perhaps an employee spoke up at their last job, and it didn't go well. Despite being in a new place, where speaking up is rewarded, they've already decided that it's a risk they're not likely to take again. Perhaps an employee is the only person of color on the team, or the only woman. In this instance, fear of a double standard might be keeping someone silent. An employee might also fear losing status. Even though they can see others on the team asking questions and admitting mistakes without retribution, there could be something in their family or cultural background that makes it difficult for them to do the same. Sadly, it's a possibility that a member of your team has been bullied, attacked, or vilified in the past, and the trauma they've experienced is simply more powerful than the incentives a leader is providing to be more vocal.

>> **Resignation to silence.** Perhaps an employee suffers from *imposter syndrome* (a form of self-doubt that causes a person to feel fraudulent about their achievements) and therefore does not believe they have anything of value to add. An environment where others are sharing their ideas and being rewarded for them could even make this situation worse. Sometimes, employees from marginalized groups have been told that to succeed, they should focus on producing quality work while calling as little attention to themselves as possible, lest they be perceived as loud or a troublemaker. Finally, an employee might have given feedback in the past and was ignored, making the effort seem futile.

REMEMBER

While many of these factors are outside of a leader's direct control, the attitudes of leadership usually have a big influence on them. Here are some leadership responses that can go a long way toward mitigating factors that undermine psychological safety:

>> Show appreciation when people do speak up, always.

>> Communicate an open-door policy for questions and requests for help.

>> Focus on solutions, not blame.

>> Reward the behaviors you'd like to see repeated.

>> Embrace messengers, even (especially) when it's bad news.

>> Explain the reasoning behind your decisions.

>> Celebrate the contributions of your team, rather than overemphasizing "fit."

Factors that cultivate trust and psychological safety

Many of the people on my team look, act, work, and think very differently than I do, but because I have established trust and safety among them, they are high functioning, collaborative, and engaged. In successfully leading change and transformations for our client organizations, I have found that the same proven strategies for building, maintaining, and rebuilding trust and safety that work for my team, also work for them.

TIP

Communicating clearly, openly, and honestly is one of the most effective ways to establish and enhance trust. Leading by example, walking the talk, and living your values must all align and be consistent. There is nothing more damaging to trust and psychological safety than to say one thing and do another. This also gets to the heart of integrity.

Apologizing when you're wrong, and seeking to first understand by asking questions and listening intently, increases your trustworthiness and sends a message to your employees that it's OK to make mistakes. It is also the most critical step to rebuilding trust when it is broken.

WARNING

Never forget that your team members and other followers are always watching and taking cues from you. Actions speak louder than words so show them that you can be trusted by being consistent and sincere in your actions and words.

Treating others with respect is another must for building trust and safety. Some examples that I employ include:

>> Extending kindness and warmth (offering a smile, greeting team members by name, asking how they are doing, speaking words of encouragement, giving hugs).

>> Having a regard for the feelings of others (I listen to understand, I position my body language in a positive way, and I respond to the specific need).

>> Showing civility (being polite and courteous, accepting differences of opinion, using an appropriate tone and inclusive language).

>> Owning up to mistakes and avoid finger pointing and blaming.

>> Following through on commitments.

TIP

If something comes up that affects your ability to keep a commitment, immediately reach out to the person, the client, or to the team, and let them know. Apologize for any inconvenience and look for ways to minimize the impact to them. Apologies and taking ownership like this go a long way to rebuilding trust and psychological safety.

Creating Psychological Safety

Earlier in this chapter I detailed the four stages of psychological safety developed by Dr. Timothy Clark. They were Inclusion Safety, Learner Safety, Contributor Safety, and Challenger Safety. This section offers some ways that leaders can create each of these in their teams. Some of them have been detailed earlier in the chapter, but it's worth reiterating their application to these four stages.

Increasing Inclusion Safety

TIP

To create Inclusion Safety on your team, it's important that you show up as your authentic self at work. Be approachable and relatable. This means sharing things about your life outside of work. Who are the important people in your life (family, friends, even pets)? How do you spend your free time? Are you a sports fan or a movie buff? What communities do you belong to? What's your cultural background? Where and how did you grow up?

Part of this disclosure is about finding common points of interest with your team members, but mostly, it's an act of role modeling. You cannot expect people on your team to be upfront about who they are if you are not as open and vulnerable with them. In this case, it is both unfair and unrealistic to ask your followers to disclose to you what you are unwilling to disclose to them.

It's also important to let your employees know what your values are and to live according to your values, consistently. Think back to Tristan, earlier in this chapter, who worked at Arrow Company. His dilemma would have been greatly helped if he had felt comfortable sharing that he had bipolar disorder with his colleagues long ago, but he didn't. Just after he joined, he overheard some crude jokes in the staff kitchen, and then noticed his own manager chuckling along. He remained silent and detached because it felt safer. In this case, the manager played a direct role in Tristan's lack of psychological safety, or didn't really value inclusion in the first place.

TIP

It helps to have supportive organizational practices. Including "Diversity" or "Inclusion" in your organization's core values is a start (but it's even better if your organization can define these values as observable behaviors and holds all employees accountable to exhibiting them). Explicit nondiscrimination policies might not have kept Tristan's colleagues from telling those jokes, but they might have prompted Tristan's manager or someone else to challenge them. An organization that invests in DEI (Diversity, Equity and Inclusion) Training, Employee Resource Groups, or other Leadership Development programs can also encourage employees to consistently be their authentic selves at work.

Increasing Learner Safety

To increase Learner Safety, a leader can be proactive about providing feedback in a timely manner. Even if your followers aren't asking questions, a leader can notice when someone on their team is stuck and needs assistance.

TIP

Offering answers or guiding the employee toward a successful outcome can go a long way toward encouraging them to come to you (or their colleagues) with questions the next time they need help. However, it's important that you do so without belittling them or making them feel as though they have been reduced in status or credibility.

Inclusive leaders can create *practice fields* for their employees. Before an important client presentation, for example, allow your employees to present to their colleagues and get feedback. These kinds of trials, dry runs, or simulations can encourage employees to take risks and learn important skills, leading to more creativity and innovation.

Increasing Contributor Safety

If Contributor Safety is lacking on your team, be on the lookout for those skills and abilities your employees have that might have nothing to do with their job description. Remember Claire, the captain of her college sailing team, who featured earlier in this chapter? It might seem as though Martha, her leader, lucked into the knowledge of Claire's unusual expertise, but in fact she learned this important piece of information because she felt it necessary to give Claire information about the team's full portfolio. Had she only shared the information she felt Claire "needed to know," it might have been months before Martha knew there was such an asset on her team.

TIP

Job descriptions can be written in a way that encourages Contributor Safety. When a role is defined as collaborative and interdependent of others within a work unit, it encourages the kind of information exchange that makes it not only safe to contribute, but necessary!

Increasing Challenger Safety

To create a sense of Challenger Safety on your team, it's important to manage their emotions and reactions. Read more about emotional intelligence in Chapter 8.

Within a command-and-control leadership style, challenges can feel like insubordination, or a lack of respect. To see how it could be done better, let's recall Kathy and Ahmad, two leaders at BoardTech who featured earlier in this chapter.

In Kathy's case, her top priority was to send out a press release that would celebrate the accomplishment of her company's Hispanic ERG. Antonio's challenge brought to light that the press release, as written, might have insulted them instead. Meanwhile, Ahmad was clear about the candidate that he wanted to hire. But more important than his own ego was hiring the best candidate for his team at that time — and he had to admit, his follower Rivka was making some excellent points to support her choice. Even if Ahmad does not change his mind, he will feel even better about the decision he eventually makes, knowing he made space for a reasonable counterargument.

Measuring Psychological Safety

Because the defining characteristic of an unsafe workplace is silence, it can be difficult to accurately measure the degree of a team's psychological safety with your five senses. Obviously, you can see when someone is shut down for asking a question, retaliated against for making a mistake, or ignored when challenging the status quo. But these situations only need to play out once for a team to cease speaking up for a long time afterwards. It's also predictable that a leader will tend to be too optimistic when diagnosing their own team in this regard, especially if they believe that a lack of psychological safety is an indicator of poor leadership on their part.

TIP

The best way to measure psychological safety on your team is acquire concrete data. If your organization conducts regular engagement surveys, here are some statements that you could include. After each statement, present your employees with a five-point scale, ranging from 1 (Strongly Disagree) to 5 (Strongly Agree). Note that some of the statements are framed positively and others negatively, to encourage careful reading!

>> When someone makes a mistake on the team, it is often held against them.

>> In this team, it is easy to discuss difficult issues and problems.

>> In this team, people are sometimes rejected for being different.

>> It is completely safe to take a risk on this team.

>> It is difficult to ask other members of this team for help.

>> No one on this team would deliberately act in a way that undermines my efforts.

>> My unique skills and talents are valued and utilized by my colleagues.

>> In this team, we use established norms to approach challenges and manage conflict.

Recognizing Best Practice Companies

In addition to what great leaders can do to create psychologically safe workplaces, it can also be valuable to note what great companies do. What follows are the stories of four companies who take the lessons of this chapter and apply them to their entire organization.

Pixar: "Fail Early and Often"

At Pixar, the film studio responsible for motion pictures such as *Coco*, *Up*, *Wall-E*, and the *Toy Story* franchise, former president Ed Catmull takes issue with the idea that mistakes and failure are necessary evils in creative endeavors. In his book *Creativity, Inc.* (Random House, 2014), he writes, "Mistakes aren't a necessary evil. They aren't evil at all. They are an inevitable consequence of doing something new and, as such, should be seen as valuable. Without them, we'd have no originality."

In fact, many variations on this theme are very popular around Pixar. For instance, Andrew Stanton (director of *A Bug's Life* and *Finding Nemo*) would often say "fail early and fail fast," or "be wrong as fast as you can."

In this way, both Contributor Safety (having an idea, no matter how zany) and Challenger Safety (recognizing that an idea isn't working) were explicitly rewarded by the organization, helping to cement Pixar's reputation as a studio that makes movies you won't find anywhere else.

WORKING WITH TRUSTED LEADERS

As you strive to be the kind of leader who fosters trust and a psychologically safe workspace, can you think of a time in your career when you worked for such a leader? Think about the following questions:

- Who made you feel comfortable hearing feedback from, or giving feedback to?

- Who seemed especially receptive to your ideas and challenges?

- What characteristics did they possess to help put you at ease?

- How did you know it was safe to be your authentic self with this person?

- Can you emulate any of these characteristics or behaviors with your own team?

Eileen Fisher: "Leadership is About Listening"

When Eileen Fisher, an American fashion designer and entrepreneur, founded the company that bears her name, she said that listening was always at the forefront of the way she worked: "Everything's about listening, that's just how I started. I started listening to buyers in a way that other designers don't. That's just very second nature to me. When we listen, things shift."

She readily admits that an overabundance of listening sometimes makes it difficult to complete simple tasks, such as staying on a strict agenda for a meeting. But, according to Fisher, sometimes when a meeting "goes off course," people on her team end up talking about what really matters.

She describes her leadership style as a focus between focus and flexibility, which allows her company to both create products that are personally fulfilling but are also what the market is looking for. Because she has always modeled listening as the primary function of a leader, this has become synonymous with the way the entire company functions.

Barry-Wehmiller: "What We Do Matters"

When Bob Chapman assumed the role of CEO of manufacturing company Barry-Wehmiller in the mid-1970s, the company was nearly a century old. But during his tenure, he transformed a local manufacturer into a $3 billion global firm, and built a culture based on human psychology.

In his book *Everybody Matters* (Portfolio, 2015), he wrote, "When we say our people matter but we don't actually care for them, it can shatter trust and create a culture of paranoia, cynicism, and self-interest. This is not some highfalutin management theory — it's biology. We are social animals, and we respond to the environments we're in. Good people put in a bad environment are capable of doing bad things. People who may have done bad things, put in a good environment, are capable of becoming remarkable, trustworthy, and valuable members of an organization."

Leaders at Barry-Wehmiller are coached to value every employee and communicate that value. "Everyone wants to contribute," Chapman writes. "Trust them. Leaders are everywhere. Find them. Some people are on a mission. Celebrate them. Others wish things were different. Listen to them. Everybody matters. Show them."

X Development LLC: "Shoot for the Moon"

X Development, LLC (formerly Google X) is an American research and development facility founded by Google in 2010. The mission of X Development is to develop *moonshot* technologies, which are defined as "radical new technologies to solve some of the world's hardest problems."

TECHNICAL STUFF

The term "moonshot" was inspired by John F. Kennedy's 1962 speech at Rice University, when he told the world about his dream to put a person on the moon before the decade was over. Famously, American astronaut Neil Armstrong took that giant leap for mankind in 1969. This was only possible, according to the leaders at X Development, because Kennedy took a courageous, audacious, and public stand.

Nothing about their mission statement supports thinking small, compromising, or taking tiny steps forward. Rather, the leaders at X Development insist on big ideas and extreme innovation. It should go without saying that the researchers at X Development therefore must be free to ask questions, contribute their knowledge, and challenge old ways of thinking. The Moonshot Mindsets, which define X Development's culture, are:

>> Aim for 10X (10 times bigger), not 10 percent.

>> Fall in love with the problem.

>> Make contact with the real world early.

>> Fuel creativity with diverse teams.

>> Tackle the monkey (the difficult but necessary part) first.

>> Embrace learning (through failure).

>> Become a chaos pilot.

>> Learn to love "version zero crap."

>> Shift your perspective.

>> Take the long view.

You can read more about these mindsets at their website: http://x.company/moonshot.

IN THIS CHAPTER

» Harnessing employee potential through coaching and feedback

» Differentiating between coaching and feedback

» Using Situational Leadership

» Steering clear of common feedback pitfalls

» Giving well-planned and well-executed feedback

Chapter **12**

Coaching and Giving Feedback

Leaders play a crucial role in unlocking the full potential of diverse talent within organizations. By prioritizing coaching and feedback, leaders contribute to the individual growth, inclusivity, and enhanced performance of their teams. And they contribute not only to the well-being of individuals but also to the overall strength and resilience of the organization.

Early in my career as a young, single woman of color I sought to move up the corporate ladder but too often found myself being overlooked and undervalued — doing the work, getting the results, but not getting noticed, promoted, or given the specific feedback to help me to grow. In fact, in several companies I was labeled as "high potential" and a "high performer" but was still not given direction or support to move to the next level — yet my peers who were white men were consistently advancing.

To harness the full potential of a diverse workforce, leaders must go beyond attracting great talent and assembling a diverse team to actively providing effective coaching and feedback. It is a proven fact that this increases creativity, employee engagement, organizational performance, retention, and collaboration across departments. In this chapter I focus on the need for leaders to provide more consistent and balanced feedback, and I provide the tactics and strategies to do so in a way that meets the unique needs of all workers. Also, I provide guidance for how leaders can have the difficult conversations that are often avoided but are so needed for the growth and advancement of their team members.

Acknowledging the Impact of Not Providing Coaching and Feedback

Unfortunately, the experience I shared at the start of this chapter is not uncommon. Too many leaders today still fail to provide coaching and feedback for many workers who look like me and those from other minority or underrepresented groups. What a missed opportunity for those companies who had someone with a strong commitment to hard work, willing to go above and beyond, craving to take on more challenging opportunities, and clients who loved working with me! But they just didn't invest in my development, nor did they provide any substantive coaching or feedback. In fact, in most cases when I left an employer to pursue other opportunities it was because I felt undervalued, underpaid, and lacked the opportunities to grow and advance from my direct supervisor.

TECHNICAL STUFF

Numerous studies conducted by reputable consulting firms shed light on similar experiences and the disparities in coaching and feedback among diverse talent. For example, according to a report by McKinsey & Company (https://women intheworkplace.com/), employees who identify as minorities are less likely to receive regular feedback compared to their non-minority counterparts. This discrepancy is alarming, given the crucial role that feedback plays in professional development and growth. Another study by Deloitte (https://www2.deloitte.com/content/dam/insights/us/articles/2725_if-you-love-them-set-them-free/DUP_If-you-love-them-set-them-free.pdf) highlights that diverse employees who receive inadequate coaching and feedback are more likely to feel disengaged and undervalued. This, in turn, has a direct impact on morale and can lead to higher turnover rates among diverse talent.

REMEMBER

It is evident that the current state of coaching and feedback practices is contributing to a significant gap in the workplace experiences of minority and non-minority employees. Moreover, the morale of employees is deeply connected to their sense of belonging and recognition. When diverse talent is overlooked in terms of coaching and feedback, it can lead to feelings of isolation and diminished morale. This, in turn, affects the overall atmosphere within the organization.

Engaged employees are more likely to contribute positively to their work environment. When diverse talent lacks the necessary coaching and feedback, both positive and constructive, they feel as though leadership doesn't care. As a result, their engagement levels decline, impacting not only their individual performance but also the collective success of the team.

WARNING

The lack of effective coaching and feedback has a direct correlation with higher turnover rates among diverse talent. Like me, employees who feel unsupported or undervalued are more likely to seek opportunities elsewhere. And when I voiced my concerns, they were either ignored or explained away. This poses a significant challenge for organizations striving to build more inclusive and high-performing workplace cultures.

I think you get the point — coaching and giving feedback is critical for leaders for several reasons. It helps to harness the full potential of a diverse workforce. It enhances employee engagement, productivity, organizational performance, and retention. It demonstrates a commitment to the professional growth of all employees, regardless of their diverse attributes. And it sends a powerful message that everyone's contributions are valued.

Understanding the Difference between Coaching and Feedback

REMEMBER

Put simply, *feedback* focuses on the past. It highlights successes and mistakes that an employee has made. In contrast, *coaching* focuses on the future. When acting as a coach, a leader works with their employee to identify potential issues and fixing them to enable better performance going forward.

Oftentimes, leaders excel in giving feedback but forget to coach their employees, hoping that simply pointing out those successes and mistakes in the past will encourage them to repeat the successes and avoid the mistakes going forward. But this approach might simplify the situation too much. An approach that includes coaching will examine what circumstances enabled those successes or precipitated those mistakes. Also, a coaching mindset is less about giving direction and more about asking questions, helping the employee make their own discoveries about why something in the past didn't work as well as they'd hoped. With the aid of patient and effective coaching, context is revealed that the leader couldn't have known, and the employee might not have realized without these important conversations.

TIP

It's important to understand why you are engaging in coaching and giving feedback. Ideally, coaching and feedback should strive to achieve the following goals:

>> **Education.** A coaching session is an excellent opportunity to teach your staff something they might not have known or been aware of before. This new piece of knowledge could be how to operate a piece of machinery, give a more effective sales presentation, or manage a difficult customer. When giving feedback, you might say something like, "You moved through your presentation very quickly. Next time, try stopping occasionally to ask your audience if they have any questions." When coaching, you might ask more questions, such as, "How did that conversation go? What do you think the customer wanted from you? What might you do differently next time?"

>> **Communication.** This is also a great opportunity for you to pass important information to your employee. This could be some insights into the company's wider strategy, or sales numbers from the past quarter, or industry trends that could have an impact on individual goals.

>> **Motivation.** No one likes to hear that they've done a task badly or need to improve. With that in mind, strive to minimize the upset when delivering bad news. As a leader, it's vital that you maintain a positive belief in your employee's abilities. If you believe they can improve, they will believe it, too. It's also important to tell your employee what they've done well. This not only protects their self-esteem but informs them how they can repeat certain behaviors to ensure future success.

>> **Creating Change.** Sometimes, feedback is given so that past mistakes will not be repeated. Ideally, your employee should leave a feedback session ready to make another attempt and do better next time. This is why it's very important to pair feedback with coaching. Point out what went wrong, then immediately follow up with "Next time, try this," or if the employee has more experience or skill, ask them what they might want to do differently the next time.

>> **Reinforcing or redefining relationship expectations.** Finally, while probably the least important reason to give coaching and feedback, regular check-ins can subtly remind staff that they have a leader, and that leader is you. While it shouldn't be necessary to blatantly assert your authority in a domineering way, the reinforcing of roles can be a valuable side effect of frequent coaching and feedback. This can also help employees who might be reticent to ask for help or request a sounding board when encountering difficulties at work. Conversely, when it's time for roles to change, coaching and feedback sessions can be an excellent opportunity to communicate that. If, for instance, an employee has managed a project well for a while and you'd like them to make more of the day-to-day decisions, you can negotiate this change during a coaching session.

Customizing Your Coaching Approach using Situational Leadership

In my career, I've worked for a few leaders that I could definitely label as *micromanagers*. I always felt as though they were looking over my shoulder, monitoring my every move, and didn't display that they trusted me. The result was dehumanizing and frustrating. I was sure that they neither valued my expertise, respected me as a member of the team, nor viewed me as an intelligent person with good judgment. It was in those times that I became disengaged, questioned my own self-confidence, and yearned for a leader who would *see me*. A leader who would tap into my potential, seek out my ideas, try them out, and yes — allow me to take risks even if that meant that they didn't work. But as I shared earlier in this chapter, when this was missing, I ultimately left for better treatment elsewhere.

Of course, there are reasons why some leaders tend to micromanage. And since becoming a leader myself, I've had to learn that some of my team members need more guidance than others. Some of them are motivated by different things. And some are at different stages in their development. But in all instances, I had to get to know them and understand each of their unique gifts, talents, development needs, and motivations. And when I did, I also had to learn to flex and adapt my leadership style in a way that would meet each of them where they were.

Whether you tend to micromanage or err on the side of giving your employees a bit too much freedom, the Situational Leadership model can help you find the balance you and your followers need. When I learned and used this model as a new people leader it enabled me to become a more effective at coaching and giving feedback.

TECHNICAL STUFF

In 1969, Dr. Paul Hersey and Dr. Ken Blanchard collaborated on a business textbook that has since become widely used. It's called *Management of Organizational Behavior* (Prentice-Hall, 1969). At the time, they called their work the "Life Cycle Theory of Leadership," but some years later it was renamed "Situational Leadership Theory." The new name tells you most of what you need to know about the model it defines: that certain kinds of leadership behaviors are suited to specific situations, and that effective leaders can't just lead in one way.

Four different leadership behaviors are described by the model. They are not dependent on the leader, but rather on the knowledge, skills, and maturity of the person or group being led. Therefore, a good leader will analyze what their followers need from them, and act accordingly.

Telling

In the first leadership style, sometimes called S1, the leader simply tells their followers what to do and exactly how to do it.

Imagine a leader who uses this approach all or most of the time. I can assure you, leaders like this exist. But for most of us, working with this kind of leader every day would be extremely frustrating, even toxic. People who are simply being tasked with very specific directions on how to do every aspect of their job lack agency. They don't feel respected, and likely feel invisible. If they know they could do better work elsewhere, they represent a real flight risk for your company. If, however, they've been talked down to for so long that they've begun to internalize this kind of poor treatment, they're more likely to stay on but be disengaged and unproductive.

REMEMBER

Sometimes, telling is precisely the right approach. When a person or a team is new to the organization, has taken on a new role, or for some other reason has no idea how to complete a task, has little confidence in themselves, or the task itself can only be done one way because of serious safety risks, this style of leadership can be not only effective, but necessary. Therefore, an inclusive leader should be able to give very specific direction in this way but should save these behaviors for only when they're truly necessary.

Selling

In the second leadership style, sometimes called S2, leaders provide direction, but more often, they describe the result they are seeking and allow their followers some leeway in how to get there. This desired end state is what the leader is "selling," using this style.

When being led in this way, followers have some agency, but the work still feels like it belongs more to the leader than to the team. After all, the leader is getting the exact product or process that they wanted. Followers may enjoy a bit more creative freedom, but anyone with a new or out-of-the-box idea probably still feels a bit stifled here.

REMEMBER

This style can be very effective when a person or a team is genuinely excited about the task at hand but lacks the experience to know what the best result should be. In these cases, they are usually quite willing to "buy" what their leader is "selling," while enjoying the freedom to get there in their own way.

Participating

In the third leadership style, sometimes called S3, leaders focus less on providing direction and more on developing relationships with their followers. While they are typically accountable for their team's work, the work truly belongs to the team. Decisions along the way are not made by the leader in isolation but might come about through consensus or by genuinely asking the team for their input.

REMEMBER

Working with a participatory leader feels more like a partnership than a hierarchical relationship, and if a person or a team is skilled and knowledgeable enough to fulfill their part of the equation, it can be an incredibly rewarding experience. Followers who succeed under this style are often able to do the work but lack complete confidence in themselves. Therefore, frequent interactions with their leader provide a mental safety net that allows them to try new things.

Delegating

In the fourth leadership style, sometimes called S4, leaders delegate all or most of the responsibility to the group. They will monitor a group's progress, but often don't involve themselves with routine decision making.

To thrive under this type of leadership style, a person or a group must have extensive knowledge, skills, and talents. They should be able to complete the task on their own and be confident in their own abilities. In addition, they should be comfortable taking full responsibility for the task, whether it succeeds or fails, and can independently course-correct when necessary.

REMEMBER

Delegating can be a challenging style for the micromanager to adopt, but when the person or group being led displays high maturity and exceptional skills, they will flourish when given the autonomy and agency to make their own way. Rather than feeling as though they are working under a leader's thumb, they own their work, which results in high engagement (and likely, high retention).

Avoiding Common Feedback Pitfalls

When giving feedback, many leaders will make mistakes. As you review this section, ask yourself if you've ever sat down for a coaching and feedback session and experienced one of these.

Being unprepared

Even if you're giving praise, you should be prepared for any coaching or feedback session. Preparation need not take a long time; often it helps to quickly review your notes just before the coaching session begins.

Preparation allows you to be specific in your feedback. Even if something went spectacularly well, what exactly did your employee do that allowed them to succeed. If something needs to change, what? Preparing for your conversation will allow you to speak to their observable behaviors, rather than the motivations you might have assigned them.

Taking time to prepare also enables you to separate what you know from what you don't, and to write down some questions you'd like to ask to get the information you need, so that your eventual feedback can be as helpful as possible.

Failing to establish trust

Receiving feedback doesn't have to be an awkward or painful experience. In my career, I've found an inverse relationship between the difficulty I have hearing feedback and the trust I have in my leader. In other words, when I trust that my leader wants me to succeed, and our regular check-ins are designed to help me do just that, I look forward to those meetings, and leaving smarter and readier than when I entered them.

REMEMBER

Inclusive leaders make the investment in getting to know their team members at a deeper level by actively listening (Chapter 7), showing empathy (Chapter 8), and asking them what support they need and what that looks like (Chapter 10). This goes a long way in building trust.

Ignoring cultural context

Imagine that you are working in a culture very different from your own, and after working hard to establish good relationships and add value to your team, your leader pulls you aside to give you some feedback. In the feedback session, you're shocked to learn that everything you've done to be seen as friendly and competent has been interpreted as arrogance and bullishness.

On the one hand, this is important knowledge for you to have. If eye contact, for example, is seen as overly defiant in this culture, that information would be important for you to know. If your efforts to be literally close to your colleagues are violating norms of personal space, you need to know that, too. But if your leader has no idea that culture is at play, the feedback you receive will probably not address cultural competence, but rather assume that you are simply boorish or rude — and it might not end up being all that helpful.

WARNING

Different cultures have unique communication styles, norms, and expectations. Leaders should educate themselves about the cultural backgrounds of their employees to ensure that coaching and feedback are culturally sensitive and respectful.

Treating everyone the same way

In Chapter 18, I make the distinction between equality and equity. While equality is often seen as a virtue, inclusive leaders strive toward equity: equal outcomes combined with respect for individual differences.

Inclusive leaders recognize that individuals from diverse backgrounds may have different development needs, so customize coaching and feedback to ensure their success. You can raise your awareness of these important issues by committing to your own diversity and inclusion training. This can help raise awareness of biases and stereotypes and provide tools for coaching and giving feedback.

Avoiding reciprocal feedback

Employees who truly trust their leaders know that they can "manage up," and give their leaders feedback of their own. Often, an employee knows what they need to succeed, and simply asking them how you could better support them will yield very valuable information that allows you to treat your followers equitably rather than equally. Inclusive leaders actively seek feedback from their team on their effectiveness as a coach and commit to making adjustments based on these suggestions.

TIP

Certain words or phrases that can affect your message. Try the following word swaps when you give feedback to make your coaching and feedback more effective:

>> **Change "you" statements to "I" statements.** "You" can sound accusatory and provoke a defensive reaction; "I" invites comparison and encourages information seeking.

>> **Change "should" or "must" to "could."** "Should" or "must" implies rigidity; "could" creates flexibility and possibility.

>> **Change "but" to "and."** "But" contradicts; "and" integrates.

Giving Great Feedback

When you need to deliver any kind of feedback, it's best to have a plan, stick to it, and follow through appropriately. The following sections detail how to do just that, and to ensure that you are clear, open, and inclusive during these important conversations.

Before the conversation

It's always a good idea to prepare for any coaching or feedback conversation, especially one that is making you a bit nervous. Jumping in without adequate preparation is much more likely to result in a bad outcome. Preparation not only yields better results but allows you to be more comfortable throughout the conversation. Before having a potentially difficult discussion with an employee, try the following steps:

1. **Examine your motives and intentions for having the conversation.** What is the very best outcome that you could hope for? Now, work backwards. What will be necessary from you, both verbally and non-verbally, to make this best outcome more probable?

2. **Assess and identify your own knowledge gaps, biases, or prejudices.** When you think about the topic at hand, what narratives are you likely to construct before having the conversation? Before having the conversation, can you validate or invalidate these narratives with trusted resources? These could include colleagues, mentors, or internet searches.

3. **Practice!** Enlist a trusted advisor, friend, or spouse to have a talk before the talk. Encourage them to give honest feedback on your choice of words, approach, tone of voice, body language, and ability to listen actively.

4. **Educate yourself on the issue that you are addressing.** Find out if your company has any policies on the topic, and look for books, videos, and articles that can give you more information.

5. **Determine the time and place for your conversation.** Ideally, the conversation should take place in a neutral spot that offers privacy, psychological safety (see Chapter 11), and minimal interruptions.

During the conversation

You can't plan for all the ways the conversation might go. Your employee might take offense at something that your partner praised you for in your practice session, or you might have missed an important nuance in your pre-discussion research. Therefore, it's important to remain open and as relaxed as possible during the conversation as well:

WARNING

» **As you open the discussion, agree on parameters and boundaries.** If possible, let your employee know that everything they say will be kept in strict confidentiality, place your phone on silent mode, and ask your employee to do the same. If it's unusual to have a conversation away from your office, explain why you've chosen a more neutral spot.

There are times when sensitive and legal situations must be reported to Human Resources and/or General Counsel. In those instances, stress that you have an obligation to notify HR but that confidentiality will be honored.

» **Grant permission for either party to make mistakes.** If your employee reacts hastily and wants the opportunity to express themselves in a different way, allow this. Let them know that this discussion is a teachable moment for the both of you.

» **Approach the conversation with humility.** Even if you've read everything the internet has to offer on a particular topic, your employee is the foremost expert on their own life.

» **Be open, authentic, honest, and coachable throughout.** This can often be achieved by using more "I" statements and fewer "you" statements. Telling your employee how they feel or what their motivations are will likely cause defensiveness or criticism but telling them how you feel is harder to argue with. (This should include how you feel about the employee's behavior but refrain from telling them if the conversation is making you a little nervous. Don't force your employee to coddle you when they're likely very uncomfortable themselves.)

» **Look for shared meaning and commonalities throughout.** For instance, your employee surely wants to succeed in their job, and they might need to hear explicitly that you have the same goal.

» **Assume positive intent.** If your employee is being coached because they've offended others in some way, realize that this might not have been their goal.

» **Practice active but humble listening.** Don't interrupt when they are speaking, stay present to the conversation, rephrase or mirror back to them for understanding when appropriate, and try not to defend your feelings or debate theirs.

» **If you make a mistake during the conversation, own it and apologize.** Rather than diminishing your credibility, a sincere apology is more likely to enhance it.

» **Don't minimize, marginalize, or trivialize their experience.** If you don't understand why a comment or situation is important to your employee, don't assume they are overreacting. Rather, entertain the possibility that there's something about the dynamic that you do not yet understand, and commit to learning what this is.

>> **As the conversation wraps up, ask them what they need from you and how you can support them going forward.** These simple questions reiterate that you value their presence on your team and can be seen as a trusted resource.

>> **Thank them for their willingness to have the conversation.** If the conversation was difficult for you, it was likely more difficult for the person in the room with less power. Even if they had little choice in the matter, participating in a feedback dialogue requires courage.

TIP

This is a lot to remember, but it boils down to this: Make the conversation about them, not about you. A leader should deliver the important message clearly but compassionately and allow the employee to process it in the way that works best for them. For some, this might include exhibiting emotional reactions, or keeping their emotions firmly in check. If this differs from your preferred style, simply focus on what they're saying rather than how they're saying it. Finally, make sure they know they have an ally in you.

After the conversation

When you have parted ways, it might be tempting to wipe your brow, breathe a sigh of relief, and be glad it's all over. But your work as a leader isn't quite done yet! After a difficult coaching or feedback discussion, make sure you do the following:

>> Follow up on any commitments made.

>> Internalize what you learned and decide how you'll apply your new knowledge.

>> Continue your learning on the topic.

>> Check in periodically to nurture the trust between you.

Take the time to reflect, commit, and practice these tips with your conversations so that you see them as a common and effective way to communicate and build stronger relationships.

REMEMBER

Feedback should be frequent and ongoing. This doesn't mean you should be constantly looking for little ways your employees could improve, which casts you in the role of the micromanaging nitpicker. Rather, your employees should always have an accurate picture of how they are doing in their role. This includes not only corrective feedback, but information on what they're doing well. Positive feedback is not only nice to hear, but incredibly valuable, as it lets your employees know what behaviors to repeat for future success.

TOP TIPS FOR PROVIDING EFFECTIVE FEEDBACK

TIP

To ensure that your feedback achieves the desired result, keep the following tips in mind.

- **Focus on a clear goal.** Whether giving positive or corrective feedback, begin your preparation by asking yourself, "What are we trying to achieve here?" This is especially important if your feedback involves one of the taboo topics discussed in this chapter. If it's helpful, state your goal explicitly to your employee. If your goal is to help your employee be a success, they should be ready to hear what's next.

- **Protect your employee's self-esteem.** Remember to always maintain a positive belief in your employee's abilities. If you honestly don't believe that your employee has the capacity to succeed at a given task, then all the feedback in the world isn't likely to change that. In that case, you should be focusing on changing their role, not sitting them down to coach. But if you are inclined to believe they can do well, it's important to always demonstrate respect for your employee. Use language that reflects that respect and monitor your body language and tone. Finally, listen to your employee when they respond to your words.

- **Focus on success.** Create a vision for what success would look like and share it with your employee. Get inspired by that vision and allow it to make a corrective conversation more enjoyable.

- **Make it interactive.** Plan your coaching and feedback sessions to be highly participatory. Interactive feedback is much more likely to be received by the employee. You can track how well your employee has received the message by tracking their non-verbal reactions and the energy they bring to the conversation.

- **Be flexible.** If you have the same feedback for two different employees, the feedback should be delivered differently. In other words, tailor the feedback to your employees, not to your comfort or ease. If the message isn't landing, try another approach until you get through. Also, be willing to consider a different way of

(continued)

(continued)

accomplishing the goal. You may have something in mind of how you want things to go, but be open to other ways of accomplishing it. Be patient with yourself and others as you grow and mature in this area.

- **Be timely.** You shouldn't wait too long to give important feedback, but neither should you rush into it. You need to be ready to deliver the message, and the other person needs to be ready to hear it. If either you or your employee are emotional or upset, wait a brief period to deliver the feedback. Some of your employees can handle a spontaneous conversation, but others will want time to gather their thoughts before hearing feedback, and this can change depending on the issue. You or your employee might not be ready to give or receive feedback immediately after an incident, but you could approach them immediately and let them know that you've scheduled a time the following day or later in the week to have a c onversation about what happened. In addition to real-time feedback, regular check-ins with your employee are valuable, and give you the opportunity to follow up.

- **Be helpful and supportive.** Speaking of follow up, this is something to continue to do until the matter is fully resolved to everyone's satisfaction. As a leader, reinforce positive results and changes when necessary, and be sure that your employee knows that you are motivated to help, not to scold.

- **Conduct regular check-ins.** Consistent communication is key to effective coaching. Leaders should schedule regular check-ins with their team members to discuss progress, address concerns, and provide feedback. These check-ins create a continuous feedback loop, allowing for timely adjustments and preventing misunderstandings that may hinder the development of diverse talent.

- **Encourage a growth mindset.** Leaders should foster a culture of continuous learning by encouraging a growth mindset within their teams. This involves promoting the belief that abilities and intelligence can be developed through dedication and hard work. By emphasizing learning and improvement, leaders empower diverse talent to embrace challenges and view feedback as an opportunity for growth rather than criticism.

- **Create mentorship opportunities.** Mentorship is a powerful tool for coaching and feedback. Leaders can facilitate mentorship programs within the organization, pairing experienced professionals with diverse talents. This not only provides valuable guidance but also opens up channels for constructive feedback and skill development.

Chapter **13**

Communicating Inclusively

L et's face it, no matter how well we attempt to understand each other, communication is complicated. And in today's hyper-connected global and diverse world, leaders must ensure that communication within their organization is inclusive and respectful of every individual. Yet, numerous companies have yet to crack the code on establishing an environment where every voice is heard, respected, and valued.

In this chapter, I explore this by being clear on what inclusive communication looks like and how it contributes to a positive employee experience and organizational performance. I also expose the non-inclusive language that leaders should avoid and provide strategies for developing and promoting more inclusive communication approaches.

Recognizing the Benefits of Inclusive Communication

Inclusivity is not tolerance; it involves actively acknowledging, respecting, and valuing differences in race, gender, culture, abilities, and more. Inclusive communication ensures that everyone can contribute their perspectives and feel like they belong.

The significance of inclusive communication cannot be overstated. It's crucial for several key reasons. First, companies want to be employers of choice and highly sought out by top talent. Second, as the marketplace and customer base expand to become more diverse, corporations must be positioned to better relate to multiple cultural backgrounds, beliefs, and needs, must reflect the demographics of their customers, and be able serve them. Third, inclusive communication encourages diverse perspectives and backgrounds which drives greater innovation, problem solving, and creativity. Fourth, it promotes greater understanding, collaboration, increases trust, and fosters a sense of belonging. And fifth, it minimizes your legal exposure — many governments and organizations have laws, policies, and regulations designed to ensure equal opportunities and that all people are treated fairly and with respect.

The choice of our language holds significant importance in ensuring a sense of belonging for all within our organization. By adopting the words that individuals use to define themselves, we establish a workplace that fosters a sense of value and embraces everyone for who they are.

Whether intentional or not, our choice of words has the power to either include or exclude others.

Understanding the Impact of Non-Inclusive Language

Have you ever felt reluctant to engage with individuals who look, think, believe, or work differently than you because you were afraid you might say the wrong thing? Reflect on how this hesitation could influence your relationship with that individual. Demonstrating inclusive communication requires a continuous commitment to educating oneself about the potential effects of our own words on individuals from marginalized social backgrounds.

REAL-WORLD EXAMPLES OF INCLUSIVE COMMUNICATION

Organizations that prioritize inclusive communication effectively attract and retain a diverse pool of talent. Employees seek an environment where they feel welcomed, respected, and empowered to actively engage. Mere policies are insufficient; it is the day-to-day communication strategies that genuinely cultivate a sense of belonging:

- Salesforce serves as an illustration of a company attributing its success in building a globally diverse workforce to its dedication to inclusivity. By implementing Employee Resource Groups (see Chapter 17) and providing training on inclusive language, they create a supportive atmosphere where individuals from various backgrounds can flourish.

- Cisco invests in comprehensive training programs that focus on inclusive communication. These programs not only address conscious biases but also delve into unconscious biases that may affect day-to-day interactions. By providing employees with the tools to communicate in an inclusive manner, Cisco aims to create a workplace where diverse perspectives are acknowledged and respected.

- P&G is known for its inclusive advertising campaigns that celebrate diversity and challenge stereotypes. Through brands such as Always, Pantene, and Gillette, the company actively promotes messages of gender equality and inclusivity. By using its marketing platforms to address social issues, P&G not only engages consumers but also communicates a commitment to fostering a more inclusive world. They also reach beyond their internal operations by actively seeking to include diverse suppliers, supporting businesses owned by minorities, women, and other underrepresented groups.

If we're honest, we can all admit that we've said things that we thought were acceptable but later found out that what was said was perceived as offensive, minimizing, and perhaps even illegal. In other words, we have all been guilty of inadvertently using non-inclusive language without realizing its exclusionary impact. Yes, even well-intentioned folk make these kinds of blunders, not to be malicious, but because we are human. Communicating more inclusively is a journey and each of us are at different mile markers on this journey. While I've been in Human Resources (HR) and in the inclusion space for more than three decades, I am still learning and evolving in my language and choice of words because I still have biases — as we all do.

Here are a few examples of my blunders. I was speaking to a large group of leaders and consistently used the term, "you guys." Yes, there were women in the group and I'm now sure it made some feel excluded. In another instance, I was working with a corporation who was focused on being more inclusive of their workers preferred pronouns, so using non-inclusive words such as "mankind," "manning the booth," "chairman," "fireman," or "policeman" might have been considered insensitive, so when I led a workshop for their staff, I proceeded with a heightened sense of caution realizing that certain expressions that are deeply rooted in societal norms may unintentionally marginalize specific groups. For example, using terms such as "mankind" to refer to humanity may inadvertently exhibit a bias towards men. Similarly, addressing groups with phrases such as "you guys," and "ladies and gentlemen" can be perceived as exclusionary to those beyond cisgender identities.

To cultivate effective and inclusive communication, our language must be attuned to diverse audiences, reflecting respect for all individuals. The use of intersectional and inclusive language becomes paramount in acknowledging differences and advocating for equal opportunities.

In group settings, I use terms like "colleagues," "friends," "team," "everyone," or "folks" because they tend to linguistically be more inclusive. The same diligence should extend to references about colleagues' loved ones, avoiding gendered terms that could be presumptive.

In referring to people with disabilities, avoiding labels such as "handicapped," and "crippled." Consider language such as "suffering from bipolar disorder" or "on the autism spectrum" versus calling people "bipolar" or "autistic," as this separates the person from the condition. Other examples include describing someone as "a person with loss of vision or a visual impairment," instead of "blind," or communicating that a person "uses a wheelchair" instead of describing them as "wheelchair-bound."

Instead of labeling someone as being from the "inner city" or "homeless," opt for terms like "under-resourced" or "a person experiencing homelessness." Why? Because when discussing individuals from varied socioeconomic backgrounds, the use of inclusive language guarantees that due respect and dignity are granted to them, irrespective of their upbringing or current residence. Furthermore, our choice of words can inadvertently reinforce socioeconomic disparities, prompting the need for careful consideration in professional communication.

And then there is the use of microaggressions, which are subtle verbal and non-verbal slights, insults, indignities, and denigrating messages directed towards others based on their group membership (find out more in Chapter 6). They are often loaded labels such as "bossy," "ambitious," and "feisty" directed toward women and can impede their progression.

Language is inherently encoded with meaning, and has the potential to unintentionally exclude people, so keeping these considerations in mind ensures the use of language that is inclusive to all. Addressing gender bias in language is crucial for promoting inclusivity. Gender gaps in the workplace are not overcome by good intentions. Each of us must acknowledge our unconscious gender biases and look at the ways those biases influence our thoughts, feelings, and behaviors.

TIP

Table 13-1 shows some examples of gendered descriptors and suggestions for using them in a more inclusive way. As you review the list, jot down those that you need to avoid.

TABLE 13-1   Avoiding gendered descriptors

Non-inclusive descriptors commonly used for men	Non-inclusive descriptors commonly used for women	Inclusive descriptors that could apply to everyone
Aggressive	Bossy	Assertive
		Confident
Ambitious	Pushy	Driven
		Goal-oriented
Analytical	Cold	Detail-oriented
		Logical
Confident	Conceited	Self-assured
		Self-confident
Experienced	Seasoned	Experienced
Independent	Isolated	Autonomous
		Self-reliant
Leader	Supportive	Collaborative
		Effective communicator
Soft	Compassionate	Caring
		Empathetic

I realize that it can be daunting to try to get it right every time, and the reality is we won't. When these blunders happen, I view them as teachable moments and lessons learned for future interactions. It's crucial to be open, flexible, and adaptable without being judgmental and thinking that "people just need to get over it." As inclusive leaders, we have to understand that what might be socially appropriate for one may not necessarily be appropriate for others. And what might work in a personal setting may not work in a professional environment.

Working With Human Resources to Promote Inclusive Language

Promoting inclusive language is not only a leadership skill and competency, but it is an important responsibility for HR too. They have a key role in fostering a workplace culture where all workers are treated with dignity, respect, a sense of belonging, and where policies, procedures, and strategies are created to enforce such behaviors. If you have an HR team, they should work hand in hand with leaders at all levels as partners in cultivating this kind of environment. If you do not have an HR department, seek advice from an HR consulting firm or become a member of an HR organization such as the Society for Human Resource Management (https://www.shrm.org/), which is the world's largest HR membership association.

TIP

Here are a few actions that HR can drive from their office; I recommend meeting with your HR team to discuss them in more detail:

>> Develop and disseminate guidelines that explicitly outline the importance of using inclusive language, avoiding stereotypes, and considering the impact of words on diverse audiences. Several guides for inclusive language can be found online, such as the one published by the Oregon Health & Science University (ohsu.edu/inclusive-language-guide/).

>> Conduct inclusion and engagement audits (see Chapter 15) to assess the employee's experience and analyze the current state of the culture.

>> Offer ongoing training sessions and workshops (find out more in Chapter 17) to educate leaders on the nuances of inclusive language and its significance in fostering a positive workplace culture. This includes fostering awareness of potential biases in language, understanding the repercussions of microaggressions, and emphasizing the use of language that reflects respect for all employees.

>> Collaborate with organizational leaders to integrate inclusive communication into leadership development programs.

>> Actively engage in ongoing dialogue with leaders to assess and address any issues related to inclusive communication.

>> Institute accountability systems to reward and penalize behaviors.

>> Create a checklist for inclusive communication.

Practicing Inclusive Communication

Becoming proficient in inclusive communication requires the cultivation of specific skills and habits.

TIP

One of the models I use is a comprehensive toolkit of practical steps for how leaders can develop their inclusive communication skills. It was created by Forbes' Coaches Council (https://councils.forbes.com/forbescoachescouncil) which is a vetted professional organization of respected business, career, and professional coaches. Their guidelines include:

>> Don't be afraid of authenticity, vulnerability or affection.

>> Begin by recognizing your unconscious biases.

>> Adjust your listening and speaking style.

>> Recognize and allow for different communication styles.

>> Stop talking, solicit engagement, and genuinely listen.

>> Remove your preconceptions and be open.

>> Focus on results.

>> Focus on building relationships and trust within your team.

>> Be adaptable.

>> Why not ask the women you lead?

>> Are you listening or are you rehearsing?

TECHNICAL STUFF

It's worth expanding on two of those guidelines:

>> **Why not ask the women you lead?** Simply said, male leaders should feel comfortable asking women about their preferred communication style. When a male leader asks a woman "How do you prefer to communicate?", it instantly breaks down any defense because it gives women a choice.

>> **Are you listening or are you rehearsing?** A common complaint by women is that they feel male colleagues do not really hear what they are saying. If you find yourself rehearsing in your mind what you want to say next instead of really listening to the person you are talking with, change it up.

TIP

Similarly, the Academy to Innovate HR (https://www.aihr.com/), an organization that provides online training programs for HR professionals, offers a list of guidelines that organizations can practice to implement inclusive communication. This list was compiled by Tess C. Taylor, an HR veteran and founder of HR Knows (https://hrknows.net/). Notice that the previous bullet list by Forbes Coaches Council was for leaders and this list is for organizations. Despite this, check out how their guidelines cover similar ground:

>> Avoid language that may be offensive or insensitive.

>> Listen to multiple perspectives and create a safe space for people to express themselves.

>> Promote inclusive language when referring to gender, race, ethnicity, or religion.

>> Be mindful of body language and facial expressions when communicating.

>> Lead by example and model inclusive behavior.

>> Adapt communication style to different groups of people.

>> Implement inclusive policies and create diversity and inclusion committees.

>> Offer inclusive communication training programs.

Inclusive communication is a fundamental aspect of navigating the complexities of our diverse, interconnected, and constantly changing world. Recognizing the importance of inclusive communication, understanding its nuances, actively cultivating the necessary skills, and paying attention to the Diversity, Equity, and Inclusion (DEI) landscape and ways that language is changing are vital steps toward building a more inclusive society. As individuals and organizations embrace the principles of inclusivity, we move closer to a world where every voice is heard, valued, and respected, regardless of differences.

Chapter **14**

Dealing with Conflict

A mong the many audiences that I speak to when I'm presenting on the topic of this chapter, I ask them to raise their hand if they like conflict. Of course, very few hands raise because the fact is, none of us really like conflict. Dealing with conflict is one of the most uncomfortable areas of a leader's job. And far too many leaders have not honed the necessary skills to effectively deal with it. But I confront conflict in this chapter. I address the reasons why we tend to avoid conflict, then detail ways to normalize conflict to enhance performance. Additionally, I explain a few models for how to deal with conflict effectively and some best practices for responding to real workplace situations.

Addressing the Reasons We Avoid Conflict

Leaders avoid conflict and uncomfortable situations at work for many reasons. For me, it used to be uncomfortable and stressful because I was afraid that the conversation could go awry — that I might say the wrong thing, feelings could get hurt, the relationship could get damaged, and it could affect my standing at work.

Many of us have been taught to avoid certain conflict by our Human Resources (HR) departments because it could lead to legal jeopardy and inconsistent practices if not handled correctly. It may be an explicit policy in the organization's employee handbook, taught in orientation sessions, or implied to leaders when HR directs them to send their team members to HR. In essence, we've learned to fear the unknown and thus we avoid it. This is especially true in today's social media environment. It's not paranoia nor far-fetched to believe that if a manager handled a conversation extremely poorly, an employee might return to their office and type up the whole story on their social media profiles and bring lots of unwanted attention to you and the company. In more extreme cases, individuals and organizations have been written up, shamed, blamed, or even sued for an insensitive and poorly handled conversation.

I don't say any of that to scare you away from dealing with conflict but to acknowledge the realities. Managing conflict is a necessary part of a leader's role and we have to lean into the difficult part of our roles just as we do the enjoyable aspects. And that means learning to handle them compassionately and inclusively so that trust is built among the team.

Normalizing Conflict as a Tool for Higher Performance

When a team or an organization is bereft of conflict, does that really mean that everyone is getting along? Or is it more likely that people are unable or unwilling to say what's really on their mind? Is the mood pleasant, are the people nice, or is it more likely that anger and resentment are present just below the surface but something in the culture keeps it tucked away from view?

Human beings are different to one another. In every group there is diversity if we look hard enough. Therefore, it stands to reason that in any human system, there will be disagreements, competing priorities, distinctive worldviews, and different ways of doing things. These differences will be increased when an organization makes strides to become more diverse in terms of race, gender, sexual orientation, religion, disability, socioeconomic status, education, background, and culture. And since there's plenty of research that shows how organizations can benefit from increased diversity — see my book *Diversity, Equity, & Inclusion For Dummies* (John Wiley & Sons, Inc., 2022) to find out more — it is easy to see why organizations that want to outperform the competition, make a profit, or change the world need to learn to manage conflict.

But conflict isn't just a by-product of diversity. In companies and industries that depend upon creativity and innovation to succeed, conflict is often the way that bold new solutions are discovered. Even if a particular conflict is more personal than professional, flexing those conflict management muscles can prepare everyone on a team to manage conflict better, setting them up for future success.

Identifying the Topics We Tend to Avoid

I've met many leaders who are excellent role models, interested in my goals, invested in my success, and full of great advice. But even they rarely enjoy engaging with their employees around a list of subjects that I call *taboo topics*. These can include (but are not limited to):

>> Race

>> Gender

>> Sexual orientation

>> Disability

>> Neurodiversity

>> Age

>> Religion and faith

>> Political affiliation

>> Body odor and grooming

>> Dress and hairstyles

>> Pay

>> Language

WARNING

Few of us have been taught how to discuss these taboo topics. In fact, many of us have repeatedly been told to avoid these dialogues at all costs. In my role as an HR officer early in my career, I admit that I made it a point to discourage these conversations because those of us in HR and in the Legal Department knew that if leaders said the wrong thing or took the wrong action, that it could put the company in legal jeopardy. For example, if a leader asked a female employee if they planned to have children and stated that it could affect their promotability if they did, it could be in violation of employment laws and regulations. Or if a leader asked an employee to remove their hijab or told another employee that they could not take time off to observe Rosh Hashanah because the leader didn't agree with their religious beliefs, that could be very problematic for the company.

These risks are exacerbated when there is conflict around the issues (for example, political differences, disagreements over what constitutes professional attire, or whether someone is being paid fairly). When you combine disagreement with discomfort, these conversations are even harder to manage.

However, in the past few years I have observed a significant shift. Companies are leaning into having conversations about these topics in a way that I've not seen in over 30 years in this industry. They call them "crucial," "courageous," and "bold" conversations and focus them on the leader's role in having them. Part of this shift is attributed to the spike in traumatic events of racial, ethnic, and religious hate crimes that occur around the world. Another contributor was the outbreak of the COVID-19 pandemic in 2020, which had devastating effects on businesses, individuals, and economies, including taking an emotional, physical, and psychological toll on millions. News outlets, talk shows, celebrities, athletes, and other famous people began to discuss taboo topics in public forums. Some even shared their personal struggles and experiences with them, which encouraged others to discuss theirs. As a result, companies required leaders to engage their workers differently, giving them permission to talk about these issues at work, and providing them with support and resources. But with their lack of experience and the fear of saying the wrong thing, they were uncomfortable and ill prepared.

REMEMBER

Our discomfort is often well intentioned. We might be consciously aware of the risks involved. We could easily hurt someone's feelings or leave them feeling insulted or offended. Of course, our fears might also be a tad selfish in nature, as any misstep might result in repercussions, ranging from a complaint to HR, being blasted on social media, or other career-inhibiting outcomes.

Because the risks are real, leaders have every right to ask themselves if such conversations are truly necessary. For instance, if your customers are uncomfortable because one of your sales associates wears a headscarf that is an important expression of their religious faith, a leader could very well just shut this criticism down; in other words, this need not be shouldered by the employee. If you are sincerely in doubt, check in with a mentor or another trusted resource.

If the conversation is necessary, you need to be prepared to step outside of your comfort zone. Talking about taboo topics requires courage and vulnerability but when handled well, can reap some important benefits. And I have found that the more you have these conversations, the better you get at having them and the more at ease you become when doing so. Additionally, you can learn a lot from others who see the world very differently than you.

Difficult or courageous conversations create further benefits, such as:

>> **Helping you to understand another person's perspective.** This new knowledge can broaden your own awareness and understanding of the complexities of racism, sexism, heterosexism, transphobia, xenophobia, Islamophobia, ageism, and other phobias and -isms.

>> **Breaking down barriers and stereotypes.** You might even think of them as learning labs for diversity and inclusion training.

>> **Strengthening or rebuilding trust between leader and follower.** This occurs when both parties come from a place of mutual trust.

>> **Exposing your own biases in ways that help you learn about yourself.** These talks can deepen your understanding of yourself and others.

>> **Demonstrating your commitment to be part of the solution and not the problem.** If you think the topic is difficult, your employee is likely aware that it's uncomfortable for many people. If you can speak about it in a true dialogue, where both parties are learning from the other, most employees will truly appreciate the effort.

The more often you engage in these dialogues, the easier it is to access the necessary courage. There's something to be said for practice, which enables you to have more effective, productive, and collaborative conversations up, down, and across organizational levels.

REMEMBER

Having courageous conversations is a part of life. When it's necessary for your employee to hear from you, even if it's a topic you'd rather avoid, these conversations are a valuable source of communication and learning. When we don't handle the conversations appropriately, it can lead to a negative outcome, far worse than anything that might result from a conversation that goes badly. But where these discussions are openly addressed, and where we can create open and productive dialogues where people feel heard, listened to, and the issue is resolved, the result can be a win–win.

TIP

Think about the last tough conversation you had. How did it go? What could you have done differently? What did you learn about yourself? What action did you take to make it better?

Seeing the Benefits of Engaging in Uncomfortable Conversations

As prickly and awkward as participating in conflict and dialogue around taboo topics might be, plenty of reasons exist to want to engage in these conversations.

Before getting into too much detail, I'd like you to stop for a moment and consider two questions:

>> What kind of leader do you want to be?

>> What kind of work environment do you want to foster?

I'm hoping you answered that first question with at least a few words similar to "bold," "inspiring," and "trustworthy." And I'm hoping your answer to the second question was not a work culture characterized by fear and walking on eggshells. If my hopes are well-founded, that's your main reason for engaging in difficult conversation in a nutshell. The benefits of being the kind of leader you imagine yourself to be and a work environment where everyone can contribute their best ideas and feel a deep sense of belonging are achievable, but they only exist on the other side of those awkward encounters.

In case you need more convincing, here are even more reasons why it's important to engage with conflict and taboo topics:

>> **Productivity.** A team or an organization that can effectively manage conflict and discuss important issues can do higher-quality work, on time, and within budget. That's not the most humanistic argument (Ill get to those next), but it's undeniably true. It takes time and energy to maneuver around topics that are so strenuously avoided they become untouchable, and that same time and energy could instead be spent on doing the work as outlined in your job description, which has a direct impact on the bottom line or mission success of the organization.

>> **Engagement and retention.** People who work in an organization equipped to have difficult conversations are often happier and more fulfilled in their work. If they're not all happy during these discussions, they're certainly better off on the other side. And, in addition to making people happy, there are financial benefits as well. The sense of inclusion and belonging that is engendered when inclusive leaders responsibly engage in conflict is directly related to being more engaged in their work, more willing to put in extra effort when required, and less likely to be actively looking for opportunities elsewhere.

>> **Psychological safety.** When employees feel as though voicing their concerns, introducing their ideas, or asking tough questions is just too dangerous, this translates to a lack of psychological safety (see Chapter 11 for an exploration of psychological safety and its benefits). Like physical safety, this allows workers to do their jobs without harm. At its core, psychological safety is about trust, and a leader's ability to engage in conflict makes them more trustworthy. Inclusive leaders who can effectively mediate and manage conflict are better able to understand differing perspectives, articulate their own biases, empathize with others, and facilitate bridge building. Conversely, when employees come to work each day in a place that doesn't feel safe, this takes a demonstrable toll on their well-being and mental health.

Interpreting Two Models for Managing Conflict

Before considering exactly how to address conflict or difficult conversations as a leader (tackled later in this chapter), it's worth taking the time to do a bit of self-reflection on your preferred styles of dealing with conflict. I find two models that define different ways of managing conflict extremely helpful.

Thomas–Kilman conflict modes

The first model of conflict management that I find useful is the Thomas–Kilmann conflict modes (shown in Figure 14-1). Ken Thomas and Ralph Kilmann are pioneers in the field of organization development, and their model has been backed up by hundreds of research studies.

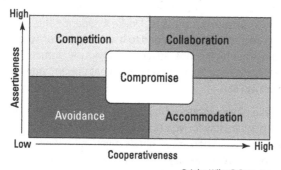

FIGURE 14-1:
The
Thomas–Kilman
conflict modes.

© John Wiley & Sons, Inc.

This model differentiates between five different strategies (or *modes*) of dealing with conflict. While most of us have a preferred strategy, don't think of these modes as a box that you are trapped in, but rather a set of tools that you can choose from, depending on the issue, the personalities, and the problem at hand.

The five strategies are as follows:

>> **Avoidance:** Since most of us don't like conflict, it stands to reason that avoiding it altogether is a popular option for a lot of people. *Avoidance* is characterized by low assertiveness, but also by low cooperativeness. Many avoiders learned this tactic at home, where harmony was valued above all else. Unfortunately, if conflict is constantly roiling beneath the surface, the harmony that results is only an illusion. Think of unresolved conflict like a stick of dynamite that is never lit, but simply stored away. Now imagine that every time conflict is avoided, another stick of unlit dynamite is stored in your mental cupboard. If you've soon got a warehouse full of dynamite stored away, it's not hard to imagine that a tiny little spark could lead to disastrous consequences. Therefore, if conflict avoidance is your preferred mode of dealing with conflict, you might be creating an environment that is just as toxic as one where everyone is fighting openly.

At the same time, it can be healthy to avoid some conflicts. For instance, if you have a team member who is constantly looking to you to manage all their conflicts for them, it might be the best idea to not get involved, lest you spend too much of your valuable time being a referee relating to squabbles that your team should be able to work out on their own. At other times, the stakes are so low that it's simply not worth having a conversation about it, and the best thing to model for your team is a healthy sense of priorities. However, if this is your constant rationale for avoiding conflict, I'd suggest reflecting on this tendency, as it might be a flimsy excuse for not doing something simply because it makes you uncomfortable.

>> **Accommodation:** When in conflict with another person, the strategy of *Accommodation* means you essentially let the other person have their way without any resistance to speak of. Unlike Avoidance, this mode acknowledges the conflict and seeks to put an end to it and is therefore characterized by low assertiveness but high cooperativeness. Obviously, someone who relies too much on this strategy can be perceived as passive and unwilling to stand up for their principles.

However, there are situations that call for Accommodation, particularly when the stakes are very low for you but higher for the other party. For instance, say you're planning an important all-hands meeting for your team. The dates available to you are in late September and late October. You prefer the September date because your favorite venue is available then, but before the decision is finalized, a member of your team reminds you that this presents a direct conflict with Rosh Hashanah, one of the most sacred dates on the Jewish calendar, meaning that any Jews on your team would either have to leave early or be late for Seder. Here, it's probably best to accommodate. Your reasons for preferring September (your favorite venue with the high ceilings and excellent pastry selection) are not as important as allowing your Jewish team members to practice their faith.

» **Competition:** When a person engages in the mode of *Competition* during a conflict, they are out to win. Characterized by high assertiveness and low cooperativeness, they believe they are right, the other person is wrong, and they are willing to take a stand to defend their position. Competition sounds very combative, and it can be — but it can also look like a leader pulling rank: "Because I'm in charge, that's why" is a classic way that conflicts can be managed through Competition. Of course, no one is right all the time, but there are those in the workplace who have a difficult time admitting they're wrong and will default to competition as a mode of managing conflict. These people are usually deeply unpopular, especially in industries or roles where people were hired because of their expertise and want their ideas to be considered.

There are times, however, when the Competition mode is absolutely the right choice. Leaders might choose to pull rank if a decision needs to be made immediately. A good leader will not make a habit of this and will communicate clearly why there is no time to discuss further so that their team is not routinely disheartened. Another time to employ Competition is when your values are at stake. If a member of your team is voicing comments that are openly bigoted and discriminatory, a strong stance should be taken. If you are sure that you are right and the stakes are high enough, this can easily be your best option.

» **Collaboration:** Defined by high assertiveness and high cooperativeness, the next mode of conflict management is *Collaboration*. Of all the strategies discussed thus far, this is the best default mode for an inclusive leader to take. It involves a lot of listening to the opposing party, understanding not only what they want but why, and a willingness for both sides to search for a resolution that is a true win–win.

While it's wonderful when people are creative, collegial, and invested in each other's success enough to come up with a solution that is even better than the original stances, sometimes Collaboration just isn't possible. Obviously, if one party is too eager to avoid, accommodate, or compete, it can be difficult to make true Collaboration work. One reason why a person might be entrenched in another mode is that they simply don't trust the other person. Collaboration requires vulnerability, and a lack of trust can make that impossible. Also, Collaboration takes time and energy, and most teams simply don't have the resources to make this their go-to strategy every time a conflict arises. But if it can work and the conflict is important enough to spend the time and energy, it can be the very best option available.

>> **Compromise:** The final mode of conflict management in the Thomas–Kilman model is *Compromise*. This mode requires each party to give up a little of what they want to reach a solution. When parties Compromise, no one gets everything they asked for, but hopefully it's a resolution that makes everyone happy, if not ecstatic. Compromise is placed in the center of the model, but it requires participants to be both assertive and not, both cooperative and not. When engaging in Compromise, it's important to know your why and be able to articulate what is important to you and what you'd be willing to sacrifice.

Ultimately, Compromise isn't as satisfying as Collaboration, but when there's a sense of urgency, it can be a solid option that, unlike Competition, leaves all parties feeling heard and at least partially validated. When one party is entrenched in Avoidance, Accommodation, or Competition, it might be easier to get them to engage in Compromise rather than Collaboration.

So which mode is best? Well, it depends on a variety of factors. Given unlimited time and resources, Collaboration is usually a solid option, but can often be derailed by power dynamics, personality traits of all involved, the interpersonal relationships (and amount of trust) between the parties, or the nature of the problem itself.

REMEMBER

Leaders have an outsized influence on the culture of their team or organization. Therefore, your followers will have a strong tendency to mirror your preferred mode of conflict management, whichever it may be. However, if you can skillfully move between the five modes of conflict, depending on the context of each given situation, your followers will model that behavior, too.

TIP

When mediating conflict on your team, try to diagnose which mode of conflict the various parties are engaging in. Before discussing the unique concerns of each side, try to get everyone on the same page in terms of how you'd like to address the situation together.

Intercultural Conflict Styles

Another model of conflict management was created in 2005 by Dr. Mitchell Hammer, the founder of several organizations that focus on intercultural competence development, and it describes a person's mindset as it relates to conflict. This model becomes important when you are engaging in or mediating culture across cultural difference, where learned mindsets might be misaligned. Often, if two people from the same cultural background are solving a problem together, they will hold the same mindsets and preferences. However, when people from two different cultural backgrounds are engaged in conflict, they would do well to understand the other's style before their different approaches cause further misunderstandings.

TECHNICAL STUFF

The model of Intercultural Conflict Styles is depicted as a quadrant, with two axes (as shown in Figure 14-2). The first measures a person's preference for either Direct or Indirect Communication. Those who prefer it when people say exactly what they mean are typically aligned with Direct Communication. Those who prefer Indirect Communication can easily perceive their literal rivals to be brusque and rude, while those who prefer Direct Communication might perceive indirect communicators to be impossible to understand, or even deceptive. The second axis in the model measures a person's preference for either Emotional Restraint or Emotional Expressiveness. Those who prefer Emotional Restraint have often been taught by their home culture to value logic over emotion, or that too much emotion can cloud a person's judgment. On the other side, those who value Emotional Expression are often taught that a cool, rational argument lacking in emotion is simply unconvincing, that you can measure the importance of a topic by how much feeling accompanies any discussion of it. Those who exhibit Emotional Restraint can often view their expressive rivals as lacking in a logical basis for their arguments and attempting to win through emotional manipulation, while those who exhibit Emotional Expressiveness might believe that their more restrained rivals are either apathetic or hiding something and therefore unworthy of their trust.

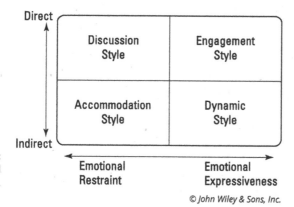

FIGURE 14-2: Intercultural Conflict Styles.

© *John Wiley & Sons, Inc.*

Within the quadrant are four conflict styles, based on their location along each axis:

>> **The Discussion Style:** When a person prefers both Direct Communication and Emotional Restraint, they are grouped in the *Discussion Style*. This style is prevalent in many Northern European nations, including Great Britain, Germany, Scandinavian countries, and among most European descendants

in the USA. While people who prefer the Discussion Style might be very animated otherwise, they adopt a slightly more restrained persona when dealing with conflict, believing that this will place a greater emphasis on their words and allow them to be better heard and understood. Saying exactly what they mean in a restrained way will, they believe, increase the chances that the opposing party will understand that the conflict is about the issue being discussed, not about the personalities involved.

>> **The Engagement Style:** When a person prefers both Direct Communication and Emotional Expressiveness, they are grouped in the *Engagement Style*. This style is prevalent in France, Russia, Spain, and Israel, and is also popular among people of color in the USA. Those who prefer the Engagement Style tend to say exactly what they mean, in very literal terms, but do so in a much more animated style, freely expressing their emotions as they make their case. For them, how they feel about an issue is just as important as what they think about it, and expressing those feelings is a sign of credibility.

>> **The Accommodation Style:** When a person prefers both Indirect Communication and Emotional Restraint, they are grouped in the *Accommodation Style*. This style is prevalent in Japan, Thailand, Malaysia, and parts of Latin America, including Peru and Costa Rica. Because of the name given to this style (and especially because it shares a name with one of the Thomas–Kilman conflict modes detailed earlier in this chapter), it might be easy to assume that those who prefer the Accommodation Style simply give up whenever conflict arises so that others can have their way. There's some truth in the idea that, compared to the other Intercultural Conflict Styles, those in this quadrant place a high value on harmony and often view preserving a relationship as more important than winning every battle that comes along. However, when immersed in these cultures, their members have just as much of a tendency to compete, compromise, or collaborate as anyone else, they just typically do so in a much quieter (they might say more polite!) way.

>> **The Dynamic Style:** Finally, when a person prefers both Indirect Communication and Emotional Expressiveness, they are grouped in the *Dynamic Style*. This style can be observed in Egypt, Saudi Arabia, Kuwait, Lebanon, and Pakistan. There is an Arabic proverb that says, "It is good to know the truth and speak it. But it is even better to know the truth and speak of palm trees." This style might be understandably baffling to those who do not have the experience to decode what's being said under the surface. Others might perceive this style as taking too long to get to the point and straying into topics that aren't relevant. It's important to remember that this is not objectively true, but rather the result of one's own cultural conditioning. To people who prefer the Dynamic Style, they are simply solving problems without stepping on any toes, and this is much more comfortable for them.

REMEMBER

None of these styles are "right" or "wrong," but simply different. It is common to believe that your preferred style is the correct one, but only because it's the one that makes you the most comfortable. Culturally competent leaders can switch styles when immersed in a culture that is not their own.

Applying Best Practices to Real-World Scenarios

Time to practice what you've read about in this chapter! To do this, I'm going to return to BoardTech, a fictional company peopled by imperfect people who make mistakes but takes inclusive leadership seriously and both educates and incentivizes its leaders to do the right thing. As you read each scenario, put yourself in the role of the leader and think about the best way for you to respond:

>> **Scenario 1:** In a senior leadership meeting to discuss the upcoming performance assessment cycle, Martin, the VP of Operations, urges his peers to consider recruiting and promoting more women in their divisions since the current representation has been stagnant for the past three years. You are intrigued by this, but Clyde, another VP, disagrees. "We hire the best and brightest," he says. "And if that happens to be men, we shouldn't lower our standards just to hire more women."

>> **Scenario 2:** Emil, a new employee who just graduated with an MBA, joined your team last month. He is excited about his new role as a Senior Project Manager and dives right in. When he attends team meetings, he is eager to share his ideas and ask questions about current processes. Andrea, who has the same job title as Emil but has been with the company for more than ten years, is growing annoyed. She has come to you to complain that "Emil just got here, and he wants to change everything. He needs to learn the way we do things around here first. I'm not the only one who feels this way."

>> **Scenario 3:** Mike has always held conservative views, but in recent years has become much more vocal. When others on the team adopt new language, he decries these changes as "too woke," and will happily engage in a verbal debate with anyone who disagrees with him. In the last few months, several members of your team have begun to decorate their workspaces with signifiers of more liberal views, while others are insisting that the political rhetoric is making the workplace uncomfortable. Rochelle, one of Mike's peers, has made a direct appeal to you as the team leader. "This is not a space for political debate," she says. "I just want people on both sides to cool it."

Do you already know how you'd like to respond, or are you stumped? Either way, take a methodical approach to these situations by asking yourself the following questions.

Do you need to engage?

While conflict avoidance can lead to toxicity if overused, the first question to ask yourself is whether you need to get involved at all. Honestly, we don't know enough about any of the people introduced in the above scenarios to definitively answer that question. It might be true that Martin, Emil, and Rochelle are perfectly capable of handling the conflict on their own. It could also be true that some or all of them could benefit from your involvement.

For the sake of the scenarios, let's assume that you do decide it would be best to participate in the conflicts presented.

What is the source of the conflict? Where do you stand?

Once you've decided to get involved, the next step is to examine the situation. In each case, can you accurately assess why people are behaving the way they are without making any assumptions? If not, the best course of action might be to begin by asking some questions to ensure your objectivity. Another question you might want to ask yourself is, "Have I already picked a side?" Perhaps Martin is a great ally for women, and perhaps Clyde is a sexist, but even so, giving Martin a chance to explain that "lowering standards" wasn't what he was suggesting could be a good way to handle a conflict and prevent it from getting heated. Perhaps Emil is simply enthusiastic while Andrea is a bit stuck in her ways, but are you aware of exactly what kinds of changes he might have proposed when you were out of earshot? Might the actual conflict be that Andrea is upset that Emil is brand new employee hired at a senior level? If so, how would that change your approach? Finally, do we know why Mike has begun to engage in political debate at work? What are your own political views? Do they make some of the characters in this scenario more sympathetic than others? What are your beliefs about discussing politics in the workplace? Are you prepared to reconcile asking people to avoid certain topics and encouraging authenticity in the workplace?

How will you engage?

What's your Intercultural Conflict Style (detailed earlier in this chapter)? To the best of your knowledge, is it the same or different from any of the other players in these scenarios? If there are differences, are you able to adjust your style to match others if necessary? What's your preferred mode of conflict management according to the Thomas–Kilman model (also detailed earlier in this chapter)? Is it the best way to engage in each of these cases, or is there a better option? In the case of equating the promotion of women in the workplace with lowering standards, your values might indicate that compromise would be detrimental, not only for you, but for all women at BoardTech. In the other two scenarios, is everyone invested in finding a win–win solution, or are some of the players just interested in having their own way? Is anyone in any of these scenarios currently feeling targeted, or might they feel that way once you intervene? How will you manage those emotional reactions?

What is the preferred outcome?

After the current or planned conversations are over, what's the outcome that you're looking for? It's best if you don't frame the optimal result in terms of winners and losers, but rather what kind of workplace culture you'd like to foster. For example, you might want to foster a workplace where leaders mitigate their biases by keeping an eye out for high-potential women that might otherwise be overlooked. By framing the outcome in this way, Clyde is not cast in the role of the villain; on the contrary, Clyde is included in this vision, and one hopes that he will do as much to promote more women in his department as Martin will in his. You might also want to foster a workplace where enthusiasm and new ideas are welcomed and discussed. In this way, Andrea is not the antagonist of the story, but perhaps someone who needs coaching or just a place to vent. Finally, you might want to foster a workplace in which people are productive, enjoy each other's company, and are free to do their best work. To get there, you will likely need to find out what motivates Mike to engage with his colleagues the way he does, if Rochelle is feeling any direct pressure from Mike to debate with him, whether she could easily avoid the conversations she'd rather not participate in, and what is motivating the new ways in which people have begun to decorate their personal workspaces.

What barriers currently exist?

After you gain the necessary information you need, but before you get to work on creative solutions, it would be wise to define the things in your workplace that can and cannot be changed. Are there written policies in your organization that mandate some behaviors and make others impossible? If there's something that is within your power to change, can you reach an agreement with all parties on how to manage it?

What are the implications globally or among multiple stakeholders?

One way to erode trust in a team is to be inconsistent. Therefore, before making a request of anyone on your team, imagine making the same request of someone else of a different level or a different identity. If the request holds up, then make it — and still you'll want to be sure that it is applied equitably across difference. Also, as you work to create your solution, don't forget to keep in mind everyone who could be affected by the decisions you make. This includes colleagues, customers, clients, vendors, future employees, other teams, even your competition.

REMEMBER

People don't have to be directly involved in the present conflict to be impacted by what they observe as you and others work toward a solution. In addition to solving a problem, effectively dealing with conflict is also an exercise in teaching yourself and others how to handle similar conflicts in the future.

4

Cultivating a Culture of Inclusion and High Performance

Diagnose whether your organization's culture is in the Red Zone or Green Zone. Discover ways to be more accountable for closing the gaps.

Measure the impact of inclusive leadership behaviors and integrate them into all aspects of operations, practices, and policies.

Adopt new ways to be an advocate and champion for inclusion across your organization.

Ask the right questions and develop the right competencies when applying an equity lens in decision making.

IN THIS CHAPTER

» Understanding what the employee experience means

» Assessing your current company culture

» Figuring out Red and Green Zones in the Culture Spectrum

» Addressing gaps through strategies and best practices

» Implementing accountability for leaders

Chapter **15**

Assessing the Employee Experience

The employee experience is multifaceted and directly impacts workplace satisfaction, productivity, talent retention, and organizational success. The term encompasses a wide range of factors that influence an employee's journey within a company, from sourcing and recruitment, to onboarding, to daily work life and professional development.

In this chapter, I detail the attributes that drive a positive employee experience and examine some trends and strategies for how best-in-class companies assess and enhance theirs. I also offer some ways that leaders can be held accountable for cultivating a positive work environment.

Defining the Employee Experience

The phrase "enhancing the customer experience" has been around for years, but the notion of the employee experience (also referred to as EX) is relatively new. So let's be clear about what it is. Several reputable global Human Resources (HR) and consulting firms that I have consulted with define the employee experience very similarly:

>> **Automatic Data Processing,** a comprehensive global provider of administration and outsourcing services, analytics, and compliance expertise defines the employee experience as "what employees see, hear, think and feel about your organization. It's how employees experience working at your company from when they join to when they retire or leave." (https://www.adp.com/resources/articles-and-insights/articles/e/employee-experience.aspx)

>> **Qualtrics,** a global experience management company says that "from the moment prospective employees look at your job opening, to the moment they leave your company, everything that the workers learn, do, see, and feel contributes to their employee experience. For your organization to master employee experience management, you must listen to your people at each stage of the employee lifecycle, identify what matters most to them, and create personalized, bespoke experiences." (https://www.qualtrics.com/lp/employee-experience)

>> **The Great Place to Work Institute,** a global leader in workplace culture, states that "the employee experience starts with the hiring and onboarding process and continues until a person leaves your company. It is how your employees experience the company, from relationships with their manager, to work accomplishments, to the technology they need to do their job successfully." (https://www.greatplacetowork.com/)

>> Glassdoor.com, one of the world's largest job and recruiting sites, defines the employee experience as "everything that people encounter, observe, or feel over the course of their time with a company. It is the sum of its parts — from the daily vibe in the workplace to the employee's purpose and place on their team and how they deliver value for their organization." (https://www.glassdoor.com/)

>> **Gallup Organization,** a global analytics firm that is most known for its research on employee engagement, defines the employee experience as "the journey an employee takes with your organization." (https://www.gallup.com/workplace/242252/employee-experience.aspx)

WHAT GLOBAL RESEARCH REVEALS ABOUT THE EMPLOYEE EXPERIENCE

Numerous studies conducted by some of the companies mentioned in the section, "Defining the Employee Experience," have consistently shown a strong correlation between a positive employee experience and increased productivity. They show that engaged and satisfied employees are more likely to contribute their best efforts, resulting in improved organizational performance. They also show that companies with a positive employee experience are more likely to be viewed as employers of choice, giving them a competitive edge in recruitment.

The Society for Human Resource Management (https://www.shrm.org/), the world's largest nonprofit membership organization that offers education, certification, and networking opportunities for HR professionals, provides valuable insights into employee experience trends through its research. According to their 2022 Employee Benefits Report, organizations are increasingly focusing on well-being programs, flexible work arrangements, and mental health support to enhance the overall employee experience. In another study by Deloitte University Press on Global Human Capital Trends, they found that almost 80 percent of executives rated the employee experience as important or very important.

A 2022 study by *Harvard Business Review* (https://hbr.org/sponsored/2022/01/how-to-attract-top-talent-in-2022) found that world-class employee experiences attract top talent through strong company branding, drive high performance through meaningful manager–employee relationships, and create valuable brand ambassadors long after employees have left your organization. They also found that world-class employee experiences can also lead employees to choose to spend their career with an organization because that organization provides them the best opportunity to develop and continually improve their workplace wellbeing.

Jacob Morgan's best-selling book, The Employee Experience Advantage (John Wiley & Sons, Inc., 2017), revealed from his extensive research that looked at over 150 studies and articles, featured extensive interviews with over 150 executives, and analyzed over 250 global organizations, that those that invest in employee experience are more productive, valuable, attractive, innovative, profitable, and have superior stock performance than those who don't.

As you can ascertain from these definitions, the *employee experience* encompasses every touchpoint that a worker has with an organization, from the initial sourcing and recruitment process to their daily work life, growth and advancement, and eventually, their exit from the company. It is also shaped by various factors, including company culture, leadership, policies and systems, and recognition and rewards.

Evaluating the Current State of Your Company Culture

In my work, I speak to many organizational leaders, whether I'm coaching them or helping them think through strategic decisions. Most of the leaders I speak to tell me that their company culture is inclusive and high-performing. But when I speak to those at lower levels of the company, there's a distinct disconnect — the same culture isn't nearly as inclusive from their vantage point, and they see lots of room for improvement in terms of company performance. They talk about not feeling welcome, or instances of unfairness that they've witnessed. This is why it's so important to assess your culture consistently and accurately and not take for granted that your view from the corner office matches the view that others may see every day.

WARNING

If you decide to embark on a journey of culture change, the change should begin at the top of the organization, among its leaders. Sometimes the change process starts more organically, outside of the *C-Suite* (the group of high-level executives who are responsible for making strategic decisions and overseeing the overall management of an organization). Either is fine. What's important is that once underway, the change process needs to include everyone. A change effort led solely by executives will likely result in something that looks like success in the boardroom, but less so outside of it. If the process itself isn't inclusive, it's unlikely that the outcome will be.Peter Drucker, an Austrian–American management consultant, explained this by saying: "Culture eats strategy for breakfast." Basically, he meant that whether your culture is classified as strong or weak, it tends to validate itself. Beliefs cause behaviors that lead to predictable outcomes and validate the original belief. If changing behavior is difficult, then changing belief is grueling, and changing the beliefs of many people at the same time can seem impossible. Not every strategy is up to the task.

TIP

If your organization is going to succeed in its effort to change your culture, you'll need to be exact — almost surgical — in your approach. You'll need to know what behaviors need to change, what beliefs those behaviors are rooted in, and what rewards, incentives and consequences you'll need to provide to allow those beliefs to change. You can assess your culture in multiple ways. The most common options include these:

>> Hire an outside firm that specializes in strategic and tactical organizational culture transformation.

>> Interview senior leaders and other key stakeholders to ascertain their views on the current state of the culture, their level of support (or lack thereof), and their input on goals and objectives for being more inclusive.

>> Have the company's HR Department conduct anonymous surveys of staff.

>> Set up individual employee interviews/focus groups at all levels to see what they think.

>> Schedule open town halls and all-staff meetings to host discussions around company culture and improvements.

Understanding where your leaders are in their development, commitment, and ability to work effectively across differences and to be more inclusive is an important step to take early in the organizational assessment process. This can take the form of conducting stakeholder interviews or using survey instruments.

TIP

Stakeholder interviews allow you to discover critical insight into what key leaders (which can include the president/CEO, board members, senior executives, and others at the highest levels of the organization) understand and how they view and prioritize inclusion initiatives and strategies. Utilizing a confidential setting, these interviews provide thoughts and insights that inform, guide, and direct efforts going forward. The following are examples of questions/prompts used in a 30–45-minute interview:

>> Describe the culture of your organization.

>> What achievements/progress has the organization made in the past 12–24 months in the area of inclusion, equity, and belonging?

>> What can the organization do differently over the next 12 months to be more inclusive?

>> What are some perceived or real obstacles in your organization that may prevent it from achieving greater inclusion?

>> As a senior leader, what role will you/do you want to play to ensure long term sustainability of inclusion initiatives in your organization?

Leadership assessments can provide a framework to gauge cultural competence among your leadership team. They give the organization and individual leaders valuable intel on how their attitudes, beliefs, and unconscious biases weave their way into the organization and teams and create formal and informal barriers to success. These surveys also provide the organization with a broad overview of leadership training and development needs.

TECHNICAL STUFF

Several of the surveys that I have used include the Intercultural Development Inventory (IDI) created by two industrial organizational psychologists, Drs. Mitch Hammer and Milton Bennett; the Inclusion Skills Measurement (ISM) Profile developed by Dr. Helen Turnbull; and the Global Diversity Survey developed by Dr. Alan Richter. Other popular tools you can use to assess leaders' differences in thinking, personality, and leadership styles include the Myers-Briggs Type Indicator (MBTI), DiSC Personality Profiles, Clifton Strengths (formerly Strengths-Finder), the Predictive Index, and the Hogan Assessments.

Checking Out the Culture Spectrum

From extensive research and assessments conducted over the past decade, I've identified six key strengths of cultures that are high-performing and inclusive. Correspondingly, there are six deficits to be found in organizations that are low-performing and toxic. I call this model the *Culture Spectrum™* and it helps change agents identify their organization's strengths and deficits during a culture change effort. It serves as a guide to categorize and understand the prevailing cultural dynamics within an organization. The spectrum spans a range of cultural orientations, but here I focus on the dichotomy between Red Zone cultures (shown on the left in Figure 15-1) and Green Zone cultures (shown on the right in Figure 15-1), as described in the following sections.

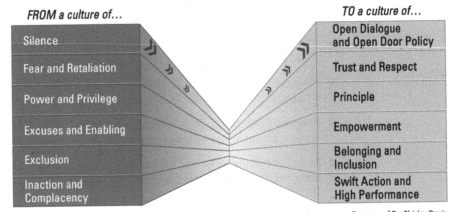

FROM a culture of...

Silence	Open Dialogue and Open Door Policy
Fear and Retaliation	Trust and Respect
Power and Privilege	Principle
Excuses and Enabling	Empowerment
Exclusion	Belonging and Inclusion
Inaction and Complacency	Swift Action and High Performance

TO a culture of...

FIGURE 15-1: The Culture Spectrum™.

Courtesy of Dr. Shirley Davis.

Exploring the Red Zone

WARNING

In the Red Zone, organizations exhibit characteristics that may hinder employee well-being and hinder overall performance. There are six clear signs that your culture is toxic and low-performing.

Silence

In organizations that put an emphasis on safety, there's a phrase you'll hear a lot: "If you see something, say something." But in many toxic, low-performing organizations, a culture of silence pervades. In these environments, people have seen that speaking up is either dangerous, or simply pointless because no one listens, and no action is taken. They might notice that those who do speak out are seen as annoyances and are routinely passed over for promotion or advancement opportunities.

Fear and retaliation

Of course, sometimes silence is caused because people have seen the immediate negative consequences that come from speaking out, or stepping "out of line" in any number of ways. These can range from using innovative and creative ways of completing routine tasks, to reporting unethical (perhaps even illegal) behavior they've observed. In fact, when a company culture is rife with fear and retaliation, unethical behavior will surely follow — because people can use it to get ahead and there will not be a price to pay. Often, these environments are especially hostile to people of color, women, LGBTQ people, people with disabilities, and other groups that can be harassed, demeaned, or discriminated against.

Power and privilege

What does the C-Suite look like in your organization? Is it overwhelmingly white and male? Are there any openly LGBTQ or people with disabilities to be found there? How does it compare to your mid-level managers or entry-level workers? Is there a noticeable lack of diversity when you compare the top levels of the organization with those they lead? If so, how do you explain the discrepancy? Unless you believe that race, gender, sexual orientation, religion, gender identity, disability or other identity markers are true indicators of talent and work ethic, there can only be one explanation: You are working in a culture of power and privilege, where the most talented people from underrepresented groups are either denied advancement or voluntarily leave your organization before you have the chance to stall their careers. Are those who look like your organization's leaders evaluated based on their perceived potential where everyone else must work to justify their place at the table. If so, this is likely a deficit in your culture that must be addressed.

Excuses and enabling

When people behave badly inside your organization, what do people — especially those with power — typically say about it? Is there an honest admission of unethical behavior and accountability for bad behavior? Or do you tend to hear a lot of excuses: "Sure, he's not easy to work for, but he brings in so much money;" "It's just the way she was raised, she probably doesn't mean it;" "It's a tough industry, you should get used to it." When a culture suffers a lack of accountability and transparency and enables unethical actors to get away with bad behavior because they are considered rockstars or have valuable connections, this is a toxic workforce, especially for those from underrepresented groups.

Exclusion

When people are excluded from a group, neuroscientists can detect activity in the same regions of the brain usually associated with physical pain. Like the experience of physical pain, the occurrence of exclusion is coded in the brain as negative, and something not to be repeated. If you put your hand on a hot stove and suffer burns, you're not likely to repeat that experience again. So too, if you are excluded from a group repeatedly, it's not likely that the incidents will give you the resolve to keep trying. It's far more predictable that you will disengage. If you are fortunate to have a healthy degree of self-esteem, you might polish up your CV and begin to look for another workplace that will be more welcoming to you, but it's also possible that you'll interpret this lack of inclusion as proof that your ideas have little merit, and you'll simply withdraw.

TIP

Consider these questions as you determine whether your culture is one of exclusion:

>> How engaged are your employees? Who's most engaged and who's least engaged, demographically speaking?

>> Does everyone feel they can have equal access to opportunities or get a seat at the decision-making table?

>> Which voices/ideas are heard loud and clear and which ones are drowned out or dismissed?

>> How much turnover do you experience, and how many dollars do you spend trying to fill the seats of people who have voluntarily separated from your organization? How do these numbers look demographically?

>> Are lively debates commonplace at your organization, or do most of your staff simply "go along to get along"?

>> What are you learning from conducting exit interviews when employees turn in their resignation?

Inaction and complacency

When you discuss inclusion inside your organization, how do people typically respond? Is there an authentic reckoning of how far we need to go and all the ways the organization hasn't lived up to their potential? Or do people just shrug their shoulders, as if culture change is too difficult to manage? Let's be very clear, the work of culture change is difficult, especially when your company is decades (or perhaps centuries) old. But an unwillingness to try to do that which is difficult not only means that inclusion will be hard to achieve, but it points to a general lack of passion and drive that can only lead to mediocrity at best, and a failing business at worst.

Stepping into the Green Zone

So how do you move from the Red Zone into the Green Zone? These cultures represent environments that prioritize collaboration, inclusivity, and employee well-being. Organizations within the Green Zone embrace diversity and equity, fostering an atmosphere of open communication and mutual respect. Leadership is often distributed across different levels, allowing for a more fluid exchange of ideas and a sense of shared responsibility.

TIP

The six strengths that signal an inclusive, equitable, and high-performing culture are essentially the opposite of the six deficits discussed in the Red Zone. As you read about them, be honest about the current state of your organization. Don't feel discouraged, if your organization is not fully in the Green Zone — most companies aren't and even those that are can slip if they start to believe their own hype and get lazy. But do take a moment to imagine how powerful your company could be and what joy you'd experience at work almost every day if this were a reality. It can be, if the work is done strategically and with steadfastness.

Open dialogue and open-door policy

In contrast to organizations where silence pervades, this kind of culture talks about the issues that are impacting the organization and the world. Ideas are brought forth, from all levels of the organization and while not every idea is acted upon, the act of bringing forth an idea is appreciated, and bold thinking is recognized and rewarded. Of course, not every important conversation can be had out in the open, but leaders have an *open-door policy* wherein staff can schedule time with their manager or leader to discuss matters large and small: how their current project is going, their long-term career goals, or elements of the organizational culture that are difficult to navigate or might be holding them back.

REMEMBER

Leaders will often see a preponderance of these conversations as a sign of weakness, but they actually point to strength. Remember that your company culture should be an open culture, and the issues that impact everyone who lives in our world will follow them into their workplace. But the ability to address them and talk about them is an asset that not every organization possesses.

Trust and respect

Unlike organizations rife with fear and retaliation, high-performing companies can have the tough conversations, because they trust the organization not to react negatively when difficult issues are brought to light. When an organization is dedicated to rooting out bad actors, it respects and appreciates those who report unethical behavior — which, by the way, is a rare occurrence in companies like this. In this kind of culture, ideas come from every corner of the company and are considered based on an inherent respect for every employee.

Principle

If your C-Suite is just as diverse as all the other levels in your organization, it's far more likely that your company is much closer to an ideal meritocracy than most others. But reacting to principle isn't automatic, or simply the result of being "good people." In an open system, resisting the systems of power and privilege that exist everywhere in our society takes work, and is often assisted by diversity hiring strategies, Business Resource Groups, robust and ongoing Diversity, Equity, and Inclusion (DEI)-related training, mentoring programs, and similar positive practices.

Empowerment

The combination of open dialogue, trust, and a strong emphasis on people will not only influence your staff away from shady behavior and toward ethical, morally sound choices, it will enable them to take their own actions in this regard, including calculated risks in the name of doing the right thing. In such organizations, mid-level employees will not hesitate to stand up, even to a high-paying client or senior leader, when demeaning or harassing behavior takes place.

Belonging and inclusion

TECHNICAL
STUFF

When Abraham Maslow, a founder of humanistic psychology, created his famous hierarchy of needs in *Motivation and Personality* (Harper & Row, 1954), he posited that our most basic needs were physiological, such as food, sleep, and safety. Belonging was the third need, followed by esteem and self-actualization. According to Maslow, our more basic needs would need to be satisfied before we could truly focus on higher needs. Today, many thought leaders believe that Maslow was wrong; they theorize that belonging may well be the primary need of human beings. At the very least, it seems undeniable that human beings require connection to be healthy and whole; in fact, in 2020 the United Nations declared the excessive use of solitary confinement a form of torture.

In any organization, people need to feel a sense of inclusion and belonging to be their most productive — even when tasks are repetitive or menial, a deep connection to the people on one's team will result in top-quality work — and an environment that values and generates mental health.

Swift action and high performance

Unlike organizations where inaction and complacency are commonplace, high-performing cultures are typified by the ability to take swift action and achieve results. This kind of company culture isn't created overnight and is only possible when all the other Green Zone attributes are in place. Employees speak up, they trust their leaders, and they trust each other. Leaders respect their staff, and decisions are made on principle. Everyone in the organization is empowered to do what is right, and there is a deep sense of connectedness and belonging. In a company like this, when swift change is necessary or desired, it's possible, because everyone is performing at the peak of their ability and able to work together at their highest capacity.

Applying Strategies to Address Gaps in the Employee Experience

TIP

What does your organization do to create a positive employee experience? What do you do as a leader do? Here are some practices you can implement; I realize that many of them seem incredibly simple, but leaders often underutilize them:

>> **Create meaning and purpose.** This is a powerful driver for employee engagement and satisfaction. Workers seek more than just a job; they desire a sense of connection to something significant and bigger than themselves. Encourage this by casting a compelling and inspiring vision for the organization. By doing so it helps employees understand how they fit into it and the broader impact of their work.

>> **Provide clear objectives and goals for achieving performance.** Ensure that these markers align with the broader mission and strategic priorities of the organization as well as with the company's values. Most importantly, be sure that you are living the values and walking the talk. Employees will see the disconnect and respond accordingly when you don't.

>> **Identify worker potential and help workers grow and develop new skills.** Recognize the strengths, talents, and aspirations of individual employees and provide them with training programs, mentorship, and clear career paths and support. Employees are more likely to thrive in an environment that offers opportunities for professional growth.

>> **Recognize and appreciate good work.** Foster a culture of appreciation and recognition. Acknowledging and celebrating individual and team accomplishments reinforces the idea that each person's work is valued and contributes to the organization's success. Workers want to hear "thank you" more than leaders think, and they like creative and fun ways to show appreciation.

>> **Give the "what" and "why" of tasks and leave the "how" to your staff.** People want autonomy and freedom to figure things out versus being micromanaged and/or prescribed that something has to be done a certain way. They also want to be asked for their input and for it to be seriously considered.

>> **Admit when you make mistakes and use them as teachable moments for the team.** Allow the team to do the same and to share their failures and how they

course-corrected. Acknowledging errors demonstrates humility, transparency, and a commitment to continuous improvement. When leaders openly admit their mistakes, it fosters a culture of accountability and trust within the team.

>> **Treat each person as an individual and appreciate their uniqueness and diversity.** Recognize differences in backgrounds, beliefs, skills, and life experiences without making assumptions or generalizations. This contributes to a positive and inclusive atmosphere, and may include offering flexible work arrangements, accommodations, or tailored development opportunities.

Demonstrating Accountability as a Leader

I believe leadership accountability is at the heart of any organization's ability to achieve optimal performance and to build a strong culture. Have you ever worked for a leader who made a mistake, a bad decision, or didn't know the answer to something, and rather than admit it, they deflected by blaming someone else, justifying it, or acting like it didn't happen? This occurs all too often and it undermines trust, engagement, and communication.

Workers today place a higher premium on their leaders walking the talk and being more accountable. At a time when we continue to experience accelerated change, increased complexities, growing pressures, and competing priorities, demonstrating accountability as a leader couldn't be more critical.

TECHNICAL
STUFF

In 2017's *The Leadership Accountability Gap* (https://www.lhh.com/lhhpenna/en/-/media/lhh/uk/pdfs/lhh-leadership-accountability-global-research-report.pdf), a global study conducted by talent management company Lee Hecht Harrison, nearly 2,000 senior HR leaders and business executives in 20 countries were asked about the state of the leadership in their organizations. They found that only 31 percent were satisfied with the degree of accountability being shown by their leaders, and as such, a leadership accountability gap exists and is dragging down many companies.

WARNING

Without accountability, even the most talented and well-intentioned leaders fail — they fail to meet their performance goals, to develop their teams, to hire top talent, to coach their employees, to communicate clearly, to optimize performance, and they fail the business overall. This is a lot of failings, but when leaders are committed to achieving optimal performance by aligning their thinking, behaviors, and attitude with their words they can avoid these kinds of failures.

I'm a big believer that leaders are the thermostat in any organization — meaning they have the power to set the right temperature and create the right environment for how things are done and how people are treated.

Let me share five behaviors that matter the most for leaders to demonstrate accountability. I've seen these make a real impact on team performance, personal relationships, and the success of the organization. Take a minute to rate how effectively you demonstrate each of the five behaviors listed in the following sections.

DEMONSTRATING ACCOUNTABILITY

I was keynoting at a global leadership conference for a *Fortune* 50 company. As the CEO was introducing the speaker for the morning, he made some remarks that he later learned had a racially insensitive connotation. There were a few audible gasps in the audience but he didn't catch it. When he sat down it was brought to his attention and he was shaken but it was too late to address it — the speaker was already on stage. Before I got up to speak that afternoon, he asked me if he could have a minute to address his comments. I said, "Of course." He apologized before his group of over 300 leaders and took full ownership for not knowing that his comments were insensitive and tone deaf. I talk more about ownership elsewhere in this chapter.

The CEO used this as a teachable moment and vowed that he would do better. He also shared how well-intentioned he was but that it was not an excuse. He said, "Even CEOs don't always get it right and when they don't, they should immediately own up to it. I expect the same from all of us." I thought, "Wow." What courage and strength he displayed. This is what "demonstrating accountability" looks like. And if more leaders acted like this, our workplaces would be much more welcoming and productive. And I might be out of a job!

And wouldn't you know that when I got up, it was the perfect segue way to my keynote topic which was on "Driving Innovation Through Inclusive Leadership." I celebrated his actions and thanked him for being the kind of leader that made their company best-in-class. I also used that incident to highlight the importance of being more aware of our blind spots (biases) and reinforced the fact that all of us have them and that that situation could happen to any of us, and then I shared a few examples of when I didn't get it right — even as the HR veteran and the DEI expert. I also explained that we are all on the journey to becoming more inclusive and learning to work more effectively across differences.

The audience's response was extremely positive and I heard leaders commenting later on about how the CEO's actions set a tone and gave them permission to do the same back in their departments. They also appreciated my response and how I provided them with strategies for how to minimize their biases and how to leverage authenticity as a strength. It was a great conference and it was made to be even more meaningful because a bad situation was turned around for good.

Consistency matters

Being predictable is okay! The reality is that employees want to be led. They want to work for a leader who provides them with guidance and helps them navigate the terrain of uncertainty and change. When people know what to expect from you and how you'll respond, it enhances engagement, increases satisfaction, and improves decision making . . . all of which lead to greater productivity.

As I was writing this book, I asked a number of people what it meant for a leader to be consistent. The most "consistent" responses were:

>> "They do what they say they're going to do."

>> "Who I see today is the same person I see tomorrow."

>> "They are steady and reliable."

>> "They communicate expectations and manage them."

>> "They do the right thing over and over again."

So ask yourself, would your direct reports say these things about you? If not, check out Chapter 7 for my helpful advice.

Taking ownership matters

Leadership accountability requires a personal commitment to honesty and integrity, and that means owning up to your part when things go wrong, admitting when you don't know something, and apologizing when you make a mistake (like the CEO in the sidebar "Demonstrating Accountability"). I don't know about you, but I've worked for those kinds of leaders who made mistakes and bad decisions and then deflected by blaming, justifying it, or denying the truth rather than admitting it. That kind of leadership undermines trust, engagement, and communication.

Here's a personal example. Recently I was expecting a member of my team to complete a project by a certain time frame that was a critical deliverable for a client. As I checked in with him on the status of the project, he responded that he hadn't received a report I'd promised to send and that it was impacting his timeline for completion. I could've sworn I'd sent it, and I insisted to him that I had. But when I checked my email, there it was, in my drafts and unsent. I had gotten distracted and totally forgotten to send it because of my hectic schedule. I went back to him immediately, told him I was sorry, and owned the fact that the project may get delayed because I didn't follow through on my end. Then I went a step further. I called the client myself to explain that we needed a few extra days to complete the project due to my hectic schedule. I didn't blame my team member; I didn't make excuses; I owned up to it. Ultimately, the project was completed on time, and the client was very pleased.

TIP

Simple phrases that can be used in these situations include:

>> "I was wrong."

>> "I made a mistake."

>> "I don't know."

These phrases are perhaps three of the most underutilized — yet among the most impactful — phrases a leader can use. So I urge you today to add those three important and impactful phrases to your vocabulary and be willing to use them.

Sound decision making matters

Every day we have to make decisions. And as leaders, those decisions can affect our direct reports, customers, colleagues, and ourselves. Unfortunately, far too many leaders are guilty of ineffective decision making or the avoidance of making decisions all together.

TIP

This is one of my strong skillsets, so let me share what works for me:

>> First, I have a group of what I call my *personal board of advisors*, people who might trust, who are smarter and more successful than me, and who have been there done that. I use them as a think tank, my sounding board, and as resources for informing my decisions. And yes, this can and has included my direct reports. Don't be too proud to ask for input and to leverage the experience of others around you!

>> Second, I always revert back to the goal and the purpose. What are we trying to accomplish and why? We should figure out what's most important, who will be affected, and what the consequences are, as this helps you make sound decisions.

>> Third, I've learned how to balance my emotions with rational thinking and a steady head, also known as emotional intelligence (see Chapter 8). This is especially important when times are hectic, stressful, or difficult. Even when I'm upset, I have learned to take a timeout before making an important decision. Making tough decisions is a part of every leader's role and you don't always have the luxury of a do-over.

> » Fourth, I finally conquered the *analysis paralysis syndrome*. Before making a decision, I used to think and think and think to the degree that it would paralyze me from making a decision in a timely manner. And you can imagine how frustrating that was for my staff and for others. So the way that I conquered it was to realize that I won't always have all of the information that I need to make a decision. I learned to lean on my personal board of advisors and to trust my experience and my gut.
>
> » Finally, I came to understand that making the decision — even if it's not the best one — is better than not making one at all.

REMEMBER

Making a decision, even if it's not the best one, is better than not making one at all.

Providing feedback matters

One of my worst experiences was working for a leader who got her thrills from criticizing, devaluing, and making people feel small. She was inconsistent in sharing feedback and rarely had anything positive to say. It was always difficult to know where you stood with her, yet she would hold you accountable for results and outcomes. Needless to say, everyone was miserable under her leadership.

Eventually, I moved on to another company. Ever worked for this kind of leader? It certainly taught me what not to do. But thank goodness for the last leader whom I had the pleasure of working with for six years. I call him my best boss ever. Contrary to the bad leader, he taught me what providing feedback effectively looked like. He created a very positive work environment. I never felt berated or marginalized by him, even when things didn't go well. In fact, he didn't even like to use the word "criticism" because it had a negative connotation. Notice that I didn't use the word either. He called it *coaching for improvement* or *corrective feedback*. And the way that he did it was to ask me how I felt things were going on a project or a task, or how did things go in a presentation, or how could I be more effective and improve. Once he heard my thoughts, then he would share his.

He also provided consistent feedback, both positive and corrective. Formally we met once a month to discuss projects and special assignments, but if I needed feedback prior to the meeting, he maintained an open-door policy. He trusted and believed in me and my work ethic and reminded me often that he hired me because of my expertise. And he relied on my expertise and experience and gave me autonomy to do my job. He consistently offered his support and reminded me that I had lots of talents and strengths to offer. It was never his way or the highway.

Under his leadership I thrived. I was fully engaged at work. I trusted him and I felt valued. I gave more than was expected. I came up with lots of creative solutions and I wanted to stay. This is what giving positive feedback looks like and it's what being an inclusive leader looks like. It's the experience that every worker wants. And I am proud to say that I have provided the same experience to my team, who often refer to me as their best boss ever. I take pride in this title and I work hard to continue to be that kind of leader.

How do you provide feedback (gain further insight into giving feedback in Chapter 12)? How are you making your team feel? Are you more like the worst boss I described or like my best boss?

Communicating effectively matters

I deliver nearly 100 presentations a year. I lead a team of global senior consultants and I interact with clients from around the world on a daily basis — clients in the board room, in the C-Suite, and those on the front lines. I'm communicating my expectations to my staff. I'm communicating my value to clients as to why they should hire me. And I'm communicating strategies and solutions in my presentations. So every day I'm conveying information. And every day I am influencing the thinking, behavior, and decisions of others. Along the way, I've picked up some ideas and best practices that I believe have contributed to my success.

TIP

First, I always recognize the who is my audience (the hearers). I acknowledge that they possess diverse experiences, expectations, learning styles, that they come from different backgrounds, and that they are different knowledge levels. So I've learned to be flexible and adaptable in my communication style, to be more relatable and impactful. Second, I practice what I call the four Cs of communicating effectively:

>> **Be clear.** People should understand the goals, direction, expectations, or why something is (or isn't) being done. Because when communication is not clear, it is hard to expect accountability.

>> **Be concise.** Get to the point and stay focused on the key message. Don't overwhelm or underwhelm with information but ensure that people understand what is expected.

>> **Be consistent.** Make sure that your words match your actions and communicate as often as you can. This establishes trust and accountability.

>> **Be credible.** Give accurate, complete, and honest information that helps others make informed decisions and take action.

Chapter **16**

Tracking and Measuring Inclusion Initiatives

very organization seeks to discover its standing in the eyes of customers, staff, and competitors. This has gained heightened significance with the emerging workforce generation, which places heightened expectations on employers to foster greater inclusion and equity.

However, it's not enough to tout your inclusion and diversity efforts if you cannot demonstrate how they are contributing to your organization's success. As a result, companies are awakening to the realization that there is substantial work ahead in evaluating and measuring the impact of *inclusion initiatives* (programs designed to increase diversity and create inclusive cultures). You have to be intentional about the metrics you use and you should only measure what matters because what gets measured, gets done . . . and what gets measured gets treasured.

Bridging the Accountability Gap

WARNING

Leadership accountability plays a significant role in shaping company culture. In fact, business leaders who possess the qualities of accountability and integrity are more likely to outperform their peers according to Professor Gary Latham of the Australian Graduate School of Management. When leaders exemplify accountability, they establish the groundwork for a positive organizational culture that values responsibility and commitment, and where mistakes are openly acknowledged with transparency. But when the leaders of an organization are not being held accountable to meet their objectives, the entire productivity and engagement of the workforce can be at risk.

Unfortunately, there's a gap in accountability where leaders are concerned. This *accountability gap* refers to the disconnection between responsibilities and actions within an organization, leading to a lack of transparency, trust, and overall effectiveness. It is a multilayered challenge that encompasses various dimensions, including ethical conduct, decision-making processes, and organizational culture.

REMEMBER

Lee Hecht Harrison, a global outplacement and Human Resources (HR) services solutions firm, released *The Leadership Accountability Gap* (https://www.lhh.com/lhhpenna/en/-/media/lhh/uk/pdfs/lhh-leadership-accountability-global-research-report.pdf) that provides valuable insights into the root causes of these issues and proposes strategies to address them. The study emphasizes the need for organizations to prioritize leadership development, foster a culture of open communication, and establish clear expectations for ethical conduct. It also identifies several key gaps that contribute to the accountability deficit within leadership roles:

>> **A breakdown in communication.** When leaders fail to effectively communicate expectations, goals, and feedback, it creates ambiguity and confusion among team members. This gap can result in misalignment between individual efforts and organizational objectives, hindering overall productivity.

>> **A decision-making gap.** Leaders are often entrusted with critical decision-making responsibilities. However, the accountability gap arises when decisions lack transparency, are made without due diligence, or fail to consider the long-term consequences. This gap erodes trust within the organization and can have detrimental effects on employee morale.

>> **An ethical gap.** Ethical lapses in leadership contribute significantly to the accountability gap. When leaders deviate from ethical standards, engage in unethical behavior, or turn a blind eye to such actions within their teams, it creates a toxic culture that erodes trust and undermines the organization's reputation.

>> **A responsibility gap.** Here, leaders must take ownership of their decisions and actions. The responsibility gap emerges when leaders deflect accountability or shift blame onto others. This undermines the credibility of leadership and fosters a culture of finger-pointing rather than problem solving.

Closing the accountability gap is imperative for fostering a culture of transparency, trust, and sustained organizational success. The consequences of an unaddressed accountability gap can be severe, including decreased employee engagement, increased turnover rates, damaged reputation, and diminished stakeholder confidence. A culture of accountability, on the other hand, cultivates an environment where individuals take responsibility for their actions, learn from mistakes, and contribute to the overall growth and success of the organization.

Recognizing the Importance of Measuring Inclusion Initiatives

The major objective of measurement is to assess your progress along your journey. For example, measuring how fast a runner completes a 100-meter dash is irrelevant if that runner's event is actually a marathon, which requires much more endurance for running at a set pace for an extended distance. So a more appropriate metric for a marathon runner is pace per mile for a certain number of miles; that stat is a better predictor of that runner's ability to successfully complete a marathon.

And so it is with inclusion efforts. You have to appropriately measure what matters — not just organizational performance, employee engagement, and a host of HR practices, but also marketing efforts, consumer behavior, and profits.

REMEMBER

Measurement is the outcome or quantification of a process. As an organizational manager and leader, you're seeking information to optimize the performance and profitability of your company. In order to do that, you have to methodically measure what matters.

Inclusion, equity, and belonging matter. In my experience, companies often track the conventional measurements of representation such as counting the number of people who belong to certain diverse groups such as women, BIPOC (that is, Black, indigenous, and other people of color), and sometimes age groups, people with disabilities, and in more recent years, people who identify as LGBTQ. And while representation matters, tracking and measuring inclusion initiatives must extend beyond counting heads, to making heads count. Why? Because top talent cares about a company's commitment to being a great place to work and working for an employer where all talent can thrive.

Nearly 80 percent of workers in a 2021 CNBC/SurveyMonkey workforce survey (https://www.surveymonkey.com/curiosity/cnbc-workforce-survey-april-2021/) say that they want to work for a company that values Diversity, Equity, and Inclusion (DEI). Additionally, according to *Diversity, Equity, and Inclusion at Work: Do Americans Really Care?*, a 2022 study conducted to over 3,000 American workers by Goodhire (https://www.goodhire.com/resources/articles/diversity-equity-inclusion-survey/), a leading provider of employment background screening services, 81 percent of workers said they would leave their job if their employer lacked a commitment to DEI in the workplace, while 54 percent said they would take a pay cut to improve inclusion and belonging at work. These are compelling stats that reveal just how important it is to track and measure your inclusion initiatives.

Looking at Ways to Measure Inclusion Initiatives

A number of metrics can help an organization gain a sense of how effective its inclusion efforts are and how all employees — especially those who are among the marginalized or underrepresented groups — are experiencing the workplace every day. As a leader, you have to be intentional about the metrics you use. In other words, you need to measure what matters. The following sections highlight a few of the most common metrics that my colleagues in HR and DEI track, as well as companies who consistently perform as best-in-class for inclusion and diversity.

Recruitment and selection

As an HR professional, I worked in and headed up recruiting for nearly ten years. I can't tell you the many times I've heard the statements, "We want to be more inclusive in our recruiting efforts, but we can't find any," and "We're only seeking the most qualified/the best and the brightest." It was as though people believed that diverse talent was lost or hidden somewhere and couldn't be found, or that the standards and qualifications would have to be lowered if a company had to hire diverse talent.

Organizations often focus on a single metric in their diversity and inclusion recruitment efforts, and that metric is underrepresented hires. And while representation matters, a number of other metrics can be tracked throughout the recruitment and selection process and can give you a full picture of the success of your efforts. Some have a direct financial impact while others impact the workplace culture.

TIP

Here are a few examples of recruitment and selection metrics you can use in your inclusion and diversity efforts:

>> **Demographics of hires (for example, race/ethnicity, gender, age).** It's important to know your starting point if you want to close the gaps in attracting and hiring talent that you don't have.

>> **Sourcing channel (for example, employee referral, online job boards, job fairs, educational institutions, partnerships, search firms, online minority groups).** Casting your net wider and broader is a great way to ensure that you gain access to more talent from underrepresented groups.

>> **Quality of hire (how long the employee remains on the job as well as the job performance of that employee).** Tracking this helps justify the cost of recruiting in more unconventional ways.

>> **Turnover rates (the number of employees who have left the company voluntarily or involuntarily) and all of the costs associated with replacing an employee.** This is an important metric to track to ensure that you don't have a revolving door. It's one thing to recruit top diverse talent but if they don't stay you have a bigger problem.

>> **Selection ratios (number or percentage of offers extended to underrepresented candidates; number or percentage of job offer declines by underrepresented candidates as a percentage of the total number recruited).** If candidates aren't accepting offers it is worth investigating why (for example, pay, the role itself, the employer's reputation, their experience in the selection process, or the company's lack of diversity).

REMEMBER

These metrics should be a part of your short- and long-term recruitment strategy, and you will need to decide which of them works best for your organization. Measure what matters.

Development, advancement, and retention

One of the most common reasons that workers report leaving their jobs is the lack of development and advancement opportunities. When my firm analyzes the data from the many inclusion and engagement staff surveys we conduct, we find even higher numbers exist among minority and underrepresented talent (10 to 15 percent higher on average) who report a lack of development or advancement opportunities. Additionally, they report higher levels of pay disparity. Moreover, women are still experiencing slower promotion rates than men. Women of color continue to lose ground at every step of the promotion pipeline and are the fastest growing group quitting their jobs and turning to entrepreneurship.

TECHNICAL STUFF

When you look at the *Fortune* 500 today, less than 50 women CEOs are represented, and the numbers are even more abysmal when you look for CEOs of color (less than 1 percent).

Not only are these realities measurable, but they result in higher turnover rates, which have a tangible impact on a company's bottom line.

TIP

Want to avoid these costs? Offer development and advancement opportunities, especially tailored for minority and underrepresented talent. This can include:

>> Mentoring and coaching programs (see Chapter 17)

>> Training and skill building programs

>> Simulations

>> Sponsorship and advocacy programs

>> Individual development plans with regular feedback (see Chapter 12)

>> *Career lattices* (the ability to move up, diagonally, or horizontally — to another department — within an organization)

>> Networking (internally and externally)

>> Participation in Employee Resource Groups (see Chapter 17)

>> Training for people leaders on such topics as: unconscious bias, inclusive leadership, how to provide coaching and feedback, leading high-performing diverse teams, allyship, fostering trust, demonstrating cultural competence, to name a few.

Each of these can be tracked and measured based on results and how they are applied on the job. Here are some examples of typical metrics for the previous bullet list:

>> The number of participants who attended training.

>> Results of evaluations and surveys about attendee's experiences and takeaways.

>> Commitments to action and testimonials about how learner's knowledge and skills were applied back on the job, and percentage increase of productivity.

>> The number of promotions per year.

- >> How performance ratings are assigned to diverse groups as compared to the majority group (usually done through calibrations by HR).

- >> Pay equity audits and external compensation benchmarking that result in pay adjustments.

- >> Employee surveys that ask questions about development and advancement.

- >> The number of people who have mentors/sponsors and how it contributes to advancement.

- >> Stay interviews (as well as exit interviews, should employees decide to leave anyway).

These are just a few metrics, but I can't stress enough the importance of reviewing and enhancing policies and strategies that will foster a culture of inclusion, create a sense of belonging, and strive to be a great place to work.

People don't leave bad jobs; they leave bad leaders and toxic cultures.

Employee engagement and job satisfaction

Employee engagement is the connection and commitment employees exhibit toward an organization when their emotional, social, and psychological needs are met. *Job satisfaction* is how employees feel about their compensation, work environment, career development, and relationship with management.

Both are important. Both can be measured.

The most common ways to measure and track these are through employee engagement surveys and focus groups. My firm conducts these by assessing a number of drivers of engagement and satisfaction such as feedback, trust, communication, leadership effectiveness, compensation and benefits, work environment, inclusion and equity, and development and advancement. These surveys can be administered once or twice a year and should be analyzed to determine how well the company's inclusion efforts are working (or not).

It is worth noting that one of the most reputable global analytics and consulting firms that specializes in measuring employee engagement is the Gallup organization. They measure engagement as highly engaged, disengaged, or highly disengaged. One of their most recent studies revealed that high worker engagement dropped from 36 percent in 2020 to 34 percent in 2021. To find out more about the 12 questions that they ask in their survey (called the Q12), you can access it on Gallup's website (https://www.gallup.com/q12/).

In addition to employee engagement surveys, you can also measure and track:

>> The number of employee complaints.

>> Worker productivity.

>> Absenteeism.

>> Customer service satisfaction.

>> Reasons why workers leave your company (using exit interviews).

>> The number of *C-Suite* (the group of high-level executives within an organization) leaders and employees who attend inclusion training and capture qualitative feedback through post-activity surveys and exit interviews.

>> The Net Promoter Score (detailed later in this chapter). It is one of the most well-known HR metrics used to determine how likely employees are to recommend the organization as a great place to work to a friend or colleague.

REMEMBER

There is no single metric that tells you everything you need to know about employee engagement and job satisfaction. What's important to keep in mind is that you want to understand what motivates your employees, what makes them feel a sense of belonging, inclusion, and connection, and what drives performance, commitment, and productivity. Knowing this will inform your decisions about how your inclusion initiatives can enhance the employee experience for those who may be least engaged and most dissatisfied.

Compensation and benefits

A key focus of inclusion is ensuring that workers have fair and equitable pay and benefits that meet their specific needs. The reality is that — according to results on hundreds of staff listening sessions, employee surveys, and focus groups my firm has conducted over the past three years — many organizations still fall short of providing pay equity and benefits, particularly for marginalized and underrepresented talent.

Here's a personal example. In some of my most demanding roles as a senior leader, I had to juggle work and my role as a mom. It was important for me to work for leaders and employers who offered flexible work arrangements, mentoring opportunities, and competitive pay. At the same time, I didn't want to be overlooked for opportunities to advance simply because I was a woman, a working mom, or a person of color. Unfortunately, I have experienced being overlooked, underpaid, and undervalued. Does my story exist in your organization?

How do you know if you have pay equity and benefits that meet the needs of all? Here are some ways to measure both:

>> Assess salary levels to ensure that employees within the same role earn the same base salaries and that their annual performance bonuses are calculated equitably.

>> Conduct industry compensation surveys to allow you to make more informed business decisions based on your industry, company size, and closest competitors for talent.

>> Survey your employees to assess their perception of pay equity and benefits within the same roles. Delineate the responses by various demographics to determine if there are inequities in any groups.

REMEMBER

If employees in your organization are being paid equitably, but competitors are able to pay more, you can still be competitive by offering other benefits. Take a look at those that target marginalized groups. For instance, employers with self-insured health plans may be able to expand coverage to cover medical travel for legal reproductive health care. Parental leave plans could explicitly include same-sex couples, or you might opt to cover gender-affirming care for your transgender employees.

Employer brand

Imagine that you are interviewing a top candidate and they ask you three questions:

>> "Tell me what it's like to work at this company? And how would women, people over 50, and people of color answer this question?"

>> "What does your commitment to inclusion look like? What kinds of programs are in place?"

>> "How do you stand out from other employers?"

How would you respond to each of these questions?

TIP

The new generation of diverse talent is more likely to ask these types of questions. They are more selective about the type of employer and leader they want to work for, as well as the kind of workplace culture they want to work in. Therefore, organizations must focus on building a strong employer brand. That starts with setting goals about the type of company they want to be known for (especially as it relates to attracting more diverse talent, customers, suppliers, donors, members, and partners), determining the brand message and reach, and then measuring and monitoring how well the employer brand is recognized and rated. Here are three common ways that organizations do this:

>> **Earning awards and being named on employer ranking lists.** Many companies seek to be named as an "employer of choice," or to appear on best employer lists. Even applicants and candidates pay attention to employer rankings such as Glassdoor.com, *Fortune* magazine's Most Admired Companies, the Great Place to Work Institutes Best Places to Work, and others.

>> **Analyzing recruitment results.** Measure your cost-per-hire to see if your employer brand efforts are paying off. If they are then you should see greater retention in your organization, and therefore a decrease in your recruitment costs. You can also track the number of diverse applicants that responded to your job postings and their responses to how they heard about the job.

>> **Tracking the employee experience.** Through focus groups, engagement, and satisfaction surveys you can assess how the staff is experiencing the workplace culture in such areas as trust, inclusion, feedback, equity, communication, compensation, and advancement opportunities. For more on this, see Chapter 15.

Another useful tool is the Net Promoter Score, which looks at how likely employees are to recommend the company as an employer; you can find out more at https://www.surveymonkey.com/mp/net-promoter-score/. You can also measure the types and quantity of complaints filed and legal actions taken by employees, and review feedback from conducting stay interviews, as well as exit interviews from employees who leave the company. Be sure to track this data by demographics so that you can assess which groups of employees have a favorable or unfavorable experience.

REMEMBER

Measuring and tracking the employer brand also extends beyond the workplace to ensure that your brand isn't tarnished by costly lawsuits and the associated legal fees, reputational damage, and the repair of it. What's more beneficial is reaching more diverse customers, vendors and suppliers, and community partners (discover more in Chapter 18).

Focusing these metrics internally and externally can help you to better respond to the questions I opened this section with. I invite you to revisit those responses now you've read the rest of this section.

Supply chain and procurement

Supplier chain programs have existed for decades and today they have evolved to include supplier diversity programs. Procurement and supplier diversity programs are an aspect of a company's outreach and reflect ethical actions and social responsibility. When an organization promotes and supports diversity within its supply chain, it demonstrates its commitment to inclusivity. It also builds trust and communicates to employees that the organization mirrors its internal actions with suppliers.

As a woman-owned and minority-owned business, I am a proud recipient and participant in a number of organization's supplier diversity programs. A *diverse supplier* is a business that's at least 51 percent owned and operated by an individual or group that's part of a traditionally underrepresented or underserved group. Those classifications may extend to small business enterprises, women, minorities, people with disabilities, and so on.

Supplier diversity programs aren't just considered the right thing to do; they're also good for the economy and the community. For example, in the United States, the National Minority Supplier Development Council (https://nmsdc.org/) reports that minority business enterprises generate $400 billion in economic output that preserves 2.2 million jobs and $49 billion in revenue for the local, state, and federal tax authorities. And the benefits aren't just economic. Supplier diversity programs also include education, training, and entrepreneurship efforts.

Evaluating a supplier diversity program normally begins with the dollars spent with diverse suppliers and ends with the impact on the community through corporate social responsibility efforts. The most common metrics that I've seen companies use to track supplier diversity programs are:

>> Tracking of the number of opportunities with small and diverse suppliers within the supply chain

>> Business-to-business joint ventures

>> Spend growth across the company

>> Number of new suppliers added to the pipeline

>> Industry growth (winning new contracts with small and diverse suppliers and expanding the footprint with key industry partners)

>> Diverse supplier spend and utilization

>> Job creation and workforce impact

There's more, but these should give you some food for thought. What I learned early on is that it's best to be strategic, calculating, and thorough rather than reporting inclusion metrics too prematurely and not having all of the supporting data.

REMEMBER

The reporting of diverse spend as a percentage of an organization's total spend is essential to the authenticity of a company's supplier diversity program.

Avoiding Common Pitfalls When Measuring Inclusion Initiatives

I have found that tracking and quantifying inclusion is challenging due to the fact that it is often articulated in qualitative and subjective terms with limited guidance on establishing and nurturing an inclusive environment. It is often unnoticed by those who benefit from it positively. In other words, only when something adverse happens and someone is offended or feels excluded does inclusion really matter. The challenge is particularly pronounced in measuring workforce representation for global organizations, which grapple with issues such as self-identification and defining underrepresented talent across different geographical locations.

REMEMBER

Even with demographic data, establishing a benchmark for "good" representation proves elusive. Selecting meaningful diversity and inclusion metrics is an art rather than a science. One of the most difficult aspects of measuring DEI initiatives is that leaders don't understand what to measure. It is often assumed that *soft skills* (such as communication, interpersonal skills, problem solving, trust, and work ethic) have little to no impact to the bottom line. This couldn't be further from the truth. Most of the metrics I detail in this chapter have a direct impact to the bottom line because they all impact how the employee experiences workplace culture. If their experience is positive, that translates to their performance. If it is negative, companies suffer in their ability to drive innovation and high performance, keep great talent, serve their customers, and remain competitive.

WARNING

As you track, measure, and report progress on your inclusion initiatives, what you don't want to do is undermine your success by making common measurement mistakes such as:

>> **Measuring components that aren't aligned with company goals, strategy, and business needs.** Remember to measure what matters to your leaders.

>> **Using flawed methodology and data.** Be sure that it is accurate, relevant, and vetted. Benchmark and compare with external sources or industry standards.

>> **Not reporting your inclusion metrics at all.** Don't assume that your executives or board members know the results and don't let your progress or successes be a well-kept secret.

>> **Assuming that everyone and every division is at the same place.** Progress will look different across the organization (from division to regional location, and across heads of the departments). Because inclusion is a journey, recognize that metrics must be local, and while they can be compared across the company, there must be some flexibility and understanding that leaders may be driving inclusion at different paces.

There is much to be measured, you just have to do it the right way.

Chapter **17**

Advocating for Inclusion

nclusive leaders are also advocates for inclusion. This means they don't just avoid negative or discriminatory behaviors, but they are proactive in their approach to ensuring that all team members experience an equitable, respectful, and safe work environment. For them, inclusion is a cause they speak about, support and defend, and influence policy and systemic changes. Not only do they advocate, but in some cases they act as allies and activists. I cover all three of these roles in this chapter, but I primarily discuss advocacy as a cause and as a leadership responsibility. I describe why it is more crucial today than ever, and explore how the role of an advocate is different from that of an ally or as an activist. Lastly, I list a number of ways that all leaders can advocate for the talent that needs it the most.

Differentiating Between Advocacy and Activism

REMEMBER

The terms "activism" and "advocacy" are often used interchangeably, but they represent distinct approaches to social change:

» *Activism* is characterized by direct and often confrontational actions aimed at challenging existing power structures and promoting change. Activists may engage in protests, demonstrations, or other forms of direct action to draw attention to injustices and demand immediate change.

>> *Advocacy* is a broader and more strategic approach to influencing policies and societal norms. It is one way to lobby for change within existing systems to bring about gradual systemic change, whether that system is a governmental agency, an industry, or an organization.

I have been an advocate for change (specifically for enabling organizations to be more welcoming, equitable, and inclusive) for over 30 years as a former chief diversity officer for several *Fortune* 100 companies and for the world's largest human resources association (SHRM), and now as a CEO of my global leadership consulting firm. As an advocate, I have lobbied for organizational policy reforms, engaged in public awareness campaigns, facilitated short- and long-term educational programs, and collaborated with key executives and other stakeholders to address issues that erode, disrupt, and even sabotage inclusion initiatives. And while I mostly worked inside the organization to effectuate these kinds of changes, I often found myself working outside of the system in an activist role. This is another way that changemakers can work for transformation.

Activism is generally characterized by seeking change from outside the system. For instance, if you've ever carried a sign and marched on behalf of a cause you are passionate about, you've engaged in activism. But activism isn't always simply a form of protest. Customer boycotts, posts on social media, or writing letters and emails to elected officials or business leaders are all forms of activism as well.

None of this makes activists unkind or advocates weak. Many (including myself) would argue that it takes both advocates, working within a system, and activists, working outside it, to create the changes we seek. For example, let's say your organization doesn't offer flexible work, mental health benefits, resources, or training, nor does it offer elder care time off, or domestic partner benefits to its employees. As advocates, your Employee Resource Groups (ERGs — more on these later in this chapter) might seek an audience with your chief human resources officer (CHRO) or the chief diversity, equity, inclusion, and accessibility officer (CDEIA) to discuss the changes they'd like to see. They would be motivated to make the company more successful by making it more inclusive for all.

In the example just described, the aim of the ERGs is to convince the CHRO and the CDEIA officers to join them in their advocacy. Toward this aim, they might argue (diplomatically, of course) that the costs generally incurred by organizations with a more inclusive benefit package are far outweighed by the cost savings of higher retention of staff and the additional customers that would be attracted by being identified as a Most Admired Company by *Fortune* magazine, or on Glassdoor.com's List of Best Places to Work, or ranked on the Human Rights Campaign's Corporate Equality Index. The advocates for change make use of the work that activists do to lobby for the changes they want to see.

For more on the business case for Diversity, Equity, and Inclusion (DEI), check out my book *Diversity, Equity, & Inclusion For Dummies* (John Wiley & Sons, Inc., 2022). The role of the chief DEI officer continues to evolve in its scope of responsibilities and its title sometimes now includes the "A" as shown in the previous paragraph ("Accessibility"). You can learn more about the changing role of the CDO in *Diversity, Equity, & Inclusion for Dummies.*

While both advocacy and activism are effective means of transforming systems, being a leader within an organization that supports and works for change makes you an advocate, by definition.

Understanding Why Advocacy Is Needed

South African Anglican Bishop and theologian, Reverend Desmond Tutu, known for his work as an anti-apartheid and human rights activist said:

If you are neutral in situations of injustice, you have chosen the side of the oppressor. If an elephant has its foot on the tail of a mouse and you say that you are neutral, the mouse will not appreciate your neutrality.

What he was getting at is simple: The status quo isn't fair. And just as injustice is the norm in the outside world, homogeneity and exclusion are the norms in our organizations. This is the result of many factors, from prevailing norms to learned biases. But a leader who does not take a stand on behalf of greater equity, inclusion, accessibility, and belonging is in fact supporting these norms. Therefore, it's impossible to escape making a choice, even by doing nothing.

One of the primary reasons why organizations need more advocacy is to foster inclusivity, equity, and diversity. Inclusive and more equitable workplaces are more innovative, creative, and adaptable. When individuals from diverse backgrounds feel valued, seen, and supported, and enjoy a sense of belonging, they are more likely to bring their unique perspectives to the table. This diversity of thought can lead to more comprehensive problem solving, increased creativity, and a broader range of ideas ultimately contributing to the organization's overall success.

Advocacy also plays a crucial role in promoting employee well-being. In a workplace where advocacy is actively encouraged, employees feel supported not only in their professional endeavors but also in their personal growth and development. This support can lead to increased job satisfaction, higher morale, and a more positive work environment. Employees who feel advocated for are likely to be more engaged, committed, and loyal to their organization.

An advocacy-driven culture can help attract and retain top talent. In a competitive job market, organizations that prioritize advocacy and inclusivity stand out as desirable places to work. Potential employees are increasingly seeking workplaces that not only value diversity but actively work towards creating an environment where every individual can thrive. By incorporating advocacy into organizational values and practices, employers can attract a diverse and talented workforce, enhancing the organization's overall competitiveness.

Leaders play a critical role in shaping the culture of an organization. When leaders take on an advocacy role, they set the tone for the entire workplace. Leaders who actively advocate for inclusion, diversity, and employee well-being, psychological safety, and accessibility create an atmosphere of trust and respect. This, in turn, fosters a sense of psychological safety among team members (which I cover in Chapter 11), encouraging them to express their opinions, take risks, and contribute fully to the organization. Moreover, leaders who advocate for all of the above contribute to the development of a more resilient and adaptable organization.

Leadership advocacy is instrumental in building better team performance. When leaders prioritize advocacy, they demonstrate a commitment to the success and growth of each team member. Leaders who advocate for their team members also create a *positive feedback loop* — as employees feel supported, they are more likely to work at their best, leading to improved overall team performance.

Leadership advocacy also builds a culture of trust and open communication. When employees see that their leaders are genuinely invested in their well-being and success, they are more likely to communicate openly, share their concerns, and collaborate effectively. This open communication fosters a positive work environment where feedback is valued, and issues and conflicts can be addressed promptly, contributing to overall team cohesion and performance. Chapter 13 provides additional tips and strategies for how to do this effectively.

WARNING

It's tempting to believe that your organization is the exception to this rule. After all, it might feel perfectly pleasant and welcoming to you, and a cursory glance around does not reveal anyone being mistreated or excluded. However, this is usually the result of power dynamics at play. As a leader, particularly if you also exhibit several identity characteristics from the majority group, there's much you don't see with a quick glance around. Assume there are things you don't see, and perspectives you don't (yet) have access to, as you work to make your team and your entire organization more inclusive.

Defining the Role of an Ally

Allies play a crucial role in promoting inclusion, equity, and a sense of belonging among team members, peers, and direct reports. Being an ally is especially crucial for people leaders and senior executives because their actions and attitudes set the tone for the entire workplace culture. When leaders actively demonstrate allyship, they contribute to a positive work environment, increased employee engagement, and improved team dynamics. To understand the role of an ally, it is essential to distinguish it from advocacy. While both terms involve supporting and standing with others, the key difference lies in the personal connection to the marginalized or underrepresented group. An advocate often emerges from within the community they are championing, drawing from personal experiences and a deep understanding of the challenges faced by their group. On the other hand, an ally is someone who, though not a member of the marginalized group, actively supports and advocates for their rights and well-being.

An ally uses their privilege to amplify the voices of those facing adversity. Allies recognize and acknowledge their own position of advantage and leverage it to dismantle systemic barriers, challenge discriminatory practices, and create an environment where everyone feels valued and included. Allyship involves a commitment to continuous learning, self-awareness, and taking concrete actions to promote a more equitable and inclusive workplace.

People leaders who are allies can realize some of the same benefits as detailed in the previous section, such as:

>> Creating a workplace culture that values inclusivity that in turn leads to higher levels of employee satisfaction, increased morale, and a stronger sense of belonging among team members.

>> Fostering trust between leaders and team members when employees see their leaders actively supporting and advocating for their well-being, making them more likely to feel valued and engaged in their work.

>> Attracting and retaining top talent in a competitive job market, where that top talent seeks workplaces where they feel seen, heard, and supported.

>> Improving team dynamics where team members are more likely to collaborate effectively, offer more creative problem solving and innovation, and achieve better team performance.

These same benefits can work for leaders at all levels and even those who are individual contributors.

Allyship is not just a moral imperative; it is a strategic investment and leadership responsibility in the long-term success and sustainability of the team and the organization.

Identifying Multiple Methods of Advocating

In addition to the work inside your own team, leaders can advocate in many ways for greater inclusion throughout a larger organization. The following ideas are by no means exhaustive but give you a good idea of the myriad ways you can be a change agent.

Launching and leading Employee Resource Groups

Employee Resource Groups (ERGs) are employer-recognized workplace groups voluntarily led by employees. These groups allow employees with commonalities to meet, support each other, and produce an outcome that helps improve your business and their job satisfaction. Also known as *affinity groups* or *Business Resource Groups* (BRGs), ERGs give employees the opportunity to build community, have discussions about meaningful topics, and share resources. ERGs can encompass a broad range of DEI-related topics and initiatives.

Employee Resource Groups are typically led by volunteers in the workforce, but often find it easier to meet their goals if they have an advocate in senior leadership. I recommend that companies who sponsor ERGs require each of them to have at least one executive sponsor.

If you are a senior leader in your company, sponsoring an ERG in your company is a great way to create a more inclusive organization. Additionally, if you are a team leader leading a diverse staff, consider joining one or more ERGs, even if you do not share the identity that the group is based on. ERGs are a great avenue for learning about identities that are not your own, and it provides an opportunity to be an ally (see the previous section). If there's a need for an ERG that doesn't yet exist in your organization, be available to assist those who seek to begin one and consider signing on as a founding member.

The following are some additional best practices regarding the formation and management of ERGs. Whether your ERGs are newly launched or have been going strong for years, consider how these ideas might improve your employee experience:

>> **Allow ERGs to be grassroots.** As much as you might recognize the need for an ERG focused on a particular underrepresented community, it's important that the group form on its own. Employees should be aware of a standard process to propose an ERG for company funding and do the work of applying for funding and recognition, making a case for their existence. The employees themselves need to have real energy around the group for it to succeed and sustain itself.

>> **Create a mission statement and goals.** This can be done as part of the application process or immediately after the ERG is recognized. A mission statement (what the group does) will guide all actions for the ERG, and goals (vetted and approved by the company) will ensure that the group is putting its budget to good use. Goals should be both ambitious but realistic, as meeting goals can be used to justify further budget allocations.

>> **Establish guidelines and a structure.** It is a good idea for all ERGs in one organization to be structured in a similar way. While some flexibility might be important, it can also be handy if the same committees exist in each ERG, perhaps based on defined practice areas at your company. That way, for instance, if new training is to be rolled out, an organization's inclusion initiatives could quickly involve the committee chairs of each ERG's learning committees.

>> **Define ERG leadership roles.** Just as consistent structure is useful when leading multiple ERGs, so is defined leadership. Each ERG should have a designated leader or co-leaders, and a similar leadership structure (such as officers and committee leads). Organizations should consider allowing ERG leaders to devote a small percentage of their working hours to the ERG, so that the work can be included in their performance assessments, and they can be rewarded for these leadership activities. It might be advantageous for the leader or other designated representative of each ERG to also sit on a *diversity council,* who attend regular (annual or semi-annual) meetings to discuss progress, new initiatives, and other related issues.

>> **Track and measure effectiveness.** It is a futile effort to expect ERGs to create and meet goals if there is no accountability to come later. Annually, ERGs should be expected to report progress against their stated goals as a requisite for future funding.

>> **Promote allyship and collaboration.** Encourage ERGs to pool their resources to co-sponsor events and allow the successful collaborations to count towards the goals of all involved ERGs. Remove any systemic dynamics that encourage ERGs to compete with one another and enforce a vision for the entire ERG program that explicitly states that ERGs are working together for a more inclusive environment for all employees of the company.

>> **Allow anyone to join.** Most organizations with a successful ERG program do not restrict allies from joining. For instance, white employees can join the Black ERG, an Asian employee can join the Hispanic ERG, men can join the Women's ERG, a cisgender heterosexual can join the LGBTQ ERG, and so on. Sometimes, allies will join an ERG because they have deep relationships (sometimes within their own families) with members of the social identity group, and sometimes, they simply want to learn. In all instances, make sure that they are inclusive. Unless an individual wants to join an ERG to actively disrupt it (this is very rare), anyone should be welcome.

>> **Align ERGs on business initiatives.** One way that ERG structures often get a bad reputation is that they can be too focused on socializing and fun events, and are seen as a drain on business resources. This can be avoided by ensuring that the DEI strategic plan for your organization has clear duties outlined for ERGs, and that these are clearly reflected in the goals for each ERG. Tying the role, responsibilities, and results to leaders' annual performance management processes also helps to keep the focus on business.

>> **Don't forget to have fun!** At the same time, networking opportunities are a big reason for employees to join an ERG, especially if they are the only person of their social identity group on their regular work team. Therefore, events that appear to be purely social can have intrinsic value. Rather than forbidding social events, seek a balance that meet the needs of both the employees and the business.

Championing Diversity, Equity, and Inclusion education

Every so often, an article will be published in the *Harvard Business Review* or *Forbes* magazine declaring that training centered on DEI doesn't work. Without reading further, a practitioner might well wonder why they are lobbying their company to pay consultants thousands of dollars a year to lead workshops designed to open minds and elicit more inclusive behaviors.

WARNING

It's important to state that *Harvard*, *Forbes*, *The Chronicle of Higher Education*, *The Economist*, and other publications aren't lying to you. They conduct research in good faith, follow the data, and report the truth of what the data revealed. Simply taking classes on diversity and inclusion will not yield a diverse workforce or an inclusive culture.

However, organizations who do DEI well don't simply rely on a workshop, conducted every few years, to transform an organizational culture. But within a culture that is doing the work and having an impact, that occasional workshop, focused on skills, real-world scenarios, with time to discuss and reflect, can have a powerful validating effect on the overall strategy, in the following ways:

>> **Increased awareness:** Diversity training can help participants appreciate differences among co-workers.

>> **Improved communication:** Diversity training can help employees enhance their interpersonal and communication skills.

>> **More inclusive hiring:** Diversity training can help leadership be more inclusive in their hiring practices and welcome a workforce with a variety of perspectives.

>> **Increased productivity:** Diversity training can help build a supportive company culture that helps everyone do their best work.

>> **Improved teamwork:** Diversity training can promote better teamwork.

>> **Prevention of civil rights violations:** Diversity training can help prevent costly and embarrassing legal troubles for your company.

>> **Increased representation:** Voluntary DEI training can improve racial and ethnic representation within companies.

TIP

As a team leader, support those team members who want to take advantage of the DEI education your company offers and encourage all team members to learn about ways they can support a more inclusive culture. Reinforce their learning by inviting them to share what they learned with the entire team. If your organization does not offer any (or enough) development in DEI, make the case for why they should invest, and be prepared to answer those skeptics who've read all the articles stating that it's a waste of resources. In fact, prepare some ideas about how education could be fortified outside the classroom, or advocate for any just-in-time solutions that could yield improved results.

Mentoring and sponsoring diverse talent

Another effective way to advocate for inclusion in your organization is to be a mentor or sponsor. The two terms are often confused, but the key difference between a mentor and a sponsor is that a *mentor* provides advice and career guidance to their mentee while a *sponsor* advocates for their protégé throughout the organization.

Mentorship

TIP

Though a mentor is typically not a mentee's direct supervisor (in fact, mentors often don't even work for the same organization as the mentee), getting to know the individual members of your team as if you were their mentor is a good idea. (Flip to Chapter 10 for advice on knowing your team members.)

Mentoring staff who are significantly different to you requires much more listening and reflection than mentoring someone very much like yourself. When mentoring across difference, the most common mistake is passing along advice that worked well for the mentor but wouldn't be effective for the mentee. Behaviors that benefit straight white men, for example, may cause a person of color, a woman, or an LGBTQ person to be perceived as aggressive, pushy, or belligerent.

REMEMBER

Mentoring diverse talent is a learning experience for both parties, and you must approach it as such. Both mentor and mentee are there to teach the other, and both will hopefully emerge with new skills and strategies.

Sponsorship

Unlike a mentor, a sponsor nearly always works within the same organization as their protégé and is either senior to them or has access to a greater network by virtue of their own role and level of influence.

Having had three sponsors in my senior roles, I found that they provided several things:

>> They spoke on my behalf when I couldn't be in the room or where important talent decisions were being made. They spoke up on promotions, succession planning, stretch assignments, and other activities that would increase my development and visibility.

>> They acted as an ally and advocate and spoke up on policies and practices that could have adversely impacted me.

>> They provided me with a safe place to share the challenges I was experiencing and coached me on how to recover when I had missteps. They also responded to their peers when those missteps were noticed, and they redirected the conversation to my strengths or lessons learned.

WARNING

To sponsor staff of diverse backgrounds, you must be aware of the barriers to success that may exist for your protégé (both generally and specific to your organization) but may not necessarily apply to you so that you can advocate for their success effectively. Unfortunately, 71 percent of self-identified sponsors in a 2019 study conducted by a global consulting firm, Coqual, reported that their protégés shared their gender or race (https://coqual.org/wp-content/uploads/2020/09/CoqualTheSponsorDividend_KeyFindingsCombined090720.pdf). Therefore, when sponsoring talented employees in your organization, pay attention to difference. If most of the leaders in your organization share your key identities, your sponsorship may be vital to helping your organization as well as your protégé by helping create a more diverse set of leaders in the future, which can only help your organization become more inclusive.

Seeking and leveraging diverse perspectives and solutions

Teams and organizations that know how to leverage diversity are smarter. Research has proved this time and time again. And yet, even in organizations with robust diversity hiring programs, sometimes the *C-Suite* (senior executive or chief-level positions) and the people leaders within the organization aren't nearly as diverse as the rest of the organization.

TIP

One powerful way to advocate for inclusion within a company is to keep an eye out for situations where a homogeneous group is making decisions on behalf of a more diverse population and seek to remedy that. For example, as a consultant, I often task my clients with finding a steering group that will work with my team to set goals, write vision statements, and create strategic plans. I always coach them to bring together a diverse group of people to make this happen. Specifically, I ask for the following types of diversity:

>> Race

>> Gender

>> Job function

>> Tenure

>> Level within the organizational hierarchy

Oftentimes, my clients are not surprised by my request to create a team that is diverse according to visible social identities such as race and gender. But the types of organizational diversity that I recommend is often a surprise to them. Without diversity by job function, however, I might be creating a DEI strategic plan for a healthcare enterprise with a bunch of administrators and no one who treats patients, or creating a vision statement for inclusion without any input from people at lower levels of the organization who are the most at risk for feeling excluded.

It's not enough just to bring together groups that look diverse (although this should always be a consideration). Depending on the decision being made, it's often important to think about other ways that diversity could make your solutions better. Of course, bringing multiple perspectives together might cause your work to go slower, but the resulting decisions will be better for more people.

Demonstrating courage in difficult and unpopular situations

Being an advocate for inclusion isn't easy. You won't always know the right thing to do. And even if you do, the work often requires courage. Inclusive leaders aren't afraid to challenge the status quo or call out deeply held and ingrained beliefs, attitudes, and behaviors that foster homogeneity and exclusion. They're willing to have tough conversations and lean into their discomfort.

On your team, you might find it necessary to have a courageous conversation with a team member about a sensitive issue such as race, gender, religion, politics, age, sexuality, disability, dress, grooming, or pay. These conversations are difficult because we've been taught to avoid them, and they can easily devolve into defensiveness, withdrawal, or hostility. They require us to step out of our comfort zone to have a discussion that might cause an emotional response. Typically, these are conversations we're not used to having and therefore we're not sure what to expect. Sometimes, we're worried that a clumsy mistake on our part might lead to someone being hurt or insulted. Other times, we suspect that the person we're speaking with doesn't think the issue is a big deal (and we must assure them it is). In an age of social media, there might be a dark fantasy in our heads that any misstep on our part will find its way into a post later that evening, with a thousand shares by the next morning. Having empathy — a must whenever you engage in a courageous conversation — means taking the perspective of someone different from yourself, and that kind of openness and curiosity can feel very vulnerable. But our fear that we'll mess up or won't be able to find the perfect word can reinforce our silence. Silence can often be perceived as complicity.

In truth, having these uncomfortable conversations can often be an important first step toward either rebuilding or strengthening trust and a culture of inclusion. While they cause a certain amount of anxiety, when handled well they can be instrumental in facilitating bridge-building across difference.

In your broader organization, you might also find it necessary to go against the grain of popular opinion to stand up for what is right. I wish I could say that doing the right thing will always yield positive results, but the truth is that taking a stand like this is risky, especially if those on the other side of the argument wield power within the organization. I can say that if you defy your values and maintain your silence in a situation that required a brave person to come forward, you'll likely regret it for a long time. When making decisions in the face of risk, it helps to be clear about your values and listen to different people within your support network who might have different perspectives to you.

There are personal benefits as well. Not shying away from difficult conversations helps you understand other perspectives and broadens your own understanding of the complexities surrounding racism, sexism, homophobia, ageism, xenophobia, and other phobias and -isms. Listening with empathy exposes your biases and helps to break down stereotypes and other barriers to understanding. As your understanding about others deepens, so does your understanding of self. Getting comfortable with the uncomfortable enables you to have more effective, productive, and collaborative conversations up, down, and across organizational levels.

Chapter **18**

Applying an Equity Lens and Inclusive Mindset in Decision Making

Many companies are actively working to improve the employee experience, striving to create a fair and inclusive environment where all workers can contribute and thrive. One crucial approach to achieving this is consistently applying an equity perspective throughout every stage of the employee life cycle. To meet this challenge, a paradigm shift is necessary — one that places DEI [Diversity, Equity, and Inclusion] at the forefront of leadership principles.

Have you ever watched a small child try on their first pair of glasses? Especially if the child was very young, they might not have been fundamentally aware that anything was wrong with their vision to begin with. A world that was fuzzy and blurry was normal to them. But as soon as they look at the world through corrective lenses for the first time, everything comes into focus. Sometimes, these children can see their parents smiling for the first time, and the smiles they give back are heartwarming.

That's what lenses are for — to help us see things we didn't or couldn't see before. Specifically, an *equity lens* involves viewing policies, practices, and decisions through a perspective of fairness and impartiality, placing special consideration on the unique needs and circumstances of different individuals or groups. An inclusive mindset entails fostering an environment where every individual feels valued, respected, and able to contribute their best.

Both concepts are interrelated, forming the foundation for a workplace culture that promotes diversity and supports all its members, and this chapter helps you to figure out the best way to lay that foundation.

Differentiating Equity from Equality

Many of us were raised with the value of "treat everyone the same" and taught that it was the best way to be fair to everyone. This value has also been embraced in workplaces around the world wherein everyone is treated the same and given the same resources. This is the definition of equality; and the tendency toward equality is almost always very well-intentioned but flawed. Why? Because every person is different, unique, and brings a variety of experiences, needs, and expectations. They have varying skills and development gaps. As a result, they don't all need the same things at the same time in the same way. Moreover, there are very good reasons for treating people differently.

In much the same way, most of us grew up learning the *Golden Rule*, which is to treat others the way we would like to be treated. Following the Golden Rule certainly prevents you from deliberately harming another person, since it's unlikely that you would like to be deliberately harmed yourself. However, the Golden Rule assumes that everyone wants to be treated the way you want to be treated and wants the same things that you want. It also inadvertently assumes that everyone sees the world the way that you do.

Here's an example: As a leader, consider that early in your career, you desired a fair amount of independence but you worked for a leader that tended to micromanage. Now that you're leading people yourself, you are careful to keep a fair distance, and not micromanage them. You feel you're doing this because you trust them in a way that you wish all of your managers had trusted you when you were starting out. But some of your employees, for a variety of reasons, might desire more coaching and feedback than you are providing. With the best of intentions, you are doing everything you can to respect your staff's space and autonomy, but some of them would be much happier and more productive if you altered your style to meet their needs.

In this instance, it would be helpful for you to practice the *Platinum Rule*, which is to treat others the way *they* would like to be treated. Obviously, practicing the Platinum Rule is more difficult, as it requires you to build a deeper and more meaningful relationship with each team member to uncover their wants and needs, rather than simply using your own preferences as a template for how you'd treat everyone else.

REMEMBER

While the Golden Rule results in equality, practicing the Platinum Rule achieves the goal of equity. *Equity* is decidedly not treating everyone the same but working toward equal access and equal outcomes among a diverse group of people.

Consider Figure 18-1 (courtesy of the Robert Wood Johnson Foundation). The top panel is a clear example of equality. Four individuals have each received a bicycle. To make things completely equal, they've all received the exact same bicycle. The individual on the left uses a wheelchair, therefore, the bicycle is completely useless to them. The remaining three individuals can ride their bicycles, but it seems clear that the tallest of the three is at best extremely uncomfortable, while the smallest is unable to reach both pedals and is likely unsafe. Only one individual (third from the left) has received a resource that truly works for them. The bottom panel shows the difference between equality and equity. In an equitable situation, all four individuals have received different bicycles, corresponding to their size and physical abilities. As a result, all four can ride safely and comfortably.

FIGURE 18-1:
Equality
versus equity.

Reproduced with permission of the Robert Wood Johnson Foundation, Princeton, N.J.

The goal of equity is to level the playing field, acknowledging and rectifying historical and systemic disadvantages. Consider a scenario where some employees want to attend a training program to enhance their skills in communication. Equality would involve providing the same training to all employees, assuming that everyone is at the same starting point. On the other hand, equity would mean tailoring the training to meet the specific needs of each employee, considering their differences in skills, experience, and learning styles.

REMEMBER

As an inclusive leader, it's not only okay for you to treat different people differently, but sometimes it's necessary to ensure full engagement, equal access and opportunities to succeed.

Understanding Why an Equity Lens Matters

The first and most obvious reason why an inclusive leader should adopt an equity lens is that it's the right thing to do. If you believe that a person's inherent identities should not be a reliable predictor of how successful they can be at your organization, then your values should make an equity lens imperative.

And as is usually the case when discussing inclusion, adopting an equity lens is also good for business. "In today's evolving world of work, fair policies and practices together with strong and deliberate DEI strategies are integral to breaking the barriers of bias and inequity that can be present in the workplace," says Alex Alonso, Ph.D., the chief knowledge officer at the Society for Human Resource Management (SHRM). "We must continue to address the root causes of bias, whether it be gender, age, race, sexual orientation or disability, while building greater equity to lead workplaces into a better tomorrow."

TECHNICAL STUFF

Together with partners at Work Equity, SHRM conducted a *National Study of Workplace Equity* in 2022 (https://www.shrm.org/topics-tools/research/national-study-workplace-equity-report), using data from more than a thousand workplaces in the U.S. In each workplace, they assigned an "Equity Score" between 1 (least equitable) and 5 (most equitable) to each of ten employment systems (such as recruitment and hiring, performance assessment and feedback, and supervision and mentoring). The system that scored the lowest was Employee Resources and Supports, with a mean score of 2.46. However, the most equitable system (Recruitment and Hiring) only had a mean score of 3.03, which signals an opportunity for much work to be done. More importantly, the study found that equity matters. It established the important relationship between the overall equity in an organization's employment systems and *organizational resilience* (the ability to anticipate, prepare for, and respond to disruptions and change). In other words, organizations with higher equity scores across all ten systems were better able to be agile, innovate, and make changes. In today's volatile and unpredictable world, that's a direct link to business success.

REMEMBER

Adopting an equity lens can have a positive impact on both leaders and their teams, in the following ways:

>> **Organizational culture:** Leaders play a pivotal role in shaping organizational culture. An equity lens and inclusive mindset contribute to the creation of a positive and inclusive work environment. When leaders actively embrace inclusion and equity, they send a clear message that every team member is valued, leading to increased morale, productivity, and overall job satisfaction.

>> **Creativity and innovation:** Diverse teams bring together a variety of perspectives, experiences, and ideas. Leaders who apply an equity lens promote an inclusive environment that encourages open dialogue, ongoing learning, and collaboration. This fosters creativity and innovation, as team members draw on their unique backgrounds and skills to solve complex problems and drive organizational success.

>> **Decision making:** Leadership decisions significantly impact an organization's trajectory. An equity lens ensures that these decisions are fair, transparent, and considerate of the diverse factors that may influence outcomes. Inclusive decision-making processes lead to better-informed choices and contribute to the long-term success and sustainability of the organization.

In addition, an equity lens can create a better working environment for all staff, which makes your company's workforce happier and more successful by improving employees'

>> **Sense of belonging:** An equity lens and inclusive mindset contribute to a workplace culture where every employee feels a sense of belonging. This sense of belonging is crucial for employee engagement, retention, and overall job satisfaction.

>> **Well-being:** Leaders who prioritize equity and inclusion contribute to the well-being of their employees. By recognizing and addressing factors that may disproportionately affect certain groups, leaders create a supportive environment that values the holistic well-being of all team members.

>> **Productivity:** Equity and inclusion positively impact productivity by reducing workplace stress, improving collaboration, and enhancing overall job satisfaction. Employees who feel valued and included are more likely to invest their time and energy in their work, resulting in increased productivity and organizational success.

Here are three common ways that companies successfully apply an equity lens to their policies and practices:

>> Flexible work arrangements:

- Equality: All employees are required to work the same hours, regardless of personal circumstances or needs.

- Equity: Flexible work hours or remote work options are offered to accommodate diverse needs such as childcare responsibilities, health concerns, or commuting challenges.

>> Professional development opportunities:

- Equality: All employees are provided with the same training opportunities, irrespective of their skill levels or career aspirations.

- Equity: Tailored professional development plans are created to address the unique goals and skill gaps of individual employees, ensuring equitable access to growth opportunities.

>> Salary adjustments:

- Equality: All employees receive the same salary increase, regardless of their performance or contributions.

- Equity: Compensation adjustments are based on performance evaluations, acknowledging and rewarding individual achievements, but also acknowledging historical inequities (for example, working to ensure that certain workers from underrepresented groups are not significantly underpaid).

Asking the Right Questions When Applying an Equity Lens

Adopting a new lens means seeing things in a different way. When you're still getting used to viewing your own leadership through an equity lens, it helps to ask yourself some key questions along the way, to ensure that you are paying attention to ensuring equal outcomes to your team, your colleagues, and your customers and stakeholders.

One of the most comprehensive frameworks on the market for assessing equity inside the workplace is from the Nonprofit Association of Oregon. They offer actionable DEI tools for leaders, managers, staff, and volunteers that can be found on their website: www.nonprofitoregon.org. They also include an *Equity &*

Inclusion Lens Guide, and a companion eCourse, *Moving Equity and Inclusion into Action*. I have adapted some of their questions along with some of my own in the following sections.

In leading people

The role of every people leader begins with the day-to-day work of interacting with direct reports, guiding their work, giving them feedback, allowing them to learn and grow, and pointing them toward success. Applying an equity lens allows you to do all of this while appreciating what makes each employee different, but without falling into the trap of playing favorites.

TIP

In your everyday interactions with the people you lead and influence, ask yourself the following questions:

>> When I interact with people, especially those who are different from me, do I ask myself:

- What assumptions or biases do I hold that might get in the way of how I work with them?

- Do I mitigate stereotypes and biases so I can see the individual in addition to their group identities?

- Am I able to respect our differences while appreciating what we have in common?

- Do I actively recognize their contributions?

- Do I lead by example?

>> Am I paying attention to those who are quiet or otherwise not expressing their ideas?

>> How do I encourage feedback and full participation from everyone on the team?

>> Have I scheduled regular check-ins with people on my team? During these conversations, do I discuss the following:

- What kind of work culture do you work best in? What ideas do you have to create that kind of work culture here?

- Do you feel connected to your team members? If not, what has been challenging for you? If so, are there things we should be doing more of?

- Where do you see yourself in five years? How can I support those long-term goals?

- Are there any professional or personal goals you have set for yourself? How can I or the organization support you in meeting those?

» Am I raising issues in a way that facilitates an open dialogue?

» Do I consider potential barriers (such as language, discrimination, various "isms") in each situation, and work to minimize them?

» If I am not sure what barriers may exist, do I ask my colleagues or customers?

» Do I discourage offensive jokes, insults, and negative comments?

» Do I recognize and build on the strengths of all team members?

» Are there procedures, policies, and practices in place that limit my capacity to be inclusive? Are there others who support my capacity to be inclusive? What action can I take to address this or bring awareness to the supportive policies?

In everyday decision making

Making decisions is an important part of every leader's job description. Unlike an individual contributor, a leader's decisions usually affect lots of other people, not just themselves. Therefore, adopting an equity lens ensures that the impact of your decisions is not harmful to those unlike yourself.

TIP

When making decisions in a leadership capacity, ask yourself the following:

» Is this decision equitable for all individuals or groups involved?

» How might this decision impact individuals differently based on their diverse backgrounds and experiences?

» Have I considered the potential unintended consequences of this decision on different groups within the organization?

» Are there barriers or biases in our processes that may hinder the inclusion of diverse perspectives?

» How can I actively involve individuals from underrepresented groups in the decision-making process to ensure a more comprehensive perspective?

REMEMBER

Bias is a form of decision-making, but a type of decision that happens so quickly, we don't often realize a decision has been made. When a leader is rushed or experiencing unusual amounts of stress, they are more likely to make decisions in a biased way. Read through Chapter 6 of this book for more information on mitigating and managing biases.

In recruiting

Almost no decision affects the future of your organization more than the people you decide to hire into your company. Whether you are in the business of providing health care to a patient population, teaching a student body, providing consulting services or thought leadership to your clients, supporting communities via a nonprofit, or selling goods and services directly to customers, the people of your organization are its beating heart. A diverse employee population paired with an inclusive work environment is the best way to achieve success against your organization's mission.

TIP

When engaged in recruiting and hiring, ask yourself the following questions:

>> Do my staff currently reflect the diversity of my customers, stakeholders, and community? Who is missing?

>> What knowledge, skills, experience, and diversity would enhance my team's capacity to be more successful?

>> Do job requirements and selection criteria unnecessarily limit who would qualify? Would anything in the job posting (such as overly masculine language) discourage specific candidates from applying?

>> Is this job posting accessible to a wide and diverse number of potential applicants? Do I encourage internal and external stakeholders to assist with outreach to help broaden the applicant pool from diverse groups?

>> Do my educational requirements present a barrier to individuals who have relevant professional experience but not the required degree?

>> How do I ensure interview panels are composed of individuals who bring diverse backgrounds, experiences, and perspectives?

>> Have I considered ways to reduce barriers in the interview process (such as physically accessible, written copies of standard questions) to make it more welcoming and friendly?

>> Do I consider that people from specific backgrounds may present interview behaviors (such as norms around handshakes and eye contact) that do not match my biases and still have the skills to do the job?

>> What checks and balances do I have in place to counter implicit biases in hiring?

Adding one token candidate from an underrepresented group rarely yields results. If only one woman, person over 55, person with a disability, or person of color is being considered for a specific job, the chances of getting hired are weaker. According to a 2016 article in the *Harvard Business Review* (https://hbr. org/2016/04/if-theres-only-one-woman-in-your-candidate-pool-theres-statistically-no-chance-shell-be-hired), the odds of hiring a woman are 79 times greater if there are at least two women being considered, and the odds of hiring a person of color are 193 times greater if at least two people of color are up for the same job.

In onboarding and orienting new talent

When talent is new, the organization who just hired them has an enormous opportunity to make a good first impression. If an employee's first days, weeks, or months on a new job are confusing, less than welcoming, or harmful in some way, it can be difficult to overcome this negative experience later on.

When onboarding new talent, ask yourself the following:

>> Am I effectively communicating my company's culture and norms (such as expectations for dress, punctuality, and communication) during this time? Am I soliciting feedback from new employees to ensure they understand?

>> Is a robust discussion of my organization's values happening? Have I defined those values in behavioral terms so that new employees know how they should behave and what they should reasonably expect from leaders and colleagues?

>> Are there "unwritten" rules or norms that some people are aware of and others not? Are these spelled out explicitly during the onboarding process?

>> Are my organization's policies and procedures easily accessible to all employees on or before their first day?

>> Have I assigned each new employee a "buddy" or informal mentor? Have I considered a system that allows a new employee to choose their own buddy from a list of potential mentors?

>> Is there a plan in place for every new employee to interact with their direct manager and team members during their first month? Are these comparable for those who work on-site and remotely?

In education and training

Leaders must invest in continuous education and training programs to cultivate an understanding of equity, diversity, and inclusion. Workshops, seminars, and online courses can provide valuable insights into unconscious biases, cultural competence, and effective communication strategies that foster an inclusive mindset.

Of course, organizations sponsor all kinds of training on many topics, not just diversity and inclusion. All employees should enjoy equal access to training opportunities and an inclusive environment in live and virtual classrooms.

TIP

When rolling out education and training in your organization, ask yourself the following:

>> Do I include equity and inclusion requirements (such as being able to reduce biases and work respectfully with people across difference) when planning or staffing for internal and external trainers?

>> Do I prioritize recruiting trainers from diverse backgrounds?

>> Will the learning objectives be designed to participants' awareness and consideration of individuals communities of diverse backgrounds?

>> Will participants develop competency and skills to work sensitively and effectively with individuals from diverse backgrounds?

>> Is a particular course mandatory for all employees? Why or why not? If particular competencies are critical, is specific outreach required to include all employees?

>> Are barriers in the classroom (such as safety, language, location, time, holidays, and accommodations) addressed?

>> Have I integrated the diverse perspectives of people who have specific equity concerns or needs (such as dietary or auditory), even if they may not be obvious?

>> When evaluating the training, do I ask whether there were any barriers to participation or whether they found the facilitator to be inclusive of all participants?

In development and advancement

Leadership teams should reflect the diversity present in the broader organization and society. By intentionally selecting individuals from different backgrounds, leaders create a more comprehensive perspective at the decision-making level, signaling a commitment to equity throughout the organization.

TIP

When developing employees for leadership positions, and making advancement decisions, ask yourself the following:

» How diverse is my leadership? Do I have the competencies or life experiences necessary to value and support the diversity of my staff or gain the trust of a diverse customer base?

» How often do I promote leadership from within my organization versus hiring senior leaders from outside? If my process leans heavily one way or the other, would a greater balance provide more access to leaders from a variety of backgrounds?

» If my leadership is more homogeneous than either my staff or my stakeholder population (which is very common), what specific steps have I put in place to diversify my leadership pipeline (either internal or external)?

» If my leadership is more homogeneous than my staff, where do the glass ceilings exist in my organization? For instance, are women, people of color, and other marginalized groups easily promoted to middle management but struggle to gain access to senior leadership positions? Have I investigated the reasons for this?

» Are opportunities for career advancement (such as education, training, work on high-profile projects, and mentoring) available to all staff, regardless of identity or remote work status?

In organizational communications

Part of building trust between an organization's leadership and its staff, or between an organization and its surrounding community, is the feeling that access to information is easy to obtain. Often, leadership teams and those focused on community engagement feel as though they are communicating frequently and transparently. But if the information is being sent but not received, all that effort might be for naught.

TIP

When communicating important messages, either internally or externally, ask yourself the following questions:

» Have I considered all relevant audiences? Who has been historically excluded from consideration?

» What specific communication strategies ensure historically excluded groups are heard and reached?

» How do the messages I am communicating foster our organizational values, including inclusion, respect, and equity?

- Are the messages I communicate inclusive, respectful, truthful, and equitable across all audiences?

- Are there concepts or terms that may be culturally specific and need to be changed to make them more accessible?

- Is the chosen medium easily accessible and understood by the full diversity of our audience? What accommodations might be possible (for example, multiple languages or embedding descriptors for graphics)?

- Have I considered what populations will be missed by only using certain methods? (Such as online, email, or social media communications)

- Have I considered if there is a budget or alternative resources for translation services?

- Do images represent the full diversity of employees and communities?

In community and customer relations

Depending on the specific mission of your organization, you may be called to interact with customers or community stakeholders to understand their perspectives. This process allows organizations to serve their communities and customers better.

TIP

When conducting community or customer relations, ask yourself the following:

- What approaches and outreach will help to ensure that those who need to be engaged are able to fully participate? How can I create opportunities for people least likely to be heard to ensure they share their specific concerns?

- Is there a history I need to consider? If there is conflict or trauma stemming from past events, how will I address it?

- When the community gathers for full participation, what steps can be taken to remove barriers such as dependent care, transportation, safety, language, accessible location, time, multiple formats, and access to technology?

- Is the environment welcoming to participants who may be reluctant to share their views? If not, what can I do to change this?

- Are the insights from marginalized groups reflected in the final report or product?

- When gathering data from customers and stakeholder communities, how will I report my findings to them and demonstrate accountability?

In marketing and branding

Your organization may offer the best goods or services in your industry, but if nobody knows about you, your chances for success are slim. Most organizations, therefore, engage in marketing and branding activities. Marketing and branding allow your company to sell more products, distinguish themselves in the marketplace, and/or create positive associations with your brand. All too often, opportunities to reach more diverse markets are thwarted by cultural ignorance or incompetence.

TIP

To ensure that your marketing and branding efforts are successfully interacting with people of various backgrounds, ask yourself the following:

>> Is the language I use in my promotional materials and communications strategy easily understood by the audiences I seek to reach?

>> Is my team representative of the diversity of the population I am engaging? What steps can I take to ensure I include a diversity of perspectives?

>> Who is best suited to conduct outreach to diverse communities and customers? If I need to engage outreach partners, how will I compensate them?

>> Are the images used reflective of the diversity of customers I seek?

WARNING

It's better to err on the side of your marketing and branding being aimed at a more diverse market rather than a less diverse market. Even if your current customer base isn't very diverse, your current (homogenous) customers aren't likely to be put off by diverse representation. However, diverse communities who don't see themselves reflected in your brand might be reluctant to become a new customer.

Developing Competencies for Applying an Equity Lens

Effectively applying an equity lens in leadership requires a combination of competencies and skills that go beyond traditional management abilities. Adopting a new lens or mindset isn't easy. There are specific competencies that are necessary for acquiring an equity lens that will be necessary before looking at your organization in this new way becomes a habit.

TIP

Review each of these competencies and reflect on how effective you demonstrate them currently:

>> **Self-awareness:** Leaders need to be aware of their own biases, assumptions, and privileges. This is crucial for making conscious, informed decisions that consider the unique needs and experiences of individuals from various backgrounds.

>> **Decentering yourself:** What makes empathy challenging is that that we've all lived our entire lives seeing the world from our own unique perspective. Therefore, placing ourselves in the center of every story is easy and automatic. This is doubly true for people who belong to one or more dominant groups (for example, white, male, heterosexual, able-bodied, and so on), since most of the stories we are told by others (including film, television, and the news) are also told from those perspectives. For example, have you ever heard a woman talk about how she had been treated unfairly in the past, and the first comment we hear from a man in response is something like, "Not all men are like that!" That response is a clear instance of a man centering himself rather than dealing with the issue at hand. Decentering might look like asking the woman how she felt, what support she might require, or simply listening.

>> **Empathy:** *Empathy* is commonly understood as the ability to put yourself in someone else's shoes to understand what they are experiencing. It is a key leadership trait that enables leaders to connect with their team members on a personal level. By understanding and sharing the feelings of others, leaders can better address the unique challenges faced by individuals and respond with compassion.

Empathy can range from a cognitive understanding of another person's feelings to a true sense of "feeling with" someone else. It's naturally easier to be empathetic toward someone who has something in common with you, but it's possible to display empathy across difference when you have taken the time to get to know someone well and have educated yourself on the differences that exist within your organization and team.

REMEMBER

Exhibiting empathy is about being fully present with other and listening for what is said and what isn't said, and about asking how you can support someone who is struggling as opposed to rushing in to solve the problem with a helpful piece of advice.

>> **Listening:** It's important for an inclusive leader who wishes to adopt an equity lens to listen well. Listening, as a competency, isn't just about hearing what people are saying. It begins with communicating your interest in the thoughts of others, so that they are willing to share with you (*empathetic listening*). Listening is exhibited when you use a person's correct pronouns, adopt language that marginalized groups prefer, and act on the issues that you know are important to them. Finally, listening involves occasionally checking for understanding and asking the right questions (*active listening*), so that you can accurately gauge what people truly need so that they may enjoy equal access and outcomes.

REMEMBER

While it's important to listen, it is always your responsibility to learn what you don't know. Therefore, take responsibility for your own education when necessary, rather than expecting your followers to teach you what you aren't aware of.

>> **Cultural competence:** Understanding and appreciating cultural differences is fundamental for leaders applying an equity lens. This involves recognizing diverse perspectives, values, and communication styles within a team and across the organization.

>> **Conflict resolution:** Leaders must have strong conflict resolution skills to address issues related to equity effectively. This includes the ability to mediate disputes, address concerns, and promote a positive and inclusive working environment.

>> **Adaptability:** Leaders should strive to be adaptable and open to change. As workplaces evolve, leaders need to be flexible in their approach to address emerging challenges and opportunities related to equity.

>> **Allyship:** Leaders can actively support underrepresented groups by using their privilege and influence to advocate for equitable policies, practices, and opportunities.

TIP

Be courageous enough to solicit feedback from your team members and/or colleagues and make the commitment to improving in the areas where you fall short.

Applying an equity lens and fostering an inclusive mindset are indispensable for leaders navigating the complexities of today's diverse workplace. As organizations continue to evolve, leaders who embrace an equity lens and an inclusive mindset will find themselves better equipped to navigate the challenges and opportunities of the future.

CONSIDERING HOW YOUR DECISIONS IMPACT OTHERS

Inclusive leaders develop the capacity to decenter themselves when necessary. This allows them to consider how their decisions will impact others, not just those who are like you. For example:

- Brett leads an organization that was founded over a hundred years ago, and whose founders and subsequent leaders are almost entirely white and male. One day, when passing through the lobby of his company's corporate headquarters, he notices that all the framed portraits that line the walls are of white men with gray hair. He wonders how this might affect women and people of color who are pass through the lobby. Are these pictures sending a message to them that is different from the message Brett and other white men receive? He reaches out to his chief marketing officer to inquire about redecorating with rotating photos of current employees that have won internal awards or led successful projects.

- Kayla works at a construction site, where she oversees a team of 20 workers. Today, there was a safety breach, and a loud siren alerted the crew to cease work until the situation could be addressed. She reflects on her last job, where two of her colleagues were profoundly deaf. She realizes that the siren would not have alerted them immediately and arranges for several bright flashing lights to accompany the sirens to ensure that any deaf crew members on the site will be protected as well.

- Maria is struggling to find a time for her leadership team, some of whom work at their regional offices, to meet in person next fall, and is in the process of socializing several possible meeting times. Before she sends an email with five possibilities, she references them against an online multicultural calendar. Immediately, she notices that two of her dates directly conflict with Rosh Hashanah and Yom Kippur. Knowing that three of the required attendees are Jewish, she immediately removes those dates from consideration, so that they will be able to mark these important holidays.

Brett, Kayla, and Maria were all able to look outside their own experiences to understand the perspectives of those unlike themselves. They realized that what worked well for them might not work well for others — and indeed, in Kayla's case, might even lead to a preventable loss of life.

5

The Part of Tens

Uncover the common mistakes to avoid while becoming an inclusive leader.

Find out common issues that inclusive leaders are challenged with.

Identify what great companies do to drive inclusion inside their organization.

Chapter **19**

Ten Mistakes to Avoid if You Want to Be an Inclusive Leader

Ever dreaded going to work because of a boss? Remember feeling stressed about your upcoming performance review? Or have you ever worked for someone and rarely or never received feedback? Ever go the extra mile to get a project completed with success only for it to go unrecognized? If the answer is yes to these questions . . . chances are you are or were working under an ineffective leader.

TIP

Based on my experience, here are ten of the most common mistakes that leaders need to avoid if they want to be a more inclusive leader. As I describe each, conduct your own personal assessment and write down those mistakes that you need to avoid. Additionally, consider how you can enhance those that you currently demonstrate.

Lacking Vision and Goals

I always say, "If you're a leader and no one is following you, you're just taking a walk." This is one of my favorite quotes to live by and one that I coach to leaders all over the world. At the core of effective leadership is casting a compelling vision for others to follow. If you don't, you will struggle to keep loyal and committed workers. And it will affect your leadership trajectory.

Vision describes what you will look like in the future (maybe three, five, or ten years from now) and sets a defined direction for the planning and execution of this.

The reality is that people don't want to follow a parked car. They want to follow a leader who knows where they are going and has an idea of how to get there. They expect their leaders to demonstrate the kind of skills and behaviors that engender followers, that will grow them into great leaders, that cultivates the kind of work environment that brings out the best in them, and that drives high performance. Moreover, they seek out leaders who are willing to help them to set goals that are achievable, and they ensure that they have the necessary tools to succeed. Don't make the mistake of "winging it" and making it up as you go. Workers see right through that and it will undermine your credibility and your impact.

Treating Everyone the Same

When leading across differences, leaders cannot assume that everyone has the same needs, skill levels, goals, beliefs, work styles, or personality. Doing so minimizes their uniqueness and overlooks the opportunity to allow them to bring their full and authentic self to work. Instead, take the time to get to know each person individually. Find out who they are beyond the project and the program, beyond the title and the position.

Do you know what they like to do outside of work, where they like to vacation, what motivates them, what support they need, where they see themselves in the future, what is the best way to communicate and engage them, and how they think and process information, and so on? This makes them feel valued and seen. My best boss "saw" me, and he showed me that he cared about me as a person. By getting to know me on a personal basis — not in a way that I felt uncomfortable or as if he was being intrusive but in a way that helped him to better understand me and my background — gave him insight into how to best support me. And he left an indelible impression.

Recognizing individual differences fosters a more inclusive environment, where each person feels valued and understood. Inclusive leaders understand that equality involves not treating everyone identically but rather acknowledging and respecting the unique qualities that contribute to a rich and diverse organizational tapestry.

Showing Favoritism

WARNING

Do you have someone on your team that you consider your go-to person? If so, ask yourself why do you prefer that person and who else might you be overlooking that can do the job as well? Favoritism in the workplace is a perilous path that can significantly undermine the principles of inclusivity. When leaders show favoritism, whether inadvertently or intentionally, they risk alienating certain team members, eroding trust, and perpetuating a disruptive work environment. This behavior can have damaging effects on morale, productivity, and overall team performance.

TIP

To avoid the perception or the reality of showing favoritism here are few tips to practice:

>> Communicate openly about what are the expectations, why certain decisions are made about special assignments, pay, promotions, and the distribution of opportunities. See Chapter 13 for more.

>> Invest in ongoing leadership development, and inclusion and unconscious bias training that exposes blind spots, stereotypes, and that teaches how to address them. These kinds of training programs help create awareness about the impact of biases on decision making and provide leaders with the tools to cultivate an inclusive mindset. See Chapter 17 for more.

>> Apply an equity lens to ensure that you are providing a level playing field for all team members. This involves being mindful of project assignments, developmental programs, and career advancement opportunities so that you are avoiding the appearance of favoritism and ensuring that individuals from all backgrounds have an equitable chance to participate, be considered, and to grow within the organization. See Chapter 18 for more.

>> Engage in open and transparent conversations and maintain an open-door policy on all issues. Provide clarity about how decisions are reached, acknowledge individual contributions, address concerns, and demonstrate a commitment to the professional development of each team member. See Chapter 13 for more.

When leaders avoid showing favoritism and provide a sense of belonging and equity, a level playing field and a sense of trust can be established.

Acting Inflexibly

A rigid approach to policies, procedures, and new ideas can inadvertently alienate individuals with diverse needs and situations. This lack of flexibility undermines the principles of inclusivity by creating an environment that stifles creativity, invokes fear, and undermines trust. It can show up as rigid work hours that do not accommodate personal needs or responsibilities to not allowing new ideas to be implemented (or shooting them down altogether) or forbidding a worker to take on additional responsibilities. Such inflexibility not only diminishes employee morale but also limits the organization's ability to attract and retain a diverse workforce.

To enhance inclusiveness, leaders must prioritize flexibility in their approach to work arrangements, policies, and decision making. They must recognize that diverse perspectives flourish in an environment that allows for various working, thinking, communication styles and approaches.

Being a Know-It-All

WARNING

Leaders who think that they are never wrong or who won't admit that they don't know it all are sadly misguided. Additionally, when leaders refuse to admit mistakes it can lead to a culture of conformity, stifling creativity and hindering the diverse perspectives that drive innovation. It can also cause employees to experience a lack of psychological safety (see Chapter 11), fearing repercussions if they question the leader's decisions or propose alternative solutions.

Employees appreciate it when leaders show some level of vulnerability and humility. Embracing humility is not a sign of weakness but of strength that builds trust, encourages innovation, and fosters an inclusive culture. Leaders who are willing to admit mistakes, acknowledge their limitations, and actively seek input from their team members create an environment where diversity of thought is valued and celebrated.

Overlooking Recognition or Reward

Everyone desires to feel valued and appreciated. Yet so often, leaders acknowledge employees only when they make mistakes. Furthermore, they tend to overlook their minority and/or underrepresented talent more than those from dominant groups. This oversight not only demoralizes individuals who may already face systemic barriers but also perpetuates a culture that fails to appreciate the full spectrum of contributions within the team. The impact extends beyond individual dissatisfaction to collective disillusionment, hindering team morale, and eroding the sense of inclusion.

To overcome this, leaders must proactively acknowledge, value, and reward diverse talent. They can establish recognition programs that highlight achievements across different dimensions of diversity. They can also conduct regular audits to identify and rectify any disparities in promotions, salary adjustments, or access to developmental opportunities. And they can highlight achievements publicly that reinforces the organization's commitment to DEI [Diversity, Equity, and Inclusion]. By publicly celebrating the accomplishments of individuals from various backgrounds, leaders send a powerful message that every contribution is essential to the organization's success.

REMEMBER

Recognition and rewards don't have to be big or showy. A simple "thank you" goes a long way. A lot of leaders insist that since employees already receive a paycheck, leaders shouldn't go out of their way to thank someone for something that is simply a part of their assigned job duties. To that, I simply shrug and ask, "Why not? Is it that difficult to say 'thank you?'" A leader should certainly save their most effusive praise for those who truly go above and beyond, but everyone on the team who contributes to a team's success deserves to be appreciated for the work they do.

Failing to Provide Feedback to All

All employees need feedback on how they are doing (positive and corrective), and they need it consistently. This tends to be one of the most underdeveloped skills of most leaders. They avoid tough conversations and don't provide the specificity that employees need to course-correct. Constructive feedback is essential for personal and career growth, yet when certain individuals are excluded from this crucial aspect of leadership, it perpetuates a cycle of stagnation and diminished opportunities.

Leaders should ensure that feedback is provided equitably and regularly, creating a culture where ongoing communication is valued. What do I mean by equitably? From my own experience, it is important to give all of your team members feedback (not just the positive, but the corrective too), especially those from underrepresented or non-dominant groups. I find too often that leaders shy away from doing this for workers who don't look, think, or believe like them simply because they are uncomfortable, or fearful that they will say the wrong thing. This can be overcome with the proper development and practice. Additionally, feedback should be approached with sensitivity, acknowledging individual strengths while highlighting areas for growth. Find out more in Chapter 12.

Overlooking Microaggressions

Microaggressions are subtle, often unintentional, discriminatory behaviors or comments that can erode the inclusivity of a workplace. Overlooking microaggressions is a grave mistake that leaders must avoid in order to maintain a healthy and respectful work environment. Chapter 6 discusses them in more detail.

Understanding, identifying, and addressing microaggressions requires a heightened level of sensitivity and cultural competence. Leaders must foster an open dialogue about these issues, encouraging employees to express their concerns without fear of retribution. By actively addressing microaggressions, leaders can set the tone for a workplace where everyone feels respected and valued.

Ignoring Psychological Safety

Leaders who fail to create a safe space for workers risk suppressing diverse opinions and fostering an atmosphere of exclusion. Leaders cannot simply order or wish that their employees feel safe and included. They must lead by example, establish trust, and create a psychologically safe workplace.

To foster psychological safety (see Chapter 11 for more), leaders should encourage open dialogue, actively listen to diverse perspectives, and create a culture where mistakes are viewed as opportunities for learning. Establishing trust and safety through consistent support, recognizing and valuing diverse contributions, and addressing conflicts promptly are vital steps in cultivating an inclusive environment where every team member feels secure to express their authentic selves.

Failing to Develop Cultural Competence

Leaders who believe they have mastered inclusivity may unconsciously become complacent and lack the ability to effectively interact with people from different cultures. Neglecting cultural competence is a mistake that can lead to misunderstandings, miscommunications, and cause a breakdown in comradery on the team.

Inclusive leaders should prioritize developing cultural competence by actively learning about different cultures, engaging with others who are different from them, fostering cross-cultural understanding, and encouraging open dialogue. By promoting cultural competence, leaders create an environment where individuals from diverse backgrounds feel valued and understood (see Chapter 9 for more on this).

Failing to Develop Cultural Competence

Chapter **20**

Ten Things That Inclusive Leaders Must Navigate

Amidst the multitude of disruptions and complexities in the global marketplace, workforce, and in our social landscape, being able to navigate a myriad of challenges is not just a virtue, it's a necessity! And it takes all of the attributes, competencies, and behaviors of inclusive leadership to recognize and respond in such a way that fosters an environment where everyone feels welcomed, valued, and accepted and where the organization can remain relevant and achieve sustained success. This chapter identifies ten challenges that inclusive leaders must navigate today and for the future workforce.

Leading through Global Socio-Political and Economic Unrest

In this era of rapid transformation, leaders are faced with the lingering effects of the COVID-19 pandemic as well as surging social, economic, and geopolitical disruptions and pressures that have fueled a sense of uncertainty and discontent among people worldwide. Consider this abbreviated list: ongoing protests; incidents of antisemitism; Islamophobia; human rights and social justice concerns; conflict around the world; the overturning of Roe versus Wade; attempts to dismantle Diversity, Equity, and Inclusion programs; rising populism, nationalism and divisive ideologies; and attempts to overthrow democracies around the world. These and many other global socio-geopolitical challenges directly affect the workplace dynamics and pose challenges to maintaining an inclusive environment. These issues have resulted in greater tensions among co-workers, increased stress and anxiety at work and at home, a rise in mental illness, suicide, and workplace violence. To this growing unrest, governments around the world have enacted new laws, bans, or changed existing policies, and increased workplace security measures in order to address these issues more effectively. Every chapter in this book has provided guidance and outlined the skills needed for how leaders should prepare to respond to these challenges.

WARNING

Organizational leaders can't afford to ignore these issues or be timid. Inclusive leaders must have a deep understanding of these external factors and be able to guide their organizations through these kinds of turbulent times. They must be able to preserve employee well-being, help them manage negative and traumatic emotions and decrease the noise that causes greater division, and create safe spaces for learning and dialogue.

Enhancing The Employee Experience

From the time an employee has initial contact with your company, to how they are hired, compensated, onboarded, developed, and rewarded, to when they leave, they workplace they have an experience. Is it positive or negative? Is it reflective of your company's brand or do you have a disconnect from what you say your company is all about from workers actually experience? If I went to Glassdoor.com and read the workers' points of view about your organization, what would the comments read?

REMEMBER

Understanding and assessing the employee experience has become a critical aspect of organizational success, as it directly influences employee satisfaction, engagement, productivity, and overall business performance. Inclusive leaders who are focused on enhancing it employ such strategies as setting a clear vision for their team, creating meaning and purpose, providing development and growth opportunities, treating every member with respect but recognizing their uniqueness, and ensuring that everyone feels heard, seen, and valued. Chapter 15 tackles this topic in more detail.

Attracting and Retaining
Top Diverse Talent

In today's competitive talent landscape, the search for skilled professionals remains intense. Top talent has many options for employment and are fully aware that they are highly sought out. Yet research continues to reveal that they are increasingly selective in the kind of workplace culture they want to work in, the type of leader they want to work for, and the kinds of perks and benefits that attract them. Moreover, the fight for top talent is exacerbated by the aging global population, artificial intelligence and automation (more on this later in the chapter), increased diversity in labor market, evolving work dynamics, and the constant pursuit of requisite skills for both immediate and future organizational growth.

Leaders can employ a number of strategies in order to attract and retain top diverse talent: diversifying their sourcing and hiring approaches, embracing more flexible work policies, considering candidates from various backgrounds and regions around the world, and employing more remote and temporary workers. Additionally, they can focus on cultivating their workplace culture to be more inclusive, providing their people leaders with more training and development in such areas as diversity, inclusion and belonging, cultural competence, managing conflict, empathy and authenticity, and emotional intelligence, all of which have risen to the top of lists that workers seek in their leaders.

Supporting Mental Health
and Emotional Well-Being

At a time when the world is experiencing accelerated change, overwhelming complexity, and working in a fast-paced and demanding environment (see the first section of this chapter), we are also seeing an increase in the emotional toll, the level of stress, anxiety, and other mental health issues that these have on employees. Inclusive leaders are needed now more than ever to ensure that the workplace is welcoming and supportive.

Inclusive leaders foster an environment free from stigma where open discussions about mental health are encouraged. They engage in active listening, demonstrating empathy and understanding towards employees' concerns. They recognize that every individual may be affected differently, so they adjust their responses to meet them where they are. These efforts contribute to cultivating a culture that not only accepts but also promotes seeking help.

Upskilling to Meet the Needs of the New Generation of Talent

In this ever-changing environment, staying pertinent isn't a choice; it's imperative! The longevity of skills is diminishing rapidly. This is where reskilling and upskilling emerges as a crucial strategy to ensure your workforce remains at the forefront. *Upskilling* is enhancing the skill set required for existing roles while *reskilling* involves providing resources for employees to acquire entirely new skills. Both of these initiatives play pivotal roles in building a thriving business prepared to confront the future with confidence.

TIP

Here are a few practical strategies that leaders can implement within their daily responsibilities: identify the key skills that your company will need today and in the next three years); offer customized career paths to meet individual development needs and align them with specific required skills (consider assigning mentors for those identified as high potential leaders for the future); create a culture of continuous improvement; and establish feedback loops to foster ongoing improvement.

Transforming Workplace Culture to be More Inclusive

Culture consists of the norms, values, behaviors, and attitudes supported by structure and strategies that an organization rewards or highly regards. It can also be illusive and invisible, yet its effect can be seen and felt. In other words, culture is like the wind: you can't see it but you experience it (feel it).

TIP

The reality is that changing a culture isn't easy, nor is it a quick fix, but I have found some effective practices that leaders have implemented to cultivate cultures of inclusion, equity, and belonging. First, evaluate and identify the current state of the employee experience, especially from those who are underrepresented in your organization, and take the necessary actions to close the gaps (find out how to assess the employee experience in Chapter 15). Second, integrate inclusion into the company values and performance goals, pay, promotion, as well as other policies and practices, and be specific about what the behaviors should look like. Third, educate leaders at all levels about inclusive behaviors to ensure that they are on the same page and have a clear understanding of their roles and responsibilities as inclusive leaders. And fourth, hold leaders accountable for demonstrating inclusive behaviors (there's more on accountability in Chapter 16).

Working with Artificial Intelligence and Automation

Automation and artificial intelligence (AI) are changing the way we work at the speed of light, and they are replacing many human tasks. While this will give us the capacity to focus on more strategic and creative tasks which only humans can do, this shift changes the skills people need today and will need in the future to succeed in the workplace. As these technologies reshape industries and redefine job roles, inclusive leaders must be proactive in implementing strategies to address the challenges and ensure a fair and equitable transition.

Inclusive leaders recognize that the evolving job market demands new skill sets, and they must come up to speed on the many facets of AI. Then they must ensure that their workforce has the necessary development and tools for success. This means allowing workers to experiment with AI and functionalities, while maintaining guardrails that protect the company's assets. Given how quickly the AI space is moving, leaders should focus on the areas where being more entrepreneurial makes sense, and maintain open communication regarding the impact of AI on their worker roles. This helps manage employee expectations, reduces uncertainty, and allows leaders to convey their commitment to supporting workers through the transition. This approach also builds trust and inclusivity, fostering a collaborative environment where employees feel heard and valued.

Managing Remote and Flexible Work

If you're responsible for overseeing a remote team, a key aspect of your role involves devising innovative approaches to keep remote employees engaged. The goal is for these team members to experience a sense of belonging equivalent to those working physically in the office — and rightfully so. While they might not have the opportunity for spontaneous chats around the water cooler, remote employees can still cultivate interest in their tasks, maintain effective communication, and derive satisfaction from their meaningful contributions to the company.

Inclusive leaders ensure that they prioritize consistent communication, hold regular check in meetings with remote team members (not only to get updates on projects but to check on them personally), facilitate social interactions such as virtual coffee breaks, or celebrations, and team builders. I've even seen leaders host virtual cooking classes where the employees showed off their skills, parties for special occasions (birthdays, births, anniversaries, and so on), and yoga, exercise, and meditation sessions. These were lots of fun and brought staff together in more personal ways to connect. For more on leading diverse and hybrid teams, check out Chapter 10.

REMEMBER

Inclusive leaders should ensure that all workers who are remote and working flexibly have quality equipment and ergonomic furniture. And they must consider the emotional and mental toll that working remotely can take, so reaffirming their support, and reminding them of the resources that are available through the company's benefit program is key. These benefits programs can range from competitive pay to non-compensatory benefits such as health and wellness programs, flexible work arrangements, recognition and rewards, tuition reimbursement, employee assistant programs (EAP), and so forth. Most companies offer two or more of these benefits.

Leading Change in Tumultuous Times

WARNING

One of my mentors used to tell me, "If you're not ready to deal with change, you're not ready to lead." Organizations today are facing rapid changes in technology, the global economy, market demands, and worker expectations. And with all of these shifts, leaders have to be able to anticipate and respond to rapidly changing conditions, recover quickly, and remain productive and positive. In other words, they must be agile and resilient. Otherwise they run the risk of becoming irrelevant.

Leading change in times of disruption is not easy and leaders have to throw out the old way of thinking and doing things to look for new possibilities and opportunities. They have to help their team understand the "why" behind the change and what it would or could mean for them and their jobs. They must tend to their emotional and psychological responses to change, most importantly, involve the team early in the process and allow their input. This garners greater buy-in and commitment to the change.

Saying the Wrong Thing

Or rather, having a fear of saying the wrong thing. Think about the climate that we live and work in . . . many have coined it an Era of Disruption, a polarizing environment, the decade of movements, and a time of the most globally diverse workforce ever. Amidst these realities, they also have to manage poor performance, disengaged workers, violations of company policies, and deal with sensitive topics such as race, gender, religion, politics, sexual orientation, disability, and the like. Chapters 12 and 13 reveal how to have more inclusive conversations. When the wrong thing is said or done, leaders can be terminated from their jobs, be featured on the news, shamed on social media, and included in legal action. At the same time, they cannot avoid taking action because that too can be harmful.

TIP

I have these tips for responding inclusively and appropriately: address the issue head on and if you were the culprit, own it and apologize; involve Human Resources; create a safe space by building trust and rapport; practice active and humble listening; suspend judgment and assume positive intent; practice empathy; and be clear about the outcomes.

Chapter **21**

Ten Practices that Inclusive Organizations Have in Common

This book is for leaders who truly want to be inclusive but aren't sure how. I hope that it not only inspires you to be more inclusive in your leadership, but also gives you the practical tools you need to put that desire into practice.

However, not everything is up to an individual leader. A significant factor in any worker's experience also comes from the organization itself. But together, an inclusive leader and a workplace that prioritizes its culture and its employees can create a workplace that welcomes all talent, treats them equitably, and fosters an environment where they can be their best. This chapter highlights organizational practices that allow workplaces to be truly inclusive.

Maintaining a Positive Employer Brand and Reputation

Being a great place to work and an employer of choice cannot be overstated. And it should not be a big kept secret from staff and from the public. In other words, organizations cannot be shy about telling their stories of success or tooting their own horns and letting the world know the good things they're doing. Why is this important? It acts as a powerful differentiator among top talent who are drawn to organizations with a reputation for fostering a positive work environment, providing growth opportunities, and demonstrating a commitment to employee well-being. Additionally, a strong employer brand helps in retaining existing talent, reducing turnover costs, and contributing to long-term organizational stability. Sustaining your place as an employer of choice must be every person's responsibility, but in particular, leaders must demonstrate the competencies and live the values of inclusion consistently.

TECHNICAL
STUFF

The new generation of talent and future leaders have been very clear that they want to work for organizations that treat people well. In fact, in a 2020 Monster poll (https://hiring.monster.com/resources/blog/monsters-2020-state-of-the-candidate-infographic/), 83 percent of job seekers from Gen Z said that a company's commitment to workforce DEI [Diversity, Equity, and Inclusion] is important when choosing an employer. They want to be accepted and valued for who they authentically are. It's not just important that *they* be treated fairly; they want a workplace that treats *everyone* fairly.

Embedding Inclusion into Strategic Priorities

I'm always puzzled by companies who say all the right things, but when it comes right down to it, they treat their people and culture as an afterthought — something to worry about after pressing business needs are taken care of.

REMEMBER

A workplace culture that values and respects *all* of its workers might be the most pressing need for your CEO to consider. Truly inclusive organizations embed inclusion into their mission, vision, values, performance expectations, development and advancement activities, marketing, branding, communications, supply chain/procurement, community outreach, and customer service philosophy.

Assessing Employee Experience

Inclusive companies value and listen to their employees to understand what their needs are, what's working, what's not working, and how they can serve them better. And they are committed to acting on the feedback because it serves as a baseline of where they are and gives guidance for where they need to go.

Many companies use an outside consulting firm with the requisite expertise in conducting assessments, audits, and surveys. The advantage is that they are a neutral third party, and that tends to invoke a greater level of participation, openness, and honesty from employees. This also allows data to remain confidential and ensures that it will be more reliable. Engagement, equity, and inclusion audits should capture respondent demographics so that the data can be analyzed and synthesized by level, tenure, and location, but also by identity markers such as race, gender, sexual orientation, age, and disability. Focus groups, listening sessions, and key stakeholder interviews are excellent ways to supplement the data in the surveys by allowing people to expound upon their answers and provide examples (see Chapter 15).

Other ways to get a sense of the current state of the workplace is to host all-staff meetings and solicit responses, use employee suggestion sites, conduct exit interviews and stay interviews, and encourage people-leaders to practice an open-door policy. Employee resource groups, which are generally organized based on common identities, interests, and/or backgrounds can be another great vehicle for feedback. For a detailed outline of how to assess an organization's culture, these my book *Diversity, Equity, & Inclusion For Dummies* (John Wiley & Sons, Inc., 2022).

Leading Change with Agility and Resilience

Organizations are facing rapid changes in technology, the global economy, market demands, and worker expectations. And with these shifts, leaders have to be able to do two things or risk becoming irrelevant:

>> Anticipate and respond to rapidly changing conditions (agility)

>> Recover quickly and remain productive and positive (resilience)

TIP

The trick is to know exactly where, when, and what you can bend in the name of agility, and where you won't move. In the areas of DEI, I suggest that your values are the place where you promote stability. An organization's values should be unshakable, not to be compromised during adversity and struggle. At the same time, a company shouldn't be led by old habits. When someone tells you that a process is "the way we've always done things," you should ask if that old way still works. Does the process remain because of company values, or because of complacency and inertia?

Educating and Developing Leaders at All Levels Consistently

All too often, when workers excel at a particular task, project, or initiative, they are promoted to a people leadership role with little or no training or recognition that this role is a fundamentally different job that requires additional knowledge and abilities on top of whatever technical and functional skills were gained in their individual contributor role.

If an organization wants to ensure that its people perform at their best it must invest in the training and development of its leaders. I employ a *build or buy* talent strategy. *Building* means growing and leveraging the collective strength among all the talent that you have within by conducting needs assessments on what skills and competencies exist in the organization, and what it wants its leaders to possess based on their strategic direction two to five years in the future. Systems and structures are then implemented that offer leaders the opportunity to learn and practice these new skills. *Buying* is about investing in external resources such as search firms, job boards, and membership organizations to source and identify diverse talent with the requisite skills you seek. Together, both of these methods can offer an organization the kind of leaders who will be prepared and ready to foster an inclusive workplace culture that enables the organization to thrive.

Removing Organizational Barriers to Equity and Inclusion

Creating a more inclusive culture doesn't just happen. There are real and perceived obstacles and barriers that must be addressed first. One of these is bias. Oftentimes, decisions we make unconsciously get in the way of our best intentions to be an inclusive leader. Another barrier comes in the form of microaggressions, those seemingly small behaviors that can have a large negative impact on your staff. Becoming aware of the biases we hold and the microaggressions we perpetuate can do a lot to allow the culture we already want to take root (as discussed in Chapter 6).

Another barrier is resistance — usually resistance to change or resistance to feedback. I've even experienced resistance to DEI efforts altogether, due to a belief that it is counterproductive and leads to reverse discrimination. It is important to address each of these with data and a compelling business case for how and why inclusive leadership drives business success. They can also be addressed through proper training and education and having open dialogue about the benefits of equity and inclusion.

Fostering Trust, Psychological Safety, and Well-Being

REMEMBER

Inclusive organizations build and maintain a culture of trust and psychological safety by acting in the best interest of both their company and their teams, and by demonstrating integrity, consistency, and transparency. Team members feel comfortable being their authentic selves, asking questions, admitting mistakes, offering ideas and suggestions, and even challenging each other (read more on psychological safety in Chapter 11). Well-being is integral to fostering inclusion. A workplace that prioritizes the well-being of its employees acknowledges their holistic needs — physical, mental, and emotional. Leaders must champion policies and practices that support work–life balance, mental health, and overall employee welfare. This investment pays dividends, as employees who feel supported in their well-being are more engaged, productive, and likely to contribute positively to the workplace culture.

Assembling and Leading Diverse Teams for Maximum Performance

If diversity is just getting lots of different people in the room, you could argue that achieving diversity is easy. And if inclusion is making sure that all people are valued and appreciated, all you need to do to achieve it is to hire a bunch of people who look, think, and act just like you . . . and that should be easy, too. It's the combination of diversity and inclusion that's challenging.

But I'd argue that a homogenous team can't be truly inclusive. It might feel inclusive, but if it's not ready to accept a new person who might challenge the prevailing norms and perspectives of the group, how inclusive can it be?

REMEMBER

Diversity not only makes inclusion possible, but it allows room for genius. A group of people who all look, think, and act alike are going to come up with solutions that just one or very few of them could have brainstormed alone. But a team that's brimming with different worldviews and lived experiences can create solutions to problems that none of them could have dreamed up by themselves — provided they're working in an environment that sees, trusts, and respects them.

Tracking, Measuring, and Holding Each Other Accountable

It's often said that what gets measured gets done. By and large, I think that's true. At work, knowing that you'll be measured and held to account for certain outcomes certainly spurs behaviors — not because workplace culture is necessarily punitive, but because measurement and accountability makes it clear that the organization is serious. Measuring how inclusive your organization is can include the quality of employee engagement surveys, performance assessment data, hiring metrics, coaching and development, promotion data, retention numbers, who has a seat at the table and who's voices are included in key decisions, and so on (see Chapter 15 for more on this).

WARNING

If your organization isn't actively tracking, measuring, and holding its leaders accountable for its culture, you might find that some of the leaders in your company are leading inclusively simply because it's important to them — but they're doing so in an organization that doesn't really value these efforts and won't know how to reward them appropriately.

Recognizing and Rewarding Top Performance

Inclusive organizations appreciate and celebrate their top performers. All organizations want to incentivize good work, but too many do so through toxic command-and-control leadership styles or harsh consequences when people fail to meet their goals.

Cultures that instead focus on recognizing and rewarding their top performers (this includes leaders who are the most inclusive in managing and leading their teams) are much more vibrant, aspirational, smarter, and quite frankly more fun to work in. Employees who know that their hard work, brilliant ideas, and loyalty will be rewarded are far more likely to go the extra mile, make valuable suggestions, and stay engaged during the tough times. More importantly, they'll do so gladly and willingly, not because they fear the consequences should they not.

Index

E

organizational barriers, to equity and inclusion, 310–311

organizational communications, equity lens and, 282–283

organizational culture, equity lens and, 275

organizational norms, 100

orientations
  of cultural competence, 137–142
  equity lens and, 280
  of new talent, 88–89

overcommunication, as a leader, 163

ownership, leadership accountability and, 238–239

P

Packaging, as one of three "P"'s of personal branding, 65

paid time off (PTO) policy, 30

participating, as a leadership style, 191

partnering, with diverse networks, 42

pay gaps, 27

performance
  as a benefit of diverse teams, 158–159
  feedback for, 127–128
  normalizing conflict as tool for higher, 208–209
  recognizing, 312
  rewarding, 312

Performing stage, of development, 154–155, 156–157

personal brands
  about, 62
  building, 62–65

personal values, establishing, 75–77

personal vision statement, 74–75

perspectives, seeking and leveraging diverse, 267–268

Pew Research Center, 14, 27

P&G, 201

phobias, 19–20

Pixar, 182

Platinum Rule, 128, 162, 272–273

Polarization, in Intercultural Development Continuum, 139–140

Polarization-Defense orientation, 139–140

Polarization-Reversal orientation, 139–140

Porter, Richard E, (author)
  Intercultural Communication, 130

Positive Psychology in Action (PPIA), 112

Power, in Culture Spectrum, 231

power distance, 134

practicing inclusive communication, 205–206

praise, 127

Predictive Index, 229–230

Preparation, as one of three "P"'s of personal branding, 65

Presentation, as one of three "P"'s of personal branding, 65

Price Waterhouse, 10, 14

Primitive Culture (Tylor), 130

Principle, in Culture Spectrum, 234

Privilege, in Culture Spectrum, 231

problem solving, as a benefit of diverse teams, 158

productivity
  conflict and, 212
  equity lens and sense of, 275
  increased, 265

progress, measuring, 32

promoting
  diversity, equity, and inclusion (DEI), 31
  inclusive culture, 43
  talent, 89–90

psychological safety
  about, 167–169
  benefits of in the workplace, 175–176
  best practice companies for, 182–184
  conflict and, 213
  creating, 179–181
  establishing, 167–184
  factors that drive and undermine, 176–178
  fostering environments of, 311
  importance of, 296
  measuring, 181
  stages of, 169–174

PTO (paid time off) policy, 30

purpose
  about, 69–70
  discovering your, 71–73
  importance of, 70–71

Q

quality of hire metric, 247

Qualtrics, 226

quiet quitting, 91, 175

R

racial diversity, 14, 27

racial minorities, 27

racism, 20

reciprocal feedback, 193

recognition
  importance of, 295
  of performance, 312

recruiting
  equity lens and, 279–280
  as a leader, 162
  metrics for, 246–247
  upgrading strategies for, 30

Red Zone cultures, 230–232

reflection, 82

relationships
  about, 134
  coaching, feedback and expectations of, 188
  management of, as an emotional intelligence domain, 115, 119–120

Remember icon, 3

remote work, managing, 303–304

representation, increased, 265

reputation
  building, 62–65
  importance of, 63–64
  maintaining, 308

research
  on benefits of empathy and emotional intelligence, 125–126
  on employee experience, 227

resignation to silence, as a factor that undermine trust and psychological safety, 177

resilience, change leadership and, 309–310

Respect, in Culture Spectrum, 233

responsibility gap, 245

Retaliation, in Culture Spectrum, 231

retention
  as a benefit of diverse teams, 159
  conflict and, 212
  improving, 45–47
  metrics for, 247–249
  of talent, 37, 90–91, 301

revising personal vision statement, 74

rewards
  about, 127
  importance of, 295
  for performance, 312

Robert Wood Johnson Foundation, 273

S

Salesforce, 48, 201
Samovar, Larry A. (author)
    Intercultural Communication, 130
scenarios, workplace, 52
selecting new talent, 87–88
selection metrics, 246–247
selection ratios metric, 247
self-assessment
    about, 54–56, 74
    for empathy and emotional
        intelligence, 121–124
    engaging in, 105
self-awareness
    as an emotional intelligence domain,
        115, 116–117
    equity lens and, 285
self-control, as an emotional
    intelligence domain, 115, 117–118
selfless leadership, 22
selfless leadership style, 59–60
self-reflection
    about, 74
    engaging in, 105
selling, as a leadership style, 190
servant leadership, 22
sexism, 20
shared goals, 127
shared values, 127
short-term focus, 100
SHRM (Society for Human Resource
    Management), 126, 204, 227, 274
Silence, in Culture Spectrum, 230–231
situational leadership model
    about, 21
    customizing coaching using, 189–191
situational leadership style, 62
Six "C"s
    about, 22, 33
    assessing, 34–35
Slow Brain, 81, 93
smart technology, future workforce
    and, 28
social awareness, as an emotional
    intelligence domain, 115, 118–119
Society for Human Resource
    Management (SHRM), 126, 204,
    227, 274
socio-political unrest, 299–300
solutions, seeking and leveraging
    diverse, 267–268

sourcing
    diverse talent, 148–150
    new talent, 87–88
sourcing channel metric, 247
specificity, in personal vision
    statement, 74
sponsorship, 265, 266–267
stakeholder interviews, 229
stakeholders, conflict and, 222
Stanton, Andrew (director), 182
*State of the Global Workplace 2023
    Report,* 46, 175
Storming stage, of development,
    152–153, 156–157
strategic goals, supporting as a
    leader, 161
strategies, applying to address gaps in
    employee experience, 235–236
succession planning, 31
supply chain and procurement metrics,
    253–254
supporting, in situational leadership
    model, 21
Swift Action, in Culture Spectrum,
    234–235

T

talent
    accessing pool of, 42–44
    acclimating new hires to teams, 150
    attracting, 301
    communicating with, 90
    developing, 89–90
    engaging, 89–90
    onboarding new, 88–89
    orienting new, 88–89
    promoting, 89–90
    retaining, 90–91, 301
    sourcing and selecting new, 87–88
    sourcing diverse, 148–150
TalentSmart, 126
targeted recruitment events, 43
Taylor, Tess C. (HR veteran), 205–206
teams
    about, 147
    acclimating new hires to, 150
    avoiding common pitfalls when
        leading, 164–165
    diversity in, 311–312
    fostering environments of trust and
        belonging, 159–160

    improved dynamics for, 135
    leading across differences and
        distances, 160–163
    leading through five stages of
        development, 151–157
    maximizing benefits of diverse,
        157–159
    psychological safety for, 168–169
    sourcing diverse talent, 148–150
teamwork
    cultural differences impeding, 36
    increased, 265
Technical Stuff icon, 4
telling, as a leadership style, 190
terminology, for inclusion, 15–20
Thinking, Fast & Slow (Kahneman), 81
Thomas, Ken, 213
Thomas-Kilman conflict modes,
    213–216
three "P"'s, of personal branding, 65
Tip icon, 3
tracking
    accountability, 312
    inclusion initiatives, 243–255
training
    equity lens and, 281
    seeking, 105
transactional leadership style, 60–61
transactional leadership theory, 21
transformational leadership style,
    21, 60
transparency
    in communication, 44
    culture of, 105
    as a leader, 163
transparent leadership
    about, 99
    analyzing effectiveness of, 100–103
    mastering, 105–107
transphobia, 20
trust
    about, 167–169
    benefits of in the workplace, 175–176
    best practice companies for, 182–184
    in Culture Spectrum, 233
    establishing, 167–184
    factors that drive and undermine,
        176–178
    fostering environments of,
        159–160, 311
    importance of, 192
    as a value, 76

About the Author

Dr. Shirley Davis is president and CEO of SDS Global Enterprises, a strategic development solutions firm that specializes in human resources strategy; talent management; leadership effectiveness; high performance; and culture transformation. Dr. Davis has over 30 years of experience in a variety of senior executive leadership roles in *Fortune* 100 & 50 corporations in financial services, banking, manufacturing, and retail sales, as well as in non-profit leadership at the world's largest human resources association, the Society for Human Resource Management. Her work has been featured by the *Wall Street Journal, Forbes Magazine,* NBC's *Today Show, USA Today, CBS News, Fox News,* CNN.com, *Fast Company, CEOWorld Magazine, Harvard Business Review,* and many others. In May 2022, her story was featured on the front page of *Oprah Daily.* As a result of her contributions and expertise in the HR, leadership, business, and DEI fields, she was inducted into *Inclusion* Magazine's Hall of Fame in November 2021, and in August 2022 in Nashville, TN she received The Golden Gavel Award, which is Toastmasters International's highest and most prestigious award given to only one person each year. Additionally, she was nominated for Forbes 2021, and 2022 Women 50 Over 50 list.

Dr. Davis has worked in more than 30 countries on five continents and delivers more than 100 speeches a year to a wide range of industries, sectors, and sizes. She continues to consult, coach, and train leaders at all levels, including corporate CEOs, C-Suite executives, and board of directors. She served on the Board of Directors and the Foundation Board for the National Speakers Association (2017–2021). She is currently a member of the NSA Million Dollar Speakers Group, Black NSA, and the Global Speakers Federation.

In 2021, she was named to the national board of the Make-A-Wish Foundation. She holds a Bachelor's in Pre-Law, a Master's in Adult Education; a second Master's in Human Resource Management, a Ph.D. in Business and Organizational Leadership, and holds more than ten certifications.

Dr. Shirley Davis is the author of the Amazon bestseller, *Diversity, Equity, & Inclusion For Dummies* (2022) and *Living Beyond "What If?" Release the Limits and Realize Your Dreams* (2021). She's also the author of *Reinvent Yourself: Strategies for Achieving Success in Every Area of Your Life* (2020) and *The Seat: How to Get Invited to the Table When You're Over-Performing but Undervalued* (2016). Additionally, she is a popular author for nine LinkedIn Learning courses on Leadership, Workplace Culture, and Business/Career Development.

She is a former Miss District of Columbia National Teenager, Mrs. Oklahoma-America, Ms. Richmond Virginia, Ms. Virginia, and in 2000 she won the national title of Ms. American United States. Among her many accomplishments and titles, the one she holds dearest is "mom" to her beloved daughter, Gabrielle Victoria. In 2023 they both launched the Dr. Shirley Davis Foundation where they give individuals and women owned and minority-owned businesses the hope and help they need to achieve their vision and goals, produce at higher levels, and experience success and fulfillment in every aspect of their lives!

Dedication

This book is dedicated to my extensive network of Human Resources professionals, Inclusion and Equity allies, advocates, and champions, and the many clients that I and my firm have had the good fortune to serve as your consulting partners, executive leadership coaches, keynote speakers and training facilitators. It has been a pleasure to work with your board of directors, senior executives, and people leaders at all levels to foster more welcoming, winning, and world class workplace cultures and it is because of those lived and learned experiences that I gained such wisdom, knowledge, and expertise to write this book.

This book is also dedicated to the many leaders who simply don't understand the significance of the leadership, accountability, and inclusion gaps that currently exist and that must be closed if you want to attract, retain, and fully engage top talent and if you want to remain relevant in the years to come. I appreciate that you decided to pick this book up to find out how you can become a part of the solution in making the world and your organizations more inclusive.

Author's Acknowledgments

This book was written based on my 30+ years of experience as an HR business leader turned corporate executive, turned CEO of a full service thriving global workforce consulting firm. Along the journey I have led many teams, reported to many types of leaders, and worked in several kinds of cultures, all of which had varying degrees of dysfunction, toxicity, and lack of inclusion but all of which prepared me to write this book. Along the way I have built an extensive network of colleagues and friends and hired some amazing talent with unique gifts, perspectives, and strengths and I recognize that I cannot achieve anything significant alone. As in this case of writing this book, I knew that it would be a huge undertaking given my hectic schedule, so I sought out someone whom I respect, trust, adore working with, and who is a phenomenal writer and thought leader. In fact, I tapped this person to work with me on the last For Dummies book I penned in 2022, *Diversity, Equity, & Inclusion For Dummies,* for his perspectives, experiences, and tips. And because of his contributions, this body of work is even more comprehensive. Let me acknowledge and introduce to you Eric C. Peterson, MSOD.

He is a recognized facilitator and educator in the inclusion space with over 20 years of experience in unconscious bias, diversity and inclusion, learning strategies, organization development, allyship, the LGBTQ community, and whiteness as a social identity. He as senior consultant on my team and also acts as an independent consultant. I had the pleasure of hiring Eric as the manager for diversity and inclusion at the Society of Human Resource Management (SHRM) and years later, I am thrilled to be working with him in this capacity as CEO of my own consulting firm. He has been a guest contributor for NBC Out and has been sourced as an inclusion expert by CNN, National Public Radio, the Washington Post, the Boston Globe, the Los Angeles Times, and others.

I can't thank the Wiley team enough, especially Tracy Boggier for seeking me out for this assignment and for the team you assembled to support me, especially Dan Mersey who guided me through the writing and editing process.

I thank God, my Creator, who has bestowed many gifts and blessings on me. I am so grateful that I wake up each day excited about living out my dreams, doing the work that I love, all while being in my happy place (by the ocean). I never dreamed that all of the experiences at work and in life (good, bad, and ugly) would be working together to prepare me to write this book at this time that will now be a road map and reference guide for leaders to use in creating more positive employee experiences at work.

Publisher's Acknowledgments

Acquisitions Editor: Tracy Boggier

Development Editor: Dan Mersey

Managing Editor: Sofia Malik

Production Editor: Saikarthick Kumarasamy

Cover Image: © Alex Zhou/500px/Getty Images